# AMERICAN INDIANS: SOCIAL JUSTICE AND PUBLIC POLICY

## * * * * *

VOLUME IX

**ETHNICITY AND PUBLIC POLICY**
SERIES

# ETHNICITY AND PUBLIC POLICY
## SERIES
WINSTON A. VAN HORNE, General Editor
THOMAS V. TONNESEN, Managing Editor

**✱  ✱  ✱  ✱  ✱**

# AMERICAN INDIANS: SOCIAL JUSTICE AND PUBLIC POLICY

EDITED BY

## DONALD E. GREEN and THOMAS V. TONNESEN

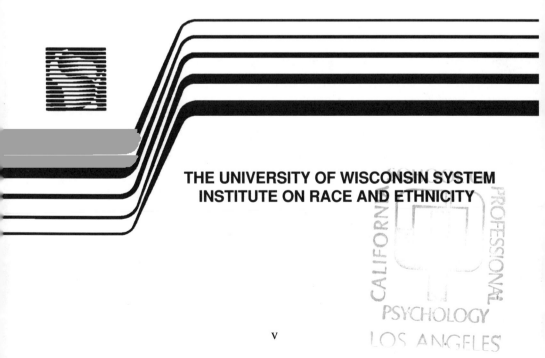

### THE UNIVERSITY OF WISCONSIN SYSTEM
### INSTITUTE ON RACE AND ETHNICITY

The University of Wisconsin System
Institute on Race and Ethnicity
P.O. Box 413, Milwaukee, WI 53201

International Standard Book Number ISBN 0-942672-16-X (cloth)
International Standard Book Number ISBN 0-942672-17-8 (paper)
Library of Congress Catalog Card Number: 91-66089

There can be no moral agreement with injustice, even though one may agree voluntarily to what is unjust. Voluntary agreement, then, may bind one particularly by standards of legal justice, but not universally by precepts of moral justice.

Winston A. Van Horne

# PREFACE

Thomas V. Tonnesen

*University of Wisconsin-Milwaukee*

It is with no little irony that this volume is appearing at about the time that the nation is preparing to celebrate the cinquecentennial of Christopher Columbus's "discovery" of America. While many in the United States and elsewhere will partake in festivities marking the introduction of Europeans to the Western Hemisphere, the year 1992 should also serve as a time for pause and reflection. Those individuals and groups who are descendants of the indigenous inhabitants of this part of the globe, and others of non-European heritage, will likely find little cause for joy.

On what is it, though, that we should reflect? In that the subject of this book is American Indians, perhaps we should start with the following: Why is it that two sets of words which appear in this book's title, American Indians and social justice, seem almost oxymoronic when combined? Should there be anything incongruous about principles of social justice being applied to American Indians? The answer to this question is obviously no, but the sad truth of their history and exploitation would have us believe otherwise.

This volume is the ninth in a series on the interplay between race, ethnicity and public policy, especially in American society. One of the premises of the series, and of this book in particular, is that the kind of public policy evidenced is key to the acquisition and continued possession of social justice. Most of us should not need to be reminded about the history and consequences of U.S. public policy vis-à-vis American Indians. Nevertheless, readers will find a good degree of history in the chapters of this book, much of it from a distinctive vantage point. But what the reader should find most important here is the discussion of various aspects of public policy—social (e.g., health care, education, employment, criminal justice, etc.) as well as legal (e.g., treaties, sovereignty, self-determination, etc.)—and their relationship to fulfilling the promise of social justice for American Indians.

This leads one to muse a bit about how public policy is formulated, especially in a democracy. Behind all public policy are private thoughts, private beliefs, private assumptions, private prejudices. It can be said that public policy is the embodiment of a nation's psyche. Ultimately, the way a democracy's electorate feels about certain issues will be reflected in that nation's public policy. This view of public policy changes it from the standard perception of a rather massive, bureaucratic, impersonal unfolding of laws, rules and regulations, for which no individual can take personal credit or must take blame, to a set of actions for which we as individuals can and should be held accountable. It is true that public policy can occasionally move ahead of a nation's private, collective sentiments. In these cases it is playing a leadership role, although it should not be assumed that the results will necessarily be benign. But eventually, if congruence is not reached between the public sphere of policy action and the private sphere of thought, the former will prove hollow and be ignored. It must be remembered that public policy is not just a function of decrees but of implementation; if a people's "heart" is not in the former, their minds and bodies will not properly perform the latter.

But what do all these ruminations have to do with the case of American Indians? The answer, of course, is plenty. The public policy of the American colonies prior to 1776, and continuing unabated in the United States throughout the nineteenth and much of the twentieth centuries, was unequivocally hostile to American Indians as a people. It also cannot be disputed, sadly, that such policies reflected accurately the prevailing, private feelings of the American majority, read whites. But perhaps by now the private view of American Indians and their plight by a sufficiently large portion of the electorate has changed enough so that public policy can begin to both adapt and lead.

Social justice is not a "zero sum" game, where if one group gains a degree of it, others must necessarily lose a corresponding amount. The problem though is that the effectiveness of the kinds of public policies discussed in the chapters which follow, items such as health care, education, employment, criminal justice, treaty rights, etc., is perceived as a function of financing—and finances are often viewed in the "zero sum" vein. Thus, some might argue, the achievement of social justice for some groups such as American Indians must wait until the pool of economic resources expands sufficiently to allow the requisite public policies to come about. This type of thinking not only presumes a finiteness of wealth and resources which does not truly exist, but it also reveals and betrays something much more important—a lack of will.

The question of will, then, returns us to the private base upon which public policy must be founded.

The means to alter the socioeconomic conditions of American Indians are within our grasp. After all, in terms of demographics, they comprise a small part of the population. Whether improvements in socioeconomic conditions can repair the psychological damage wreaked on American Indians over the centuries is another question, but as Donald Fixico demonstrates in his chapter, they are an amazingly resilient people whose strong sense of group identity has served them well. The real question regarding the ills that plague the American Indian population and their achievement of social justice is whether, *privately*, the American people have the will and desire to bring about change. If they do, the necessary conditions will be evidenced on the *public* plane. Come to think of it, perhaps a variation of the "zero sum" game does apply to social justice; for it can be argued that social justice denied to one is social justice denied to all. The editors and contributors to this volume hope that its passages help lead to this collective, private realization in some small way. If so, then the year 1992 would truly be one to celebrate.

As always, there are individuals whose contributions must be acknowledged, for their "behind-the-scences" work and support were indispensable to the publication of this volume. We must first begin with Winston Van Horne, the director of the University of Wisconsin System Institute on Race and Ethnicity and editor of the first eight volumes in the *Ethnicity and Public Policy* series. We are grateful for the confidence in our ability to edit this volume that he has evidenced, and for his advice in shepherding the book to its conclusion.

Over the years, the stellar job that Joanne Brown does in her role as copy editor has now become routine, but this makes her efforts no less appreciated. When Linda Jallings, our friend and colleague from UW-Milwaukee's Printing Services, left her position in the past year for greener pastures, anxiety struck us over working with a new person. This feeling soon proved to be unfounded as Jane Turner immediately calmed our fears and showed her skill and expertise in guiding the book through its publication and printing phases.

Lorraine Colotti and Dick Meier of Wiscomp, and its director, Susan Cox-Anderson, have all taken great care in seeing that the typesetting turned out just right. This statement is especially applicable to Tim Greenya, who played his keyboard like a virtuoso. The four of them could start a successful business conducting seminars on customer relations. The role played by Stephanie Lam of our office was second to none. Her command of the word processor and ability to decipher editorial changes, as well as her research skills, all contributed mightily to the finished product. Two other staff members of the Institute, Judy Treskow and Thelma Conway, the latter who is responsible for the sales of volumes in the series, cannot go unmentioned.

Although the individuals whose names follow did not write or typeset a single word for this book, their contributions cannot merely be termed auxiliary, neither to the success of the *Ethnicity and Public Policy* series nor to the interests and activities of the Institute. At the institutional level, John Schroeder, Ken Watters, George Keulks and Bob Jones have all evidenced sincere concern for the welfare of the Institute and a keen understanding of its mission. The outgoing president of the University of Wisconsin System, Kenneth Shaw, and his acting successor, Katharine Lyall, have always been more than supportive, as has Al Beaver of UW System Administration. A special nod must be given to Stephen Portch, the new vice president for academic affairs of the UW System, whose attention to the work of the Institute in the early days of his tenure was not only most appreciated, but bodes well for the Institute's continued leadership in the field of racial/ethnic studies within Wisconsin and beyond. With all of these individuals in our corner, the future can only be bright.

# CONTENTS

# INTRODUCTION

---

## Donald E. Green

*University of Wisconsin-Milwaukee*

The need to review and assess the American Indian experience in this country in terms of social policy and social justice is great as we progress through the last decade of the twentieth century. This book contributes to this substantial task by asking eight scholars of the American Indian experience to focus on selected substantive areas of interest in this field and both review social policy that has affected the lives of American Indians, and assess the degree to which these policies have helped to achieve social justice for this unique American minority group. In doing so, it is our hope that these reviews and assessments will produce at least a tentative answer to the important question of how well social policies have worked to ensure social justice for American Indians.

Russel Barsh provides an important discussion of the mechanisms of social control used by both Indian and white societies prior to the formation and adoption of the Constitution of the United States. Rather than engage in a debate over whether one society had the most influence over the other, he takes the position that neither society emerged from the colonial experience unchanged. From this perspective, Barsh details the process by which Indian and white societies in the colonial period transformed each other. He demonstrates how coming to understand the respect for individual liberty prevalent in Indian societies helped the Europeans to recognize its relevance for the new political order they would create in North America. On the other hand, Barsh also highlights the role that the European emphasis on mercantilism and trade played in the assimilation of Indian societies. Perhaps most interesting, however, is his conclusion that while the colonists came to better understand their own oppression by the state (i.e., the King) in their efforts to transform Indian societies, Indians have become less aware of their oppression by inherently assimilative institutions which only create an illusion of independence.

Sharon O'Brien compares the conflicting views of social justice held by American society and Indian societies, and presents an historical account of Indian attempts to achieve social justice in the face of considerable legal and legislative efforts by the federal government to destroy tribal sovereignty and assimilate Indians into mainstream American society. No doubt a provocative conclusion for many policymakers, O'Brien places the struggle of American Indian people to maintain their cultural heritage and political sovereignty in the context of the international community. By doing so, she proclaims the right of all indigenous people to achieve social justice through the recognition and protection of their sovereignty and the concomitant right to govern themselves.

The chapter which follows by Paul Stuart provides us with a framework for understanding the American Indian quest for true sovereignty in terms of the emergence of a number of self-determination movements within the few past centuries. Drawing on the philosophical works of Dov Ronen, Stuart suggests that the contemporary manifestation of these movements is that of ethnic self-determination, which has emerged as a result of external domination, successes of earlier self-determination movements of the nineteenth and twentieth centuries, and a more sympathetic world view seen in part through the eyes of the United Nations. Unfortunately, the discussion demonstrates that while the world political climate may be more favorable to these movements than in the past, many of the goals of the American Indian self-determination movement are apparently incompatible with those of United States federal Indian policies in general, and the organizational structure of the Bureau of Indian Affairs (BIA) in particular.

An account of the history of the Indians of the western Great Lakes region of the United States is outlined in the chapter by Donald Fixico. What some will find most surprising about these people is the persistence of their sense of Indian identity in spite of the numerous federal policies of assimilation and the destruction of Indian culture over the last two hundred years. Fixico details some of the internal and external factors that have shaped the identities of the western Great Lakes Indian tribes, and presents a typology of American Indian communities today which draws our attention to their unique cultural diversity.

Jennie Joe provides us with an historical overview of the process by which the federal government has become increasingly involved in providing health care services to Native Americans, in spite of more recent efforts to redistribute some of the financial burden to other levels of government, particularly the states. She argues that while the various levels of government debate in legal and political arenas over the question of whether health care to American Indians and Alaska Natives should be viewed as an entitlement, questions of eligibility and jurisdictional issues, not to mention financial status, continue to inhibit the ability of Indian people to receive adequate health care.

The past and current status of American Indian educational efforts in the context of the political, social, legal and economic relationships between Native Americans and various levels of government in the United States is the focus of the chapter by John Tippeconnic III. He also identifies a concept that is crucial not only for the future of Indian education, but for virtually all of the aspects of the American Indian experience presented in this book — the importance of equity, as opposed to the concept of equality, in efforts to achieve social justice for American Indians. This idea is presented in his discussion of a continual problem, noted by several of the contributors to this volume, with the many evaluations and assessments of the position of American Indians relative to other groups on any number of sociodemographic characteristics and social indicators. That is, all too frequently American Indians are either excluded from these comparisons, or they are included in categories labelled "other." Given the size of the American Indian population today, however, probably any effort to win a political numbers game is doomed for all but a limited few geographical areas with large concentrations of Native Americans. Because of the unique historical, political and demographic status of American Indians then, it seems paramount that social policies aimed at benefiting this minority group be based on what is fair and just in the context of past efforts to subjugate and destroy Indian cultures, rather than merely on what is equal in relation to other racial/ethnic groups in the United States today.

The book then proceeds with a chapter by Gary Sandefur that reviews some of the economic conditions of American Indians. It contends that while there has been considerable attention directed toward economic development from both federal and tribal governments in the last two decades, the underlying rationale for these efforts has been to provide better work opportunities for American Indians, especially those who reside on reservations. In spite of less than encouraging data on American Indian employment and earning power, Sandefur argues that the complex maze of federal, state and tribal governments, departments and agencies which administer programs directed toward economic development and work opportunities for American Indians has made considerable progress over the past several years. Based on this contention, he suggests that the federal government should continue its current policy of self-determination, but with adequate funding. In addition, he argues for government policies that maintain a commitment to affirmative action, and devote more resources to public sector job creation on reservations, rather than development per se, to effectively deal with American Indian economic problems.

The chapter on American Indian criminality reviews the limited number of studies on the etiology of and social reaction to crime among American Indians. Unfortunately, in relation to those studies that make up the bulk of criminological research on these issues, studies of American Indian criminality generally have not moved beyond simplistic univariate and/or bivariate analyses, and are based on limited samples with few comparisons across different tribal groups and regions of the country. The apparent lack of interest among criminologists regarding this minority group is perhaps more surprising given that available official data on arrests and incarceration rates suggest that American Indian criminality is greater than that for whites, and is either comparable to or greater than that for other ethnic groups in the United States. For example, when considering alcohol-related crimes, American Indians have the highest rates of offending among all racial groups. Moreover, unlike the well-established crime patterns for whites, blacks and Hispanics, data on American Indian criminality suggest that rates of offending in rural areas are equal to or greater than those for urban areas. This anomaly in the criminological literature begs for a more thorough understanding than what is provided by some of the more widely cited theories of criminality, which focus on factors related to so called "urban street crime." The chapter concludes with an attempt to frame future studies of Indian criminality within the broader sociological theories of conflict and internal colonialism.

This volume does provide evidence that some social policy decisions directed toward American Indians have been successful in improving their living conditions. Jennie Joe informs us that many of the major health problems American Indians have faced historically have decreased dramatically. Deaths from infectious diseases such as tuberculosis, gastrointestinal diseases, pneumonia and influenza have dropped by over 70 percent since federal responsibility for the health care of Native Americans was transferred to the U.S. Public Health Service in 1954. The number of Indian children who die at birth also has declined significantly. The mortality rate for American Indian infants has declined from 62.7 to 14.6 per 1,000 live births since 1954.

John Tippeconnic III details some information concerning the slowly improving educational status of American Indians. The percentage of American Indians who graduated from high school increased from 51 percent in 1970 to 60 percent in 1980. Moreover, the number of American Indians in higher education has increased significantly in the past decade. Native American enrollments in colleges and universities across the United States increased from 76,000 in 1976 to approximately 90,000 in 1986. Included in this figure are 5,000 Indian graduate students and 1,000 Indian students attending professional schools of medicine and law.

Many consider economic development to be the key to providing work opportunities for American Indians in general, and in particular for those who live on reservations. In this regard, Gary Sandefur notes that in 1984, the Bureau of Indian Affairs spent approximately 60 million dollars, roughly 6 percent of its overall budget, on economic development and employment programs. The Department of Labor spent 87 million dollars in fiscal year 1983 on Comprehensive Employment and Training Act (CETA) programs through Indian tribes, and in fiscal year 1984, Jobs Training Partnership Act programs spent 76 million dollars to create employment opportunities for American Indians. In fact, in spite of a consensus among Indian and non-Indian policymakers that social policies directed toward economic opportunities for Native Americans have not worked, Sandefur argues that Indian people have made considerable progress over the past several decades. For example, he notes that American Indian male weekly earnings have grown from 63 percent to 84 percent of white male earnings between 1959 and 1979.

Of course, the contributors to this volume do not present a rosy picture solely, for the overall living conditions of many American Indians are still quite disturbing. Joe notes that Native American life expectancy is six years less than that of any other minority group in the United States. In addition, more Indians die as a result of motor vehicle accidents than all other minority groups. She estimates that there are 0.6 Indian Health Service physicians to every 1,000 Indian patients, compared to a ratio of 1.6 physicians to every 1,000 patients in the general population. Perhaps even more troubling, she suggests, is the fact that while indicators of the health status of American Indians dramatically call for more funding to help mitigate these severe conditions, Indian health care programs across the country are facing drastic cuts.

Tippeconnic offers some selected educational data that starkly demonstrate the crisis in Indian education today. Among Indians 25 years of age and older who reside on reservations, 16.2 percent have completed less than 5 years of schooling. While 66 percent of the total U.S. population 25 years of age and older are high school graduates, 56 percent of American Indians in general, and only 43.2 percent of reservation Indians, have graduated from high school. The American Indian dropout rate for high school sophomores is 29.2, compared to 13.6 for the general population. The picture for higher education is equally unsettling. Only 8 percent of Native Americans have 4 or more years of college, compared to 16 percent for the total U.S. population. College dropout rates for American Indians are estimated to range from 45 to 62 percent.

Sandefur presents U.S. Census figures on American Indian employment rates that point to their continued exclusion from the labor force in surprising numbers. Over 13 percent of the national Indian population aged 16 and older, and over 27 percent of the reservation Indian population, were unemployed in 1980. These figures compare to unemployment rates by race for similar age groups of almost 12 percent for blacks, 8.9 percent for Hispanics, and 5.8 percent for whites. Native American women in particular appear to have fared poorly in measures of earning power in the last several decades. Sandefur notes that the weekly earnings of Indian women have remained virtually stagnant over the past three decades in comparison to white males. Since 1959, American Indian women have continued to received approximately half of the earnings of white males.

No assessment of the degree to which American Indians have achieved social justice in the United States would be complete without some discussion of their continual efforts to gain true sovereignty and the right to self-determination. As some of the book's contributors have discussed, while Indians were sovereign people at the time of the first European contacts, and thus were able to determine and meet their political, social and economic needs, the history of Indian/white relations since this first contact has been that of a continual process of exploitation and the subjugation of Indian cultures.

The above is not meant to imply that attempts have not been periodically made to reestablish tribal sovereignty and self-determination for American Indians, as many contributors to this volume document. The current U.S. policy toward American Indians has come to be known as one of self-determination, and throughout this book there are references to efforts which appear to have been successful in this regard. Joe notes that as of 1985, 6 of the 51 hospitals, and 50 of 124 health centers devoted primarily to Indian clients are being administered by tribal governments. Tippeconnic indicates that there are 20 tribally controlled community colleges in the United States, which have over 4,000 Indian students currently enrolled. Sandefur notes that tribes throughout the country have developed and now control numerous business enterprises, ranging from bingo parlors and convention centers to lumber and pencil companies.

However, as Stuart has pointed out, while numerous social policies have been proposed and implemented in the last two decades that were directed toward the goal of Indian self-determination, they have fallen short of truly achieving it. For example, funds made available to the tribes under this policy have been tied to specific programs which for the most part have been established without the benefit of an "Indian perspective" in general, and outside of the reservation context in particular. Not only is this kind of social policymaking inherently destructive of Indian self-determination efforts, Stuart argues, but it also has been destructive of Indian governments themselves by encouraging conflicts among "traditionalists" and "modernists" over the importance of these various programs for the aspirations of each group. Moreover, as Barsh so astutely points out, it can be argued that efforts to achieve tribal self-government can also be viewed as a veiled attempt to foster "real assimilation" by giving Indians business and civic experience, thus having them function as "real Americans" and not American Indians. He and other contributors to this volume note that even the language of the Indian movement for "sovereignty" has assimilationist overtones because of its linkages to European political theory. In fact, Barsh suggests that in many respects distinct "Indian jurisdictions" within the United States may only preserve the appearance of respect for indigenous law, especially when the most distinctive differences between them and the rest of the United States are such things as the ability to operate a high-stakes bingo hall or avoid paying an added tax on cigarettes.

As O'Brien states, however, true sovereignty may still be the key to the realization of social justice for American Indians. With the recent events in Eastern Europe, and the prospects for even more drastic changes in political power in what we now know as the Union of Soviet Socialist Republics, her ideas concerning the potential for the unification of all indigenous peoples in their struggle for self-determination may prove even the most skeptical wrong. If nothing else, this volume surely reflects the tenacious will of Indian people to retain their identities and cultures in the face of the enormous obstacles which have been placed — or perhaps the better word is forced — upon them. Given this most remarkable history, it is probably still too early to make a final assessment on the American Indian struggle to achieve social justice, but not so to be optimistic about their chances.

# "INDIAN LAW," INDIANS' LAW, AND LEGALISM IN AMERICAN INDIAN POLICY: AN ESSAY ON HISTORICAL ORIGINS

Russel Lawrence Barsh

> The World at the first was made on the other Side of the Great Water different from what it is on this Side, as may be known from the different Colours of our Skin and of our Flesh; and that which you call Justice may not be so amongst us; you have your Laws and Customs, and so have we.[1]

The history of Indian-white relations on this continent has largely been seen in terms of the inexorable penetration of Indian society by white laws and the concomitant subjugation of an ever greater expanse of Indian life to external regulation. Even our judges have come to describe Indian status as a matter of "residual sovereignty" — that is, what is left over in the lee of intermittent congressional and, more recently, judicial encroachments.[2] While a great deal has been written over the past twenty years tracing the course of this assimilative process,[3] chiefly in legalistic terms, an essential aspect has been almost completely overlooked. Neither the indigenous legal order, nor the legal order introduced from European soil, remained static. One did not simply replace the other. Rather, they transformed each other.

Bruce Johansen[4] has shown how some of the chief architects of the American constitutional system were deeply influenced by their experience with indigenous political ideas and institutions. This went beyond the mere borrowing of mechanical elements, such as the device of checks and balances,[5] to the principles underlying the whole political edifice: the absurdity of kings, the contractual character of free societies, the equality of all men[6] regardless of their economic status. Europeans, and especially Euro-Americans, saw their own cultures and institutions through the eyes of an alien civilization, revealing hitherto unrecognized contradictions. Just as contact with the Islamic world five centuries earlier stimulated the renaissance of European mathematics and natural sciences[7] and thus helped undermine the old religious order, the invasion of North America helped to subvert the established political order. Nor was this a one-way process. Conflicts with Europeans stimulated state building among indigenous Americans, which was subversive to the latter's established political order.[8] Europeans, moreover, dedicated themselves passionately to recreating Indian society into a model — and thus vindication — of their own ideals.

This essay will depart from the usual conventions of studies on Indian law and policy by ending, rather than beginning, with the adoption of the Constitution. The Constitution was by no means cut from whole cloth but culminated two centuries of experimentation, and this is equally true for Indian matters. The draftsmen of the Northwest Ordinance and the Indian Trade and Intercourse Acts stood in the shadow of the colonial experience, and made frequent use of seventeenth- and eighteenth-century precedents. Integrating tribes into the national legal framework through the successive implementation of treaties, trade, and political reorganization was already an established pattern by 1700. Even the debate over the locus of responsibility for managing this process — that is, between the federal and state levels of government — was anticipated both in issues and results by the consolidation of imperial control over Indian policy in the eighteenth century.

### Aboriginal Law

> Concerninge ther lawes my years and understandinge, made me the less to looke after bycause I thought the Infidels wear lawless.[9]

Generalizations, for a continent of rich cultural and economic diversity, can be hazardous. For three centuries, however, European observers were fairly consistent in identifying certain underlying characteristics of indigenous American laws and government. Perhaps they were simply the characteristics most perplexing — and therefore most interesting — to Europeans themselves, who were in a difficult period of emerging from religious and political absolutism. Regardless of what Europeans may have overlooked, or misunderstood, they were unquestionably influenced by what they perceived as the native "genius" of the continent.

The earliest English explorers reported exactly what they had expected to find — a rude miniature of Europe. "The forme of this Common wealth is a monarchiall governement," Captain Smith wrote to his countrymen. "One as Emperour ruleth over many kings or governors."[10] Yet it was clear from the outset that "the King is not known by any differenc from other of ye chefe sort in ye cuntry but only when he cums to any of ther houses they present him with copper Beads or Vittal, and shew much reverence to him."[11] As English settlers repeatedly failed to obtain any consistency or organized support from these "kings," they gradually realized that indigenous government was very different from their own.

Edmund Burke was among the first Englishmen to recognize that the preservation of individual "liberty in its fullest extent" was the foundation of indigenous law. "To this they sacrifice everything," he concluded. "This is what makes a life of uncertainty and want, supportable to them."[12] Burke also appreciated the role played by child-rearing. Indian children were "indulged in all manner of liberty" and, remarkably, were spared beatings:

> Reason, they say, will guide their children when they come to the use of it; and before that time their faults cannot be very great; but blows might abate the free and martial spirit which makes the glory of their people, and might render the sense of honour duller, by the habit of a slavish motive to action.[13]

While the authority of Indian leaders accordingly was "rather persuasive than coercive," order was nonetheless maintained:

> The want of laws, and of an universal strong coercive power, is not perceived in a narrow society, where every man has his eye upon his neighbour, and where the whole bent of everything they do is to strengthen those natural ties by which society is principally cemented.[14]

In other words, social discipline was a function of the existence, and continual renewal, of ties of kinship and responsibility. "As for justice, they have not any law, neither divine nor human, but that which Nature teacheth them — that one must not offend another," observed French lawyer Marc Lescarbot in 1606, after a visit to New France. "So have they quarrels very seldom."[15]

A more critical assessment of the same facts came from Burke's contemporary, William Douglass, a colonial physician. While among other societies "an absolute compelling power is lodged somewhere," Indians governed themselves merely by "persuasion":

> Strictly speaking, they seem to have no government, no laws, and are only cemented by friendship and good neighborhood; this is only a kind of tacit federal union between the many tribes, who share the general denomination of a nation; every individual man seems to be independent and *sui juris*.[16]

Disputes were therefore settled through the mediation of kinsmen within closely-related communities, and by negotiations, under threat of revenge if necessary, between more distantly-related communities. Father Louis Hennepin remarked that

> [t]heir old men, who are wise and prudent, watch over the public. If one complains that some person has robb'd him, they carefully inform themselves who it is that committed the theft. If they can't find him out, or if he is not able to make restitution, provided they can be satisfied of the truth of the fact, they repair the loss, by giving some present to the injured Party, to his content.[17]

English society was not altogether different from this until the consolidation of central administration following the Norman conquest.[18] Only two centuries before Jamestown, the maintenance of order in Britain still largely depended on the principle of joint liability, which can be highly effective in a rural, sedentary and tribal (that is, kinship-based) society, and upon the negotiation of settlements, which can be unavoidable in a society lacking central power. Norman coroners held the entire village responsible for a breach of the peace, and resolved most matters on either an inquest — little more than delegating the decision to a local committee of neighbors — or "wager of law," a contest of raising supporters on either side of a dispute. As commerce and urbanization began to produce transient, unrelated town populations, a system of frankpledge served as a kind of artificial family to maintain a basis for joint liability.

As early forms of industrialization further eroded private responsibility for public order, state power, in the form of the King's judges and jails, grew in response to the perceived threat from the transient poor, who, it was believed, could be controlled only through the fear of terrible punishments. As the number of penal laws and their cruelty increased without apparent effect, public officials also turned to "transportation" as a remedy: the poor and undesirable were simply exported to the colonies, where they would have to work or die. While welcomed by merchants and tradesmen as a necessity, the growth of coercive state power was obviously also a potential threat to freedom and property. As such, seventeenth- and eighteenth-century society was preoccupied simultaneously with the use of law to control the rabble, and the use of law to limit itself. Law was emerging as a necessary evil.

This view was exemplified in the contemptuous reaction to European laws by Adario, the Huron chief of Louis-Armand Lahontan's 1703 *Dialogue*:

> Lahontan. But in regard that the good of the Society consists in doing Justice and following these Laws, there's a necessity of

punishing the Wicked and rewarding the Good; for without that Precaution Murthers, Robberies and Defamations would spread every where, and in a Word, we should be the most miserable People upon the face of the Earth.

　　Adario. Nay, you are miserable enough already, and indeed I can't see how you can be more such. What sort of Men must the Europeans be? What species of creatures do they retain to? The Europeans, who must be forced to do Good, and have no other Prompter for the avoiding of Evil than the fear of Punishment.[19]

When the first Englishmen arrived, Indians tried to assimilate them into the indigenous legal system by making them kinsmen. Thus Powhatan declared Captain John Smith to be a chief, "that all his subjects should so esteeme us, and no man account us strangers nor Paspaheghans [enemies], but Powhatans, and that the Corne, weomen and Country, should be to us as to his own people."[20] After the seizure of Pocahontas in 1612, Powhatan refused any negotiations with the English until her marriage, two years later, to Rolfe, which temporarily restored peaceful relations. "Intermarriage had been indeed the Method proposed very often by the Indians in the Beginning," Robert Beverley recalled in 1705, "urging it frequently as a certain Rule, that the English were not their Friends, if they refused it."[21]

Although tribal leaders sometimes interceded for whites accused of killing Indians, satisfied that the act had been in revenge, the English steadfastly refused to accept payment of restitution for men killed by Indians.[22] An illustration of conflicting notions of the aims of law comes from seventeenth-century Connecticut. The murderer of a Moheagan sachem had taken refuge with the Podunks, and the Moheagans complained to the English magistrates at Hartford. The Podunks had their own grievances against the Moheagans, and a hearing was held. The Moheagans demanded ten men as restitution, but the Podunks said this was exorbitant since the killing had been in revenge for the death of the murderer's uncle, and offered instead to pay in wampum. The Moheagans admitted they could settle for six men. The English then proposed that they follow the English practice and execute the murderer, but the Podunks responded by leaving that night, explaining that the man had too many relatives. Frustrated, the English refused to intervene further.[23]

When it became a military necessity to engage the more powerful tribal confederacies as allies, however, English settlers learned to adapt to Indian diplomatic procedures, which stressed reconciliation and symbolic restitution. Thus when agents of Maryland and Virginia came to New York to negotiate an alliance with the Iroquois in 1682, the Oneida and Cayuga chiefs explained that

[t]he Evills done by our young Indians in your Country by killing
and plundering wee do not allow of; it is against our will, and are
sorry for its being rashly done by our Indians, desired that the
harm done be dugg into the ground, and do wipe off the tears and
blood; do give two belts of Peak, one for the Oneydas, and another for the Cayugas.[24]

The two colonies initially balked, then accepted as additional compensation some beaver pelts after warning that they would not be so toler-
ant in the future. Subsequent treaty conferences were no less preoccupied with reciprocal accusations and token payments, however.[25] As
long as disputes could be settled at this diplomatic level, each nation
remained free to punish — or forgive — its own people under its own
internal laws.[26]

### Mercantilism and Trade

I know of but two methods to be used with these heathen; they
are to be held by Love and Fear.[27]

It is essential to draw a connection between "mercantilism," the system of economic theory of the Europeans who colonized the Atlantic
seaboard, and the development of Indian administration. The merchant economists argued that the state could strengthen its balance of
trade by regulating internal economic conditions — above all, the price
of labor.[28] This stimulated a variety of schemes to restructure the
English (and later, American) economy by taxes or decrees, which
helped entrench the idea of law as a form of social planning. Mercantilism also promoted the idea that other societies could be influenced indirectly through trade, even to the point of creating empires through economic inducements rather than war.[29] Correspondingly, it was taken
as axiomatic that trade breaks down the barriers of nationality and
religion, leading to peace as well as prosperity.[30]

Rationalism, utilitarianism, and the legal order went hand in hand.
"Obedience to Discipline and the Laws"[31] was essential to a world in
which commerce could flourish unhindered by prejudice or war. An
Elizabethan merchant neatly summed up the aspirations of the age:

When marchants trade proceedes in peace.
And labours prosper well:
Then common weales in wealth increase.
As now good proofe can tell.[32]

Laws should therefore, as far as possible, be "uniform, equable, and
universal," and designed "to conform to the system of our commerce,

and not destructive of it."[33] A diversity of legal regimes, however "natural" in relation to different geographical and cultural circumstances, would "render property precarious"[34] and frustrate the levelling power of economic self-interest.

Colonial officials were therefore frustrated with Indians' initial lack of interest in trade, and delighted when they "beg[an] more and more to affect English fashions,"[35] which of course made them far more vulnerable economically. As early as 1620, Virginia was ordering specially-patterned beads from London for the Indian trade, and the following year brought Italian glassblowers over to the colony solely for this purpose.[36] Great care was taken that the Indians not have the opportunity to see how the beads were made, however, lest they value them the less.[37] The number of licenses was limited and prices strictly fixed to avoid "bringeing down the vallew of o[u]r Trucking stuffe amongst the Indians."[38] Trade in food was increasingly discouraged for fear that it would make the English dependent on Indians. Indeed, the Virginia Company briefly studied the possibility of deliberately destroying all the Indians' cornfields to "force them to have their dependencie uppon us, for foode & Clothinge," and so have to labor for the English for wages.[39]

Trading for English technology was also carefully restricted. Among the items deemed "dangerous" to fall into Indian hands were horses,[40] boats,[41] and firearms and ammunition.[42] Significantly, however, dispensations were made for friendly individual Indians, especially cooperative chiefs.[43] Restrictions on this branch of trade were therefore used not only to protect the peace and safety of the colonists, but as an economic incentive to attract Indians to English laws and institutions. "Bows and Arrows are grown into disuse, except only amongst their Boys," William Byrd was able to report. "Nor is it ill Policy, but on the contrary very prudent, thus to furnish the Indians with Fire-Arms, because it makes them depend entirely upon the English, not only for their Trade, but even for their subsistence."[44]

Similarly, allowing freedom of movement and providing work opportunities for Indians were often used as incentives to assimilate. Virginia permitted five or six Indians in each town provided they "doe service in killing of Deere, fishing, beatting of Corne and other workes," and issued a limited number of "Badges of Silver, Copper or Brass" to friendly tribes as safe-conducts.[45] Massachusetts Bay restricted trade to those Indians who "doe live wthin the view, & under the eye and protection, of the English," and permitted only Indian apprentices and servants to remain in town.[46] Connecticut allowed Indians to live among the settlers only "in case they are willing to submit to the ordering and govrment of the Englishe," and in Providence, Rhode

Island, only Indians "as have served with ye English" were allowed to hunt or fish near settlements.[47] Despite such restrictions, Indians did find regular employment as "domestic servants, labourers, sailors, whalers, and other fishers" throughout the colonies.[48]

"We use no other artifice to keep the Indians in our interest," William Douglass boasted in 1760, "but, by underselling the French, and giving a higher price for Indian commodities."[49] Trade was far more effective than missionaries, he maintained, although he saw merit in Christianity bringing Indians to be more "worldly," i.e., materialistic, and teaching them "good manners."[50] A New York merchant agreed: "The Principles to be laid down in the Management of our Indians, are, first, by all means to endeavour to under-sell the French; and the next is, to do Justice to the Indians in those Sales."[51] New York Governor Thomas Pownall concluded that trade was "the only real and permanent motive of their attachment to us." Happily, there was a "reciprocation of wants" between Indians, whom he viewed as chiefly hunters, and the English, who were farmers and manufacturers.[52] It thus served the "composite interest" of both peoples to maintain this division of labor through a strict division of land and regulation of trade.

## Restructuring Indian Government

> The Countrey is not so good, as the Natives are bad, whose barbarous Savagenesse needs more Cultivation then the ground it selfe.[53]

Among the stated aims of the Virginia Company, England's first official venture on American soil, was leading the Indians "to human civilization and to quiet and peaceful gov[ernmen]t."[54] The notion that the Indians' problem was their lack of proper laws was widespread. "All Nations of men have the same Natural Dignity, and we all know that very bright talents may be lodg'd under a very dark Skin," the Virginian planter William Byrd concluded. "The principal Difference between one People and another proceeds only from the[ir] Different Opportunities of Improvement."[55] The utilitarian idealism of the early settlers appears vividly in the language of a patent granted to William Clayborn by the Virginia Company in 1626, for

> an assured way and meanes, he beleveth himselfe to have invented for safe keepinge of any Indyans, wch he shall undertake to keep for guides allways ready to be ymployed, and yt he hopeth to make them serviceable for many other services for ye good of the whole Colony.[56]

The colony gave Clayborn an Indian "for his better experience and tryall of his inventions."[57]

As long as neighboring tribes retained the power to disregard English laws, economic incentives were employed to encourage assimilation on an individual basis. Thus Virginia's governor proposed in 1621 that "the best meanes bee used to draw the better disposed of the Natives to Converse with o[u]r People and labor amongst them wth Convenient reward," so they could become "fitt Instruments" of the assimilation policy.[58] The Company quickly set about recruiting a cadre of young Indians to replace the old chiefs. "If you intreate well and educate those wch are younge to succeede in the governement in yor Manners and Religion, their people will easily obey you and become in time Civill and Christian."[59] Funds were raised and an estate planted to support an "Indian college" in 1619, with the plan of training young Indians in English trades, but the tribes refused to cooperate, being "very loathe" to surrender their children.[60]

At this early stage of relatively balanced power, integration of the tribes into the English legal system frequently was achieved by treaty. Typical was the 1644 "submission" of the Narragansetts "to be ruled and governed according to the ancient and honorable lawes and customes" of England, which nonetheless provided that it not apply to disputes among Indians, for they were better "able to judge in any matter of cause in that respect" themselves.[61] The Narragansett treaty had another interesting effect: the tribe used it as a defense against the authority of any colony except Rhode Island.[62] Thus the issue became not merely a choice between English and Indian law, but between the laws of different English communities.

The attention paid to native chiefs affected their views of themselves, as well as their relations with the English. Anas Todkill complained in 1612:

> As for the coronation of Powhatan, and his presents of Bason, Ewer, Bed, Clothes, and such costly novelties; they had bin much better well spared, then so ill spent: for we had his favour much better onlie for a poore peece of Copper, till this stately kinde of soliciting made him so much overvalue himselfe, that he respected us as much as nothing at all.[63]

Powhatan soon used his monopoly of English trinkets to lord over his people, "to whom he flings some beads & even honors a few by personally presenting them with beads calling their names."[64] He also tried to involve the English in terrorizing his enemies, which they were only too willing to do.

The growing English military and economic presence brought Indian leaders "to find by experience," as Governor Pownall viewed it, "the necessity of a civil union of power and action," and thus to imitate English state structures.[65] For the English interest, he argued, it was "absolutely necessary" to co-opt this process along the lines followed by the French:

> Observing the want of subordination among the Indians; the French made a number of sachems, to whom they give medals, and appoint them to preside as chiefs, leaders, counsellors, speakers, &c.: some over eight, some over ten villages, and so one as their influence extends: being easily, by presents and money, possessed of these medal-chiefs; they thus easily acquire a more uniform and stable management of their Indians, than the Indians even know amongst themselves.[66]

Extending English laws to Indian lands would complete the transformation, for "while we are undertaking the protection of the Indian country and hunting grounds, we are actually becoming possessed of the command of the country."[67]

From a very early date, certainly preceding the establishment of Indian "reservations" or "plantations" as such, the English took every opportunity to intervene in the selection of tribal leaders. At first, it was a matter of encouraging the election of the most cooperative candidates. Thus we find, in the Massachusetts court records, this account from 1654:

> Whereas Showanan, sagamor of Nashaway, is lately dead, & an other is now suddainly to be chosen in his roome, they being a great people, who have submitted to this jurisdiction, this Court doth order, that Mr Increase Nowell & Mr Eliott be sent unto them to direct them in their choyce, their eyes being uppon 2 or 3 which are of the bloud, one whereof is a very debaust, drunken fellow, & no friend of the English; another of them is very hopefull to learne the things of Christ; if therefore, these gent. may, by way of persuasion or counsell, not by compulsion, prvayle wth them for the choyce of such a one as may be most fitt, it would be a good service to the country.[68]

Indians could not have been ignorant of the fact that their choices would affect their relationship with the English, and as they became more dependent on English goods and protection, all pretense of an independent election disappeared. Colonial officials simply issued letters of authority to whomever they pleased.

Connecticut commissioned a "Governor" and "Assistants" for the Pequots, for example, authorizing them to appoint a constable, draw up laws and levy taxes, and set up a committee of Englishmen "to assist by Advice" — while warning at least one traditional chief not to "meddle" with this arrangement.[69] Once recognized by the colony, chiefs were held personally responsible for any disputes, and punished for unreported dealings with other tribes.[70] Their lands were often placed under the supervision of English "trustees" with power of attorney.[71] This forerunner of today's reservation system may be distinguished from the institution of "praying towns," which were more structured experiments in creating model societies around Christian missions and schools.[72] In seventeenth-century terms they were "tributaries,"[73] or provinces, of colonial governments, anticipating the "domestic dependent nation" characterization which the U.S. Supreme Court would bestow in 1831 on tribes brought under United States influence by treaty.[74]

## Conforming to Law

> [T]he law is undeniable that the indian may haue the same distribusion of Justice with our selues: ther is as I humbly conseiue not the same argument as amongst the negroes for the light of the gospell is a begineing to appeare amongst them — that is the indians.[75]

Early treaties usually called on Indians to conduct themselves "according to the Laws of this Government," or to submit to "punishment according to Law."[76] Colonial courts accordingly asserted jurisdiction over a wide variety of controversies involving Indian defendants,[77] including capital offenses[78] as well as debts and contracts.[79] Legislation likewise prescribed equal punishment for whites and Indians in most things,[80] and Connecticut even provided for a court interpreter.[81] The result was not perfect equality in outcome, however. As Indians lacked the money to pay restitution or costs, they might be imprisoned as debtors or sold for relatively minor offenses.[82]

To the extent that Indians accepted courts as the arbiter of justice, they placed themselves under English laws. It was thus an essential point of seventeenth-century policy to persuade Indians to file suits at law, rather than demand diplomatic negotiations, when any conflict arose with whites. Both trespass[83] and personal injury[84] suits were common. New York provided by 1675 that "in all Cases the Magistrates through the whole Government are required to do Justice to the Indyans as well as Christian,"[85] and to the same end Pennsylvania directed magistrates "to Demeane themselves without a just Cause of Offence to the Indians."[86] The triumph of these efforts appears in the extent to which Indians increasingly used colonial courts against one another, even over the ownership of land, thus rebuilding their own internal social relations upon the English framework.[87]

Their relative powerlessness nonetheless compelled Englishmen to bend as well, even in questions with Christian foundations. The rule of *Calvin's Case*[88] was that the common law instantly filled the vacuum upon the annexation of a pagan country. Of course, the practical effect of this transposition of rules was to restructure local land tenure and commercial law along English lines, making land a commodity to be traded under English forms, and subjecting the local population to English forms of contract. Early settlers realized that this automatic transposition of English law to Indians would not only be viewed as unjust by Indians, but could trigger hostilities as well. They adopted instead a policy of gradualism which embodied two elements: the temporary establishment of a separate legal regime for Indians, and the use of example and teaching to bring Indians into line with English institutions.

Examples can be found of town magistrates ordering speedier trials because Indian litigants were reluctant to give up their hunting for too long, and justified because they were "ignorant of ye law."[89] Ignorance of the law was sometimes pleaded by Indians as a defense, with varying degrees of success, as for example when several Schuykill Indians prosecuted for drunkenness hoped the English would "pardon it and not putt them in the stocks, for they knew no better, and the Christians did sell them the Liquor."[90] The death sentence of Tom Indian for rape was commuted to transportation for ten years on the grounds of ignorance.[91] And when Quinapintt broke Newport jail and fled home to Narragansett, the Rhode Island Assembly,

> having a respect unto, or a due sence of the Indians ignorance of the English lawes, which untill they shall be more acquainted with, may be an occasion of some extravagancies or misdoeings in regard of the differing manners and customes of the English and them. That therefore it is thought good to mitigate some of the rigor that might be used against Quinapintt, in hopes of his future reformation and good behaviour.[92]

Virginia's first code of laws, adopted in 1619, provided that while the theft of an Englishman's canoe would be deemed a felony punishable by death, theft of an Indian's canoe would require the payment of "valuable restitution,"[93] which conformed more closely with the Indians' own sense of justice. Another calculated exemption from standard legal practice was the injunction against "trusting Indians" — that is, against allowing Indians to incur debts. English creditors were sometimes deprived of any remedy, or even fined for this practice, on the grounds that it was "extremely prejudiciall to the English and allmost destructive to the Indians."[94] A modern parallel can be found in the rule that contracts involving Indian lands or funds must be approved by the Secretary of the Interior, or else they are voidable.[95]

In some colonies, special courts or commissions were initially established to hear any disputes among Indians, or involving Indians and whites, since the Indians "could not understand the way of our proceedings."[96] Virginia sometimes arranged for chiefs to sit as associates with English judges in order to help negotiate restitution.[97]  Massachusetts Bay authorized sachems to try minor cases under the supervision of special sittings of the English courts, which were directed to help the Indians "understand o[ur] most usefull Lawes, & those principles of justice & equitie whereuppon they are grounded."[98] Thus their aim was not only to resolve disputes, but also to transform the Indians' conception of lawfulness. Consistent with this, it was often provided that English law would apply to crimes among the Indians themselves only if the offender was not first punished by his own people.[99] The same approach was taken by Congress in the Major Crimes Act two centuries later.[100]

A more thorny problem was posed by the use of Indian witnesses at trial. Traditional English thinking viewed pagans as incapable of giving evidence, since only the fear of God could be relied upon to ensure truthful testimony. Efforts to suppress the liquor trade would have been defeated, however, if evidence provided by Indians was excluded, since it was usually the only evidence available. The governor of Pennsylvania, in remarks to the assembly, reasoned that "tho' they were not under the same Conscientious Obligation, as Christians are, to speak the Truth, yet they might be obliged to do it through the Terrour of some punishment."[101] Rhode Island had initially forbidden the use of Indian witnesses, but soon relented and provided that they might testify under severe penalties for perjury.[102]

The applicability of English law to the Indians frequently was questioned. In a Rhode Island land dispute, for instance, the white defendant pleaded adverse possession against the Indian landowners. He prevailed on appeal, the provincial assembly reasoning that

> though it may be granted, that it might not be intended, nor once thought on, when the several statutes of limitations were first made, that they should extend to Indian sachems' land; yet, after the Indian sachems had subjected themselves and their lands to the crown of England, to be protected, ruled and governed by the English laws then undeniably those statutes must extend both to the Indian sachems and their lands also.[103]

As the seaboard tribes' military and economic power waned, however, colonial judges relied more on the formalities of law than on considerations of what would be considered just by the Indians.[104]

The official policy of legal integration was not always popular with ordinary settlers, who harbored less idealistic sentiments regarding Indians. When John Elkin and two companions were prosecuted for the shooting of a Yoacomoco chief in 1642, the Maryland jury returned a verdict of not guilty,

> explaining themselves that they delivered that verdict because they understood the last not to have been committed agst his Lo[rdshi]ps peace or the kings, because the party was a pagan, & because they had no president in the neighbour colony of virginea, to make such facts murther.[105]

The governor strictly advised them that "those Indians were in the peace of the king & his Lo[rdshi]p & that they ought not to take notice of what other colonies did, but of the Law of England." On further reflection, the jury proposed that Elkin be acquitted for self-defense. The jurymen were eventually attainted, and one was fined for having "in an insolent manner upbraided & reproached the whole Court in these or the like words, viz., that 'if an Englishman had been killed by the Indians there would not have beene so much words made of it' or to the effect."[106]

While the settlers restrained themselves from imposing English law on Indians generally, they were strict in requiring Indians to respect English law when visiting English settlements, even to the extent of punishing Indians who happened to "labor or play" on the Sabbath within town limits.[107] This town-countryside distinction for jurisdictional purposes, which presaged the nineteenth-century legal notion of "Indian country,"[108] was reinforced by orders excluding Indians from living in or passing through English settlements,[109] by the subsequent establishment of reservations, and finally by the establishment of an Indian frontier along the height of the Appalachian Mountains.[110]

The French observed the English settlers' efforts to incorporate the Indians into colonial legal systems with amusement and satisfaction. Thus de Villebon, commander of Acadia, wrote home in 1694 that all the tribes of New England would soon join France, so enraged were they with the Bostonians' trial and hanging of an Indian who killed another in a drunken quarrel.[111] At the same time, de Villebon was quick to demand the recall of a French missionary who, offended by the tribal-law divorce and remarriage of one of his converts, beat the man nearly to death.[112] When the Indian tribes of New France and Acadia later fell under English control, they were appalled at demands that they "submit" to the laws of a foreign power — demands never made by their former allies.[113]

**Land Tenure and the Family**

> We have only one custom among us, and that is well known to all;
> this river, and all that is in it are mine.[114]

When the first English arrived they found well-defined town territories, each consisting of a patchwork of active and fallow fields, separated from one another by stretches of forest.[115] The aboriginal Atlantic seaboard economy was seasonal, with the summer planting seasons spent in the towns and winter hunting conducted from scattered and isolated cabins in the mountains.[116] Captain John Smith observed that "each household knoweth their owne lands and gardens, and most live of their owne labours."[117] Douglass agreed that tribal territories had "natural boundaries"[118] and, while he tried to argue that Indians lacked any genuine rights of possession or use, conceded that they were "very jealous of their hunting and fishing grounds or properties."[119] Roger Williams reckoned that "the natives are very exact and punctual with the bounds of their lands, belonging to this or that prince or people, even to a river, brook, &c."[120]

Although as pagans Indians did not, by traditional English principles, have any title to land that could be recognized by the common law, it was impossible to ignore their claims until European power had far exceeded the limits of Indian resistance. Settlers accordingly adapted English practices to Indian ones, and usually tried to satisfy all Indian interests before asserting a complete and exclusive title.[121] Ironically, respect for Indian title was also dictated by the necessity of maintaining respect for property generally. Counsel for the Indians in a 1767 New York land dispute argued that

> [u]pon the first Discovery of this Country, and at the Time of Constituting this Province, that particular Spot of Earth, about which the present Dispute is Conversant belonged to the Tribe of Wappinger. It was then by Prime-Occupancy (if no Other way) their undeniable Right, and Property. And methinks it must be granted that the Right and Property being once vested in them, must stil remain in them unless there has been a legal alteration of the Same.
>
> This, I believe, will hardly be denied; for 'tis a well known maxim in Law, "That Property is never to be violated." This is what the Law abhors.[122]

After the Revolution, Euro-Americans again found it necessary to recognize Indian title as the foundation for establishing their own.[123]

The earliest land negotiations seem simply to have accorded Englishmen the right to settle among the Indians temporarily, on otherwise uncultivated ground.[124] Even at a later date, after the introduction of formal deeds, tribes frequently expressly reserved their planting, hunting and fishing rights.[125] Deeds, moreover, were often followed some years later by new ones "confirming" or "explaining" the originals.[126] Possession was thus a matter of continual renegotiation and, often, fresh compensation. The Indians' notion of these transactions is reflected in a Rhode Island deed in which the Indian grantors pledge not to sell the same parcel to anyone except the same grantee.[127] Paper was nevertheless useful as a bargaining point; thus we find a settler seeking confirmation deeds from the Indians because his originals "grow ould and torne," or anxiously pleading for confirmation of his plot by the town "or Elce it may be Taken away by ye Indians they haveing ye Books."[128]

The most frustrating problem for the English was ascertaining who had the right to sell. Initially they assumed that this power rested with the "kings" or chiefs, but this simply led to disputes with other Indians. Efforts were later made to include as many of the "cheefe owners" as possible in the sale, including neighboring chiefs, or to obtain the consent of the whole tribe at an assembly called for that purpose.[129] Although the right of individuals to compensation for the sale of their own gardens or houses was recognized,[130] individual sales might be set aside for failure to show the consent of the chief.[131] Then there were disputes over which chief was responsible for a particular tract, often resulting in a "cleanup" deed covering every possible remaining claimant.[132] In one poignant case, the Massachusetts council found the tribes so "litigious and doubtfull amongst themselves" that it ordered them to work out the question of ownership among themselves.[133]

The need for a regularization of practice was obvious, but difficult to satisfy as long as the tribes held title under their own laws. Granting land back to the tribes under English law was the solution ultimately adopted, because it identified the Indian owners and, in some cases, appointed English trustees with the power to lease or sell.[134] Land could then pass by sale or inheritance entirely within English forms and rules. But this also completely restructured the tribal economy by individualizing the control of land, often in leaders appointed by the English. The Indian farm economy thus became simultaneously capitalistic and aristocratic.

A particularly tragic case of this involved Thomas Ninigret, heir to that Ninigret who negotiated with Roger Williams over the purchase of Rhode Island a century earlier. "Having been unhappily engaged in several law suits," he persuaded the assembly to release him from restrictions on the alienation of reserved lands. A few years later, however, several Narragansetts complained that he was selling their homes out from under them, with the result that many "must either starve, or become a town charge." A committee of inquiry confirmed that, by custom, most of the tribes' lands had been "set off to particular persons or families." Thomas' debts, it was therefore proposed, should be paid from his personal estate alone. But this proved to be insufficient, so the tribal council asked permission to negotiate a sale of the river frontage, upon which "all the said tribe depend for their fishing."[135]

However legitimate the early English purchases may have been, once settlers had obtained an agricultural foothold, they triggered a series of ecological changes which quickly devalued the remainder of the tribes' lands. English livestock, particularly their near-wild hogs which "run where they list, and find their own Support in the Woods," destroyed unprotected Indian fields.[136] Indian farmers were sometimes prosecuted for killing rampaging animals, and other times for not fencing their fields.[137] English hunting, much of it for sport,[138] took such a toll on wildlife in some provinces that quotas for deer had to be imposed before 1700.[139] "The English have taken away great part of their Country, and consequently made every thing less plenty among them," Robert Beverley mused, and at the same time "multiply'd their Wants, and put them upon desiring a thousand things, they never dreamt of before."[140] The result was a growing load of Indian debt, mostly financed through the mortgage or sale of their remaining land.[141]

New York's Governor Pownall shrewdly observed that the French, whose interest was chiefly trade, respected the indigenous tenure system and "the Indians did easily and readily admit them to a local landed possession: a grant, which rightly acquired and applied, they are always ready to make; as none of the rights or interests of themselves are hurt by it."[142] The English, however, insisted on obtaining exclusive rights to land, something which the Indians realized was inherently adverse to their survival. "This," Pownall went so far as to claim, "is the sole ground of the loss and alienation of the Indians from the English interest."[143]

Aboriginally, women controlled farmland and agriculture. There are references in early deeds to the need for approval by the Indian grantor's sisters, for example, or to the right of an Englishman to Indian land through his marriage to an Indian woman.[144] The European restructuring of land tenure, as well as the growth of the fur trade as a source of Indian income, necessarily undercut the foundations of women's status. It is striking, in view of the great number of "Indian Queenes" and "Squaw sachems" encountered in seventeenth-century English records, that scarcely any women later appear as litigants or as officers of Indian town governments. Colonial officials dealt almost exclusively with the men, enhancing their access to wealth and political influence.

Many early English writers deplored what they perceived as the exploitation of Indian women by Indian men. The women, explained Purchas' *Pilgrimes* in 1606, "doe all their druggerie."[145]

> Their husbands hold them in great slavery, yet never knowing any other, it is the lesse grievous to them. They say, Englishman much foole, for spoiling good working creatures, meaning women: And when they see any of our English women sewing with their needles, or working coifes, or such things, they will cry out, Lazie squaes![146]

Other observers disputed this. While Indian women "have generally the laborious part of the oeconomy," Burke wrote, "yet they are far from being the slaves they appear, and are not at all subject to the great subordination in which they are placed in countries where they seem to be more respected."[147] Englishmen simply could not come to grips intellectually with this situation, resulting in amusing inconsistencies in their efforts to describe the status of women in Indian society. After repeating the complaint that Indian women "do all their work," for instance, a seventeenth-century minister admitted they "also keep all the money."[148]

While there is little direct evidence of the impact of these differences on the internal organization of the Indian communities under English jurisdiction, there can be little doubt that granting land to men, and administering inheritance under patrilineal rules familiar to Englishmen, would tend to disrupt the indigenous matrilineal clan system. When Congress was debating the proposed allotment of Indian lands nearly two centuries later, there was explicit recognition of this fact. Noting that "the Indian laws cut off the male members of the family entirely from the inheritance," an argument was made for individualized patrilineal inheritance:

> [T]he dissolution of the Indian family relationship is the dissolution of all tribal relationships; it is the abrogation of the tribal institution. As long as that tribal institution continues it will hold to what it is based upon, and that is the commune in all that relates to land.[149]

### The Exchange

> I am an Indian, and don't pretend to be exact in my Language: But I hope the Plainness of my Dress, will give him the kinder Impressions of my Honesty.[150]

Why should the aristocratic Virginia planter, Robert Beverley, introduce himself to his readers in these words? Or the Bostonian rebels, on their way to dump the King's tea, dress themselves in buckskins?[151] Over the course of nearly two centuries of Indian administration, the colonists had not only learned a great deal about social engineering, but had come to see themselves and their own society in an entirely new light. Their relationship with the mother country was, they realized, not altogether different from the Indians' "dependency" on themselves. They were the objects of a scheme of planned social and economic evolution, conceived for the benefit of others. Indeed, the perspicacious Pownall, in his last comments on the American situation before the war, was to argue that, until the colonies harmonized their interests with those of England, they "cannot be trusted with their own internal will" but must ever remain "under pupillage."[152]

The collision of Europe and North America must be understood in the context of the political developments which were taking place in the seventeenth and eighteenth centuries on both continents. Europe was dominated by absolutist states, recently fragmented from a regional theocratic empire, which were beginning to make grudging concessions to the forces of popular resistance and a rapidly-evolving merchant class. It was a centralized political order breaking down. North America was inhabited by a great diversity of segmentary societies, extremely jealous of their independence. Under the growing threats of invasion and war, both internal and external, however, these societies were beginning to reform their loosely-organized old leagues, originally developed for peaceful relations and trade, into defensive, statelike coalitions. Indigenous America was therefore a highly decentralized political order coalescing into states. Each civilization was approaching the other, and was thus able to discover some of its own aspirations and ideals reflected in the other's "genius." Each supplied the other with necessary concepts for its future survival: in the simplest terms, democracy and authority.

At the level of law, the reciprocal influences of tribal and European thought were equally pervasive, but perhaps less obvious. Euro-American jurisprudence naturally was infected with the general spirit of popular democracy which inspired the United States' new institutions. As Perry Miller has observed,[153] early efforts to bring the legal process within the grasp of ordinary citizens, such as the movement for codification, were uniquely American reactions to the aristocratic inheritance of the common law. Similarly, but nearly a century later, the Indian tribal courts, established as part of the reservation administrative system, gradually replaced the indigenous tradition of particularism in the resolution of disputes.[154] This was done under the idea of legal universality or generality — that is, that there ought to be general rules applicable equally to everyone.[155] It was for this same preoccupation with "the sacredness of law, which makes society independent of individual caprice," that even India's great critic of the West, Rabindranath Tagore, praised the British raj.[156]

More fundamentally, however, the political struggle between Europeans and indigenous Americans left both civilizations with an entirely novel, powerful, and potentially dangerous jurisprudential axiom, which Morton Horwitz refers to as "instrumentalism."[157] This is the idea that the ultimate aim and justification of law reside in its ability to plan human conduct and transform society. Law here is no longer a ritual for the reconciliation of disputes, but the operating manual for a progressive society. Judges are no longer peacemakers, but social planners; legal argument is no longer to concern itself with abstract logic, but rather with considerations of economic efficiency. Essential to this view, of course, is the psychological assumption that human behavior can be modified under a rational regime of rewards and punishments, as well as the political assumption that legislatures and judges can properly be entrusted with this responsibility.

How did instrumentalism arise? The more obvious answer was its association with rationalism in eighteenth-century economic thought[158] and the rise of utilitarianism in early nineteenth-century liberal social theory.[159] Somewhat less obvious was the effect on European thought of a great deal of practical experience in trying to administer and transform, culturally and economically, the ever-growing number of encircled Indian communities in the New World. Long before instrumentalism (or utilitarianism) emerged as an acceptable basis for the governance of European societies, Euro-Americans were experimenting with the manipulation of Indian societies, trying to recreate in miniature their own ideal of social order. At the same time, tribes falling within the reach of European empires quickly recognized the facility of a centralized legal order for mobilizing power, and thus rigidified their own institutions. Both civilizations moved toward a middle ground of more democratic European states and more statelike indigenous societies, each more instrumentalist than its predecessor.

It should perhaps also be borne in mind that controlling the white population of the colonies was often as challenging a task as trying to administer the Indians. As one early Euro-American writer admitted, "colonies have an incidental good effect, they drain from the mother-country the disaffected and the vicious" as well as the surplus poor,[160] hence the novel and experimental character of many of the white settlements' own forms of government.[161] The entire colonial project was suffused with a sense of freedom to pick and choose among the Old

World's traditions while inventing new ones. Thus, for example, the leadership of Massachusetts Bay appointed a committee in 1651 to "p[er]use" Gerard de Malyne's great treatise on commercial law, *Lex Mercatoria*, "& to extract from thence such lawes as might be suteable for o[ur] use in this common wealth."[162] The entire colonial project was accompanied by a rash of publications advocating social engineering.

"It would be a very strange Thing," wrote a New York merchant in 1751, "if six Nations of ignorant Savages should be capable of forming a Scheme for such an Union, and be able to execute it in such a Manner, as that it has subsisted Ages, and appears indissoluble; and yet that a like Union should be impracticable for ten or a Dozen English Colonies."[163] Indeed, in 1744 during treaty negotiations with representatives of Virginia and Maryland, an Iroquois spokesman, Canassatego, admonished the colonies in these terms:

> We have one Thing further to say, and that is, We heartily recommend Union and a good Agreement between you our Brethren. Never disagree, but preserve a strict Friendship for one another, and thereby you, as well as we, will become the stronger.
>
> Our wise Forefathers established Union and Amity between the Five Nations; this has made us formidable; this has given us great Weight and Authority with our neighbouring Nations.
>
> We are a powerful Confederacy; and, by your observing the same Methods our wise Forefathers have taken, you will acquire fresh Strength and Power; therefore whatever befalls you, never fall out one with another.[164]

These were fateful words. In the summer of 1775, at Albany, on the eve of the Declaration of Independence, representatives of the newly-formed General Congress of the Twelve United Colonies, soon to become the United States, recalled Canassatego's advice and told the Iroquois they had resolved to follow it.[165] Barely twenty years later, the Americans had won the war against Britain and severely divided the Iroquois' own confederacy.[166]

The American republic that emerged proudly claimed the status of "a new order for the ages" — a new social order that had invented itself, rationally and purposefully. The audacity of the myth of American autogenesis, from an Old World perspective, is evidence of the great intellectual distance Euro-Americans already had travelled, and of the significance of the different experiences of European and Euro-American life. For the next century, Europe studied white America's emerging institutions and mores with the same curiosity as it had formerly tried to analyze the social and political world of indigenous Americans.

## The Formalities of Power

> The conduct of the United States Americans towards the natives
> was inspired by the most chaste affection for legal formalities.
> . . . It is impossible to destroy men with more respect for the
> laws of humanity.[167]

From the start, Indian policy was preoccupied with appearances. As
the Restoration economist Charles Davenant maintained, "Opinion is
the principal Support of Power, and States are seldom any longer
Strong or Wise, than while they are thought so by their
Neighbours."[168] William Byrd observed of Penn's colonists, that "tho
they paid but a Trifle" for Indians' lands, it "has procured them the
Credit of being more righteous than their Neighbours," and kept the
loyalty of the tribes.[169] Because it was so successful, this approach has
been followed ever since.

The new American government turned to the West with the same
tools that had prevailed over Indian resistance in the East. The three
legs of federal constitutional authority over Indian affairs — the commerce clause, the treaty power, and the property clause — reflect the
progression of trade (economic dependence), diplomacy (submission to
"protection"), and the reservation system (socioeconomic reorganization) that was followed by the colonies. The rhetoric of "sovereignty"
or "self-determination," which has been popular in national policy debates since the 1960s, does not negate the fact that tribal self-government was intended, in the words of its twentieth-century architect,
Commissioner of Indian Affairs John Collier, to give Indians "business
and civic experience" so that they would be prepared for "real
assimilation."[170]

Nor does it reverse the extent to which this aim has already been
achieved, and this is reflected in the great similarity of law and institutions between reservations and their white neighbors. Even the language of the Indian movement for "sovereignty" models itself on European political theory.[171] While preserving the appearance of distinct
territorial governments, contemporary Indian tribes are in danger of
fading away into irrelevance, offering less and less of a genuine alternative for their own citizens. Maintaining separate jurisdictions pre-
serves the appearance of respect for indigenous law, and for the right of
individuals to assimilate voluntarily if they choose. But when the most
remarkable difference between the reservation and neighboring communities is the operation of a high-stakes bingo hall or the absence of a
tax on cigarettes, the image of the seventeenth-century "praying

town" is difficult to dispel, except that there are now new gods to study and serve.

From Indians, and the experience of struggling to transform Indian society, English colonists came to a better awareness of their own oppression. As they have become more deeply embedded in Euro-American society, however, Indians appear to have grown less aware of their oppression, confusing institutions of assimilation with the exercise of independence. In part, this demonstrates the power of the illusion created by legal formalities; in part, also, the power of material self-interest, which manifests itself today in a white-collar version of the "Indian trade." The patterns of interaction established in the seventeenth century have not changed materially, nor has the ultimate aim of Indian policy — to "cultivate" the savage and make him "useful to the country." We simply have allowed ourselves to believe, through historical myopia, that the existence of separate jurisdictions, respect for treaties, and a system of protective laws are not inherently assimilative.


### Looking Ahead


> Well, world. What's to be done?
> We just wait and see
> what will happen next.[172]

The power of history lies in its revealing the natural consequences of complex human events which, had they not occurred before, would almost certainly be unforeseeable, if not inconceivable. The collective memory of a society, like the memory of an individual, becomes more useful with age. We live in an era of increasing choices and declining understanding, however, in which youth and novelty are preferred. Historical myopia is embraced out of fear of being held back, in our forward plunge, by the past.

It is, of course, impossible to redress fully the wrongs of the past. Those who were most guilty are now beyond the jurisdiction of any court, and those who suffered the most are no longer in a position to enjoy compensation. Without denying the moral satisfaction which may come from confession and repayment on the behalf of one's ancestors, the best justice that we contemporaries can do in such cases is to avoid repeating them. Future generations should not need to make the same apologies. History is therefore unavoidable, not as an assignment of rights or claims, but as the map of the minefields ahead.

Doing justice to the American Indian past means, above all, freeing ourselves from it and making new choices. Truncating the history of

Indian policy so that it appears to "begin" with the first Indian Trade and Intercourse Act in 1790 conveniently deprives us of the knowledge that we are repeating an experiment already once tried. This may flatter our desire for novelty, but it creates a dangerous illusion of progress.

Is change possible after all this? Would Indian leaders in the seventeenth century have behaved differently had they known what we know now? Would it have done them any good? Social and economic conditions may determine the universe of political options, but within that universe there remain choices. In the long run of human existence, perhaps, it will all end the same. In the short term of human lifetimes, however, such choices can either cause or avoid a powerful amount of suffering.

Two societies which understand "justice" in fundamentally different terms can never fully reconcile their grievances. In this respect, the historical convergence of political and legal ideals among indigenous and immigrant Americans may be viewed as a blessing. The transformation of indigenous civilization which began four centuries ago has succeeded too well. It will ensure that twentieth-century tribes probably will succeed in achieving their twentieth-century conception of justice, which is the sharing of power and wealth among groups within the framework, fabric and ethos of the contemporary American state, but they will not do so as fundamentally *different* groups. Whether this is perceived as justice by Indians of the twenty-first century will depend upon their conception of history.

## NOTES

[1] From a speech by Gachradadow, a Cayuga chief, at the Treaty of Lancaster in 1744. Carl Van Doren, ed., *Indian Treaties Printed by Benjamin Franklin, 1736-1762* (Philadelphia: Pennsylvania Historical Society, 1938), p. 63.

[2] Russel L. Barsh, "Is There Any Indian 'Law' Left? A Review of the Supreme Court's 1982 Term," *Washington Law Review* 59: 4 (September 1984): 863-892; William C. Canby, Jr., "The Status of Indian Tribes in American Law Today," *Washington Law Review* 62: 1 (January 1987): 1-22.

[3] See, e.g., Vine Deloria, Jr., and Clifford M. Lytle, *American Indians, American Justice* (Austin, TX: University of Texas Press, 1983); Wilcomb E. Washburn, *Red Man's Land/White Man's Law: A Study of the Past and Present Status of the American Indian* (New York: Charles Scribner's, 1971).

[4] Bruce E. Johansen, *Forgotten Founders: Benjamin Franklin, the Iroquois, and the Rationale for the American Revolution* (Ipswich, MA: Gambit, 1982).

[5]Which, although attributed to the Six Nations by some authors, had British roots as well. Russel L. Barsh and James Y. Henderson, *The Road: Indian Tribes and Political Liberty* (Berkeley, CA: University of California Press, 1980), pp. 4-5.

[6]The role of women in Indian political culture was conveniently omitted from Europe's borrowings. See, generally, Paula Gunn Allen, *The Sacred Hoop: Recovering the Feminine in American Indian Traditions* (Boston: Beacon Press, 1986), pp. 30-42.

[7]The impact of Islamic thought may actually have been less revolutionary. After all, Islamic scholars had been working from translations of Greek and Latin classics, a shared heritage with Europe, and Islam itself shares historical and philosophical roots with Christianity.

[8]Rennard Strickland, *Fire and the Spirits: Cherokee Law from Clan to Court* (Norman, OK: University of Oklahoma Press, 1975); John P. Reid, *A Law of Blood: The Primitive Law of the Cherokee Nation* (New York: New York University Press, 1970); Anthony F. C. Wallace, *The Death and Rebirth of the Seneca* (New York: Random House, 1969); Russel L. Barsh, "The Nature and Spirit of North American Political Systems," *American Indian Quarterly* 10: 3 (Summer 1986): 181-198.

[9]Henry Spelman, the cabin boy Captain Smith left as a "present" with Powhatan. Edward Arber, ed., *Travels and Works of Captain John Smith, President of Virginia, and Admiral of New-England, 1580-1631* (New York: Burt Franklin, 1965), p. 110.

[10]Arber, ibid., pp. 26, 79. Also see Clayton C. Hall, ed., *Narratives of Early Maryland, 1633-1684* (New York: Charles Scribner's, 1910), p. 365; Thomas Lechford, *Plain Dealing: or, Newes from New-England* (London: Nathaniel Butler, 1642), p. 49: "They are governed by an absolute tyrannie."

[11]Arber, op. cit. note 9, p. 113.

[12]Edmund Burke, *An Account of the European Settlements in America*, 3rd ed. (London: Dodsley, 1760), p. 175. Also William Knox, writing in 1763: "They are a free People, and jealous of their Liberty." Thomas C. Barrow, "A Project for Imperial Reform: 'Hints Respecting the Settlement for our American Provinces,' " *William & Mary Quarterly* (3d ser.) 24: 1 (January 1967): 108-126 at 113.

[13]Burke, ibid., p. 176. Early explorers described severe initiation ceremonies designed to "release Youth from all their Childish impressions, and from that strong Partiality to persons and things, which is contracted before Reason comes to take place." Robert Beverley, *The History and Present State of Virginia* (Chapel Hill, NC: University of North Carolina Press, 1947: repr. of 1705 ed.), p. 209.

[14]Burke, op. cit. note 12, pp. 181-182.

[15]Marc Lescarbot, trans. P. Erondelle (1609), *Nova Francia: A Description of Acadia, 1606* (New York: Harper Brothers, 1928), p. 264.

[16]William Douglass, *A Summary, Historical and Political, of the First Planting, Progressive Improvements, and Present State of the British Settlements in*

*North America* (London: Dodsley, 1760), p. 160. Likewise, Cadwallader Colden, *The History of the Five Indian Nations Depending on the Province of New York in America* (Ithaca, NY: Cornell University Press, 1958: repr. of 1727 and 1747 eds.), p. xx: "Each Nation is an absolute Republick by it self, govern'd in all Publick Affairs of War and Peace by the Sachems or Old Men, whose Authority and Power is gain'd by and consists wholly in the Opinion the rest of the Nation have of their Wisdom and Integrity. They never execute their Resolutions by Compulsion or Force upon any of their People. Honour and Esteem are their Principal Rewards, as Shame & being Despised are their Punishments."

[17]Louis Hennepin, *A Discovery of a Vast Country in America* (Toronto: Coe Publishing Co., 1974: repr. of 1698 ed.), p. 513.

[18]See, for example, Tacitus' assessments of the Britons and Germans in his *Agricola*, chapter 12, and *Germania*, chapter 11. The social character of medieval English law is discussed in greater detail in Russel L. Barsh and J. Youngblood Henderson, "Tribal Courts, the Model Code, and the Police Idea in American Indian Policy," *Law and Contemporary Problems* 40: 1 (Winter 1976): 25-60.

[19]Louis-Armand Lahontan, *New Voyages to North-America* (London: H. Boxwicke, 1703), vol. 2, p. 123.

[20]Arber, op. cit. note 9, pp. 25-26.

[21]Beverley, op. cit. note 13, p. 38. William Byrd shared his opinion, adding that: "A sprightly Lover is the most prevailing Missionary that can be sent amongst these, or any other Infidels." William K. Boyd, ed., *William Byrd's Histories of the Dividing Line betwixt Virginia and North Carolina* (New York: Dover, 1967), p. 3.

[22]Henry R. McIlwaine, ed., *Minutes of the Council and General Court of Colonial Virginia* (Richmond, VA: Virginia State Library, 1924), pp. 478, 483; Susie Ames, ed., *County Court Records of Accomack-Northampton, Virginia, 1632-1640* (Washington, D.C.: American Historical Association, 1954), pp. 57-58.

[23]J. Hammond Trumbull and Charles J. Hoadley, eds., *The Public Records of the Colony of Connecticut* (Hartford, CT: Brown & Parsons, 1850-1876), pp. 302-306.

[24]John R. Brodhead, ed., *Documents Relative to the Colonial History of the State of New York* (Albany, NY: Weed, Parsons, 1853), vol. 3, pp. 321-324.

[25]See Van Doren, op. cit. note 1, *passim*; Wilbur R. Jacobs, *Wilderness Politics and Indian Gifts: The Northern Colonial Frontier, 1748-1763* (Lincoln, NE: University of Nebraska Press, 1967).

[26]U.S. Congress, *American State Papers: Documents, Legislative and Executive, of the Congress of the United States: Indian Affairs* (Washington, D.C.: Gales & Seaton, 1832-1861), vol. 1, p. 617: "We wish likewise to enjoy our own laws, and you yours, so far that if any of our people Indians should commit a crime to any of their brothers the white people of the United States that he may be punished by his own nation, and his chiefs make good all damages; and

likewise on the other part if any white person should commit a crime to any Indian, that we, the Indians, are not to take revenge on the person, but to resign him up to justice, and there let him be punished according to the laws of the nation."

[27] *Minutes of the Provincial Council of Pennsylvania from the Origin to the Termination of the Proprietary Government* (Philadelphia: Joseph Severns & Co., 1852), vol. 1, p. 463: "They will never feed you but for feare." Susan M. Kingsbury, ed., *The Records of the Virginia Company of London* (Washington, D.C.: Library of Congress, 1906-1936), vol. 3, p. 18.

[28] "Private advantages are often impediments of publick profit." Samuel Fortrey, *England's Interest and Improvement* (London: John Field, 1663), p. 3. Similarly, Josiah Child, *Brief Observations Concerning Trade and Interest of Money* (London: Calvert, Mortlock, 1668); F. Hall, *The Importance of the British plantations in America to this Kingdom With the State of their trade and methods for improving it,* (London: J. Peele, 1731), pp. 1-2. There was a running debate on the role of the scarcity of land in the price of labor, which of course influenced the policy of overseas colonization. Jacob Vanderlint, *Money answers all Things: or, an Essay to Make Money Sufficiently plentiful Amongst all ranks of People* (Baltimore: Johns Hopkins University Press, 1914: repr. of 1734 ed.).

[29] E.g., Nicholas Barbon, *A discourse of Trade* (London: Thomas Milbourn, 1690), pp. 40-41, 47-48.

[30] Boyd, op. cit. note 21, p. 270.

[31] Charles Davenant, *Essays upon I. The Ballance of Power, II. The Right of Making War, Peace, and Alliances, III. Universal Monarchy* (London: James Knapton, 1701), p. 267.

[32] John Brown, *The Marchants Avizo* (Cambridge, MA: Harvard University Press, 1957: repr. of 1589 ed.), p. 5.

[33] Thomas Pownall, *The Administration of the British Colonies,* 5th ed. (London: J. Walter, 1774), vol. 1, pp. 34-35, 38-39.

[34] Ibid., vol. 1, pp. 105-106.

[35] Kingsbury, op. cit. note 27, vol. 3. p. 446. Indians may have been reluctant to trade at first for strategic reasons. E.g., ibid., vol. 3, pp. 167, 247. But colonial officials also feared too much dependence on buying food from the tribes. Ibid., vol. 3, pp. 172-495. See Smith's descriptions of the anxieties and risks of early trade in Arber, op. cit. note 9, pp. 10, 12, 27, 126.

[36] Kingsbury, op. cit. note 27, vol. 3, p. 300; also vol. 1, pp. 484, 493. They soon became uncooperative, however, and were sent home. Ibid., vol. 4, pp. 23, 108, 565.

[37] Ibid., vol. 3, p. 495.

[38] Ibid., vol. 4, p. 275; also vol. 3, p. 495; Trumbull and Hoadley, op. cit. note 23, vol. 1, pp. 19, 204; Nathaniel B. Shurtleff, ed., *Records of the Governor and Company of the Massachusetts Bay in New England* (Boston: William White, 1853-1854), vol. 1, pp. 55, 196, 322; vol. 2, p. 138; A. J. F. Van Laer, ed.,

*Minutes of the Court of Albany, Rensselaerswyck and Schenectady* (Albany, NY: University of the State of New York Press, 1926-1932), vol. 1, pp. 75, 148, 172; vol. 2, pp. 336, 403. As early as 1609, the Virginia Company feared it had already devalued copper as a trade good by selling it too cheaply. Kingsbury, op. cit. note 27, vol. 3, p. 18.; Arber, op. cit. note 9, p. 100. For early examples of fixing the price of corn, see Nathaniel Bouton, ed., *Documents and Records Relating to the Province of New Hampshire* (Concord, NH: George E. Jenks, State Printer, 1867-1877), vol. 1, p. 139. For fixing the price of beaver pelts, see Shurtleff, op. cit., vol. 1, p. 81; Kingsbury, op. cit. note 27, vol. 4, p. 275.

[39]Kingsbury, ibid., vol. 3, pp. 704-707, 709.

[40]E.g., John Cox, Jr., ed., *Oyster Bay Town Records* (New York: T. A. Wright, 1916-1924), vol. 1, p. 659; Trumbull and Hoadley, op. cit. note 23, vol. 1, p. 284; Shurtleff, op. cit. note 38, vol. 3, p. 398.

[41]E.g., Trumbull and Hoadley, op. cit. note 23, vol. 1, p. 284; Shurtleff, op. cit. note 38, vol. 3, p. 416. Charles J. Hoadley, ed., *Records of the Colony or Jurisdiction of New Haven* (Hartford, CT: Case, Lockwood, 1857-1858), vol. 2, p. 217.

[42]E.g., Kingsbury, op. cit. note 27, vol. 3, p. 170; Trumbull and Hoadley, op. cit. note 23, vol. 1, pp. 52, 79, 242, 349, 529; Hoadley, op. cit. note 41, vol. 1, pp. 60, 206, 219; Bouton, op. cit. note 38, vol. 1, p. 139. There were also laws against teaching Indians how to use guns, e.g., Shurtleff, op. cit., note 38, vol. 1, p. 392, or the sale of iron to Indians, Trumbull and Hoadley, ibid., vol. 1, p. 74. The Virginia Company not only forbade showing Indians how to use guns, but engaging in any "Smythey, Carpentry or such like" in the Indians' presence "as they may learne therein." Kingsbury, ibid., vol. 3, pp. 21, 93. Even the Company's bows and arrows were hidden so that the Indians would not see the manufacture of steel arrowheads. Ibid., vol. 2, p. 100.

[43]E.g., Shurtleff, op. cit. note 38, vol. 1, pp. 127, 181, 252; vol. 2, pp. 36, 44, 48, 148, 163; vol. 3, pp. 65, 164, 235; vol. 5, p. 304. Restrictions on the sale of liquor were often requested by the tribes themselves. See, for instance, *Provincial Council of Pennsylvania*, op. cit., note 27, vol. 1, p. 105, and vol. 2, pp. 26, 141; Van Laer, op. cit. note 38, vol. 2, p. 76; John R. Bartlett, ed., *Records of the Colony of Rhode Island and Providence Plantations, in New England* (Providence, RI: Providence Press Co., 1856-1865), vol. 2, p. 128.

[44]Boyd, op. cit. note 21, p. 116.

[45]Kingsbury, op. cit. note 27, vol. 3, p. 165; Beverley, op. cit. note 13, p. 190.

[46]Shurtleff, op. cit. note 38, vol. 3, p. 80.

[47]Trumbull and Hoadley, op. cit. note 23, vol. 1, p. 139; also Horatio Rogers, et al., eds., *The Early Records of the Town of Providence* (Providence, RI: Snow & Farnham, 1893-1895), vol. 17, p. 18. The same restrictions applied to Indians wishing to lease land, Trumbull and Hoadley, ibid., vol. 1, p. 149.

[48]Douglass, op. cit. note 16, pp. 177, 188. See, e.g., the many Indian employment contracts in William J. Weeks, ed., *Records of the Town of Brookhaven* (New York: Derrydale Press, 1930-1932).

[49]Douglass, op. cit. note 16, p. 159. Douglass also reasoned, quite pragmatically, that "pinching" laborers' wages was justified as it would reduce the price of exports and hence stimulate trade. Ibid., p. 227. See, too, Hall, op. cit. note 28, p. 59: "We can supply them with all they want cheaper than the Spaniards can."

[50]Douglass, op. cit. note 16, p. 233.

[51]A. Kennedy, *The importance of gaining and preserving the friendship of the Indians to the British interest, considered* (New York: James Parler, 1751), p. 12. Kennedy argued for free trade, as opposed to the traditional monopoly of traders' licenses, but also for strict government price ceilings. President Washington adopted this approach in a 1793 address to Congress: "Next to a rigorous execution of justice on the violators of peace, the establishment of commerce with the Indian nations in behalf of the United States, is most likely to conciliate their attachment." *State Papers and Publick Documents of the United States* (Boston: T. B. Wait, 1817), vol. 1, p. 42.

[52]Pownall, op. cit. note 33, vol. 1, pp. 226-227; vol. 2, pp. 219-220. As early as 1609, one Virginia Company publicist was cheerfully predicting that civilizing the Indians "will cause a mighty vent of English cloths." George Louis Beer, *The Origins of the British Colonial System, 1578-1660* (New York: MacMillan, 1922), p. 72.

[53]Edward Waterhouse, writing in an official 1622 publication of the Virginia Company. Kingsbury, op. cit. note 27, vol. 3, p. 549.

[54]Ibid., vol. 4, p. 368. See, too, John Bargrave's plan, "by gentle usage," to establish a hegemony over the nearby tribes and enable Virginia "to give lawes" to the Indians. Ibid., vol. 4, p. 436.

[55]Boyd, op. cit. note 21, p. 122.

[56]McIlwaine, op. cit. note 22, p. 111.

[57]Ibid.

[58]Kingsbury, op. cit. note 27, vol. 3, p. 470.

[59]Ibid., vol. 3, p. 19.

[60]Ibid., vol. 1, pp. 220, 307-310, 587; vol. 3, p. 128. The Company responded by giving orders to obtain Indian children "by just means," by "purchase" if necessary. Ibid., vol. 3, pp. 14, 165. William Byrd was to complain a century later that educated Indians not only tended to relapse to their old ways, but "some of them too have made the worst use of the Knowledge they acquir'd among the English, by employing it against their Benefactors." Boyd, op. cit. note 21, p. 118.

[61]Bartlett, op. cit. note 43, vol. 1, pp. 134-136. Also Shurtleff, op. cit. note 38, vol. 2, pp. 38, 40, 55, and 73; *Provincial Council of Pennsylvania*, op. cit. note 27, vol. 2, pp. 15-18; Trumbull and Hoadley, op. cit. note 23, vol. 1, p. 359; Hoadley, op. cit. note 41, vol. 1, pp. 1-7.

[62]Bartlett, op. cit. note 43, vol. 1, pp. 136-140. By the same token, the tribes in treaty relations with the Massachusetts Bay refused to deal with Rhode Island. Ibid., vol. 1, p. 322.

[63]Arber, op. cit. note 9, pp. 121-122.

[64]Ibid., p. 112.

[65]Pownall, op. cit. note 33, vol. 2, pp. 212-215.

[66]Ibid., vol. 2, p. 225.

[67]Ibid., vol. 2, p. 217.

[68]Shurtleff, op. cit. note 38, vol. 3, pp. 365-366.

[69]Trumbull and Hoadley, op. cit. note 23, vol. 2, pp. 39, 56, 66, 256; also pp. 228, 299. Virginia ordered the Chickahominies to restore their "king" to his power and privileges, for "if they Deny the Same . . . the English will take it Amisse the said [king] being alwaies a faithful friend to the English." McIlwaine, op. cit. note 22, p. 425. Also, Rhode Island refused to grant the Narragansett chiefs commissions as justices of the peace. Bartlett, op. cit. note 43, vol. 7, pp. 17-18.

[70]Trumbull and Hoadley, op. cit. note 23, vol. 1, pp. 19, 371, 529; Shurtleff, op. cit. note 38, vol. 2, p. 139; vol. 3, p. 436. "When dealing with unacculturated Indians, the colonists preferred to reinforce the authority of the sachem, since it provided accountability." James W. Springer, "American Indians and the Law of Real Property in Colonial New England," *American Journal of Legal History* 30: 1 (January 1986): 25-58 at 40.

[71]Bartlett, op. cit. note 43, vol. 5, pp. 25, 37, 156, 222.

[72]See, generally, Yasu Kawashima, "Legal Origins of the Indian Reservation in Colonial Massachusetts," *American Journal of Legal History* 13: 1 (January 1969): 42-56. They were so successful that Ninigret, of the Narragansetts, complained that other tribes were being "forced from their religion" by overzealous praying Indians.

[73]As described by W. Stitt Robinson, "Tributary Indians in Colonial Virginia," *The Virginia Magazine of History and Biography* 67: 1 (January 1969): 49-64. This relationship included, in many instances, payment of taxes, e.g., Rogers, et al., op. cit. note 47, vol. 13, pp. 45, 48; vol. 17, pp. 168, 209; Trumbull and Hoadley, op. cit. note 23, vol. 1, pp. 14, 17, 52; Beverley Fleet, ed., *Virginia Colonial Abstracts* (Richmond, VA: Mimeograph, 1938-1948), vol. 21, pp. 20, 22, 58.

[74]The legal origins of this terminology are discussed in Russel L. Barsh, "Indigenous North America and Contemporary International Law," *Oregon Law Review* 62: 1 (1983): 73-125 at 104-105.

[75]Affidavit on behalf of "Mall Indian," Ipswich court, 1660. George F. Dow, ed., *Records and Files of the Quarterly Courts of Essex County, Massachusetts* (Salem, MA: Essex Institute, 1911-1926), vol. 2, p. 240.

[76]Bartlett, op. cit. note 43, vol. 1, pp. 107-108; *Provincial Council of Pennsylvania*, op. cit. note 27, vol. 2, p. 16.

[77]Bartlett, op. cit. note 43, vol. 1, p. 498; vol. 2, pp. 283, 405, 428; Shurtleff, op. cit. note 38, vol. 1, pp. 88, 143, 209; vol. 3, p. 395. Generally, see Yasu Kawashima, "Jurisdiction of the Colonial Courts Over the Indians in Massa-

chusetts, 1689-1763," *New England Quarterly* 42: 4 (December 1969): 532-550; and James P. Ronda, "Red and White at the Bench: Indians and the Law in Plymouth County, 1620-1691," *Essex Institute Historical Collections* 110: 3 (July 1974): 200-215.

[78]E.g., Bartlett, op. cit. note 43, vol. 2, pp. 485, 519; McIlwaine, op. cit. note 22, pp. 380, 518; Fleet, op. cit. note 73, vol. 17, pp. 7-15; William H. Browne, et al., eds., *Archives of Maryland* (Baltimore: Maryland Historical Society, 1885-1972), vol. 10, pp. 293-296; vol. 49, pp. 481-491.

[79]E.g., "Lower Norfolk County Records 1636-1646," *Virginia Magazine of History and Biography* 39: 1 (January 1931): 1-20 at 9; Fleet, op. cit. note 73, vol. 2, p. 113; vol. 11, pp. 8, 45.

[80]E.g., Bouton, op. cit, note 38, vol. 3, p. 16 (murder); Trumbull and Hoadley, op. cit. note 23, vol. 1, p. 513 (theft and burglary); Shurtleff, op. cit. note 38, vol. 1, pp. 91-92 (adultery).

[81]Trumbull and Hoadley, op. cit. note 23, vol. 1, p. 175.

[82]E.g., Browne, et al., op. cit. note 78, vol. 41, p. 186. Also see Bartlett, op. cit. note 43, vol. 1, p. 412, directing the courts to sell any Indian who cannot pay costs. A great deal of Indian land was also sold to satisfy judgment debts. Springer, op. cit. note 70, p. 47.

[83]E.g., Trumbull and Hoadley, op. cit. note 23, vol. 1, pp. 165, 171; Shurtleff, op. cit. note 38, vol. 1, pp. 92, 100, 133, 249; vol. 3, p. 233; McIlwaine, op. cit. note 22, pp. 365, 369, 381 (". . . the titles of both the said Indians and Savage to be Doubtfull, Yett in respect the Said Indians have always beene in peace with us, it is necessary that they be Secured in their possessions.").

[84]E.g., Shurtleff, op. cit. note 38, vol. 1, p. 91; vol. 3, p. 386; *Provincial Council of Pennsylvania*, op. cit. note 27, vol. 1, p. 147; Van Laer, op. cit. note 38, vol. 2, p. 335; Dow, op. cit. note 75, vol. 2, p. 240 (damage to trap lines). See Browne, et al., op. cit. note 78, vol. 4, pp. 122, 254-255, 260, for the case of an Englishman prosecuted and executed for killing an Indian. The court was still afraid that the tribe would seize his property for restitution.

[85]Cox, op. cit. note 40, vol. 1, p. 667. Also see the case of Robert Crose, who was put in the stocks "for his barbarous and inhuman act of digging up the grave of the Sagamore of Agawam and carrying his skull upon a pole." Dow, op. cit. note 75, vol. 3, p. 420.

[86]*Provincial Council of Pennsylvania*, op. cit. note 27, vol. 1, p. 117; Shurtleff, op. cit. note 38, vol. 3, pp. 281-282. (Indians to have the same access to courts "as the English.")

[87]E.g., Trumbull and Hoadley, op. cit. note 23, vol. 2, p. 31; Shurtleff, op. cit. note 38, vol. 3, p. 272; Bartlett, op. cit. note 43, vol. 4, pp. 229-233. Also see Rogers, et al., op. cit. note 47, vol. 17, p. 266 (debt). Compare Marc Galanter, "The Displacement of Traditional Law in Modern India," *Journal of Social Issues* 24: 4 (October 1968): 65-91.

[88]77 *English Reports* 379 (1608).

[89]*Provincial Council of Pennsylvania*, op. cit. note 27, vol. 1, p. 147; Rogers, et al., op. cit. note 47, vol. 2, p. 101.

[90]*Provincial Council of Pennsylvania*, op. cit. note 27, vol. 1, p. 373. On the other hand, some colonies, in apparent desperation, ruled that Indians are to be presumed guilty when accused of damaging English livestock. Trumbull and Hoadley, op. cit. note 23, vol. 1, p. 19; Hoadley, op. cit. note 41, vol. 2, p. 67.

[91]Shurtleff, op. cit. note 38, vol. 5, p. 25.

[92]Bartlett, op. cit. note 43, vol. 2, pp. 295-297.

[93]Kingsbury, op. cit. note 27, vol. 3, p. 172.

[94]Trumbull and Hoadley, op. cit. note 23, vol. 1, p. 95; vol. 2, p. 252; Van Laer, op. cit. note 38, vol. 1, p. 280; vol. 2, p. 37; Bartlett, op. cit. note 43, vol. 4, pp. 233, 344.

[95]Appropriations Act, 16 Stat. 544-571, March 3, 1871 (41st Congress, 3rd Session).

[96]Bartlett, op. cit. note 43, vol. 2, pp. 362, 393, 509; also Trumbull and Hoadley, op. cit. note 23, vol. 2, pp. 37, 82, 88, 157, 225.

[97]"Indian Affairs in Lancaster County," *William & Mary Quarterly* (1st ser.) 4: 3 (January 1896): 177-179 at 178.

[98]Shurtleff, op. cit. note 38, vol. 2, p. 188; vol. 3, p. 105.

[99]Trumbull and Hoadley, op. cit. note 23, vol. 2, p. 117; also vol. 2, pp. 178, 188, 191.

[100]Originally adopted as section 9 of the Appropriations Act, 23 Stat. 362-385 at 385, March 3, 1885 (48th Congress, 2nd Session). It is now codified at 18 U.S.C. 1153.

[101]*Provincial Council of Pennsylvania*, op. cit. note 27, vol. 2, p. 48. Likewise, Rogers, et al., op. cit. note 47, vol. 3, p. 38; Cox, op. cit. note 40, vol. 1, p. 669.

[102]Bartlett, op. cit. note 43, vol. 1, p. 413; vol. 2, pp. 500-503, 509.

[103]Ibid., vol. 4, pp. 229-233.

[104]Indeed, some colonies subsequently imposed discriminatory, shorter statutes of limitations for real actions on Indians, e.g., two or three years. McIlwaine, op. cit. note 22, pp. 400, 504.

[105]Browne, et al., op. cit. note 78, vol. 4, pp. 173, 176-177, 180-184.

[106]Ibid., p. 184.

[107]Trumbull and Hoadley, op. cit. note 23, vol. 2, p. 61. Or in Massachusetts, to "pform outward worship to their false gods, or to ye devill." Shurtleff, op. cit. note 38, vol. 2, pp. 176-179; vol. 3, p. 98. One of John Smith's first orders was for the Virginia Company's employees to kill the Indians' "priests" if they had occasion. Kingsbury, op. cit. note 27, vol. 3, p. 15. On the social impact of English jurisdiction, see Yasuhide Kawashima, "Forced Conform-

ity: Puritan Criminal Justice and Indians," *Kansas Law Review* 25: 3 (Spring 1977): 361-373.

[108]See, generally, Robert N. Clinton, "Criminal Jurisdiction Over Indian Lands: A Journey Through a Jurisdictional Maze," *Arizona Law Review* 18: 3 (1976): 503-583.

[109]See notes 45, 46 and 47.

[110]Wilbur R. Jacobs, ed., *The Appalachian Indian Frontier: The Edmond Atkin Report and Plan of 1755* (Lincoln, NE: University of Nebraska Press, 1954). This culminated in the Royal Proclamation of October 7, 1763, strictly forbidding any further settlements in the West. The proclamation was openly defied by colonial officials and was one of the grievances leading to the Revolution. Thad W. Tate, "The Coming of the Revolution in Virginia: Britain's Challenge to Virginia's Ruling Class, 1763-1776," *William & Mary Quarterly* (3rd ser.) 19: 3 (July 1962): 323-343 at 337-338, 341.

[111]John C. Webster, ed., *Acadia at the end of the Seventeenth Century: Letters, Journals and Memoirs of Joseph Robineau de Villebon* (Saint John, NB: New Brunswick Museum, 1934), p. 75.

[112]Ibid., p. 50.

[113]L. F. S. Upton, *Micmacs and Colonists: Indian-White Relations in the Maritimes, 1713-1867* (Vancouver, BC: University of British Columbia Press, 1979), pp. 36-38. For a contemporary British official's assessment of French diplomatic superiority, see *The Papers of Sir William Johnson*, prepared for publication by the Division of Archives and History (Albany, NY: University of the State of New York Press, 1921-1965), vol. 4, p. 275, and vol. 9, pp. 125-132.

[114]George Copway, *The Life, History, and Travels of Kah-Ge-Ga-Gah-Bowh, A Young Chief of the Ojebwa Nation*, 6th ed. (Philadelphia: James Harmstead, 1847), p. 22.

[115]Hall, op. cit. note 10, p. 340; Arber, op. cit. note 9, pp. 111-112.

[116]Beverly, op. cit. note 13, pp. 141-156; Arber, op. cit. note 9, pp. 111-112.

[117]Arber, ibid., p. 66.

[118]Douglass, op. cit. note 16, p. 152.

[119]Ibid., p. 155.

[120]Roger Williams, "A Key into the Language of America: Or an Help to the Language of the Natives, in that part of America, called New England," originally published in 1643. *Collections of the Massachusetts Historical Society* (1st ser.) 31 (1810, for year 1794), pp. 203-233. So, too, Alexander Whitaker, *Good Newes from Virginia* (London: Felix Kyngston, 1613), p. 26, although he was certain they were servants of "the divell."

[121]See, generally, Springer, op. cit. note 70.

[122]Oscar Handlin and Irving Mark, eds., "Chief Daniel Ninham v. Roger Morris, Beverly Robinson, and Philp Philipse — An Indian Land Case in Co-

lonial New York," *Ethnohistory* 11: 3 (Summer 1964): 193-246 at 227. Also see the discussion of the *Moheagan Indians* case in Russel L. Barsh, "Behind Land Claims: Rationalizing Dispossession in Anglo-American Law," *Law & Anthropology* 1 (1986): 15-50 at 17-18.

[123]Barsh, ibid., pp. 19-20.

[124]Arber, op. cit. note 9, p. 49.

[125]E.g., Bartlett, op. cit. note 43, vol. 1, p. 464; Shurtleff, op. cit. note 38, vol. 2, p. 159; Weeks, op. cit. note 48, pp. 23, 47, 97.

[126]E.g., Bartlett, op. cit. note 43, vol. 1, p. 18; Shurtleff, op. cit. note 38, vol. 5, p. 39; Cox, op. cit. note 40, vol. 1, p. 355.

[127]Weeks, op. cit. note 48, vol. 1, p. 160; Rogers, et al., op. cit. note 47, vol. 17, p. 68.

[128]Bartlett, op. cit. note 43, vol. 1, p. 13. But in Cox, op. cit. note 40, vol. 1, p. 355, the grantee argued that, despite the lack of words of bargain and sale in his Indian deed, "ye Indeans So far as I understand have never made any Sales for Lives but of custom wch is their Lawe pass ye right of theirs, Heirer &c wth their owne, unlesse they make any expresse exception," concluding "I shall be Sorry yt such as prfess ymselves Christians shall teach Heathens Less Honesty under prtence of teaching them more Law."

[129]E.g., Cox, ibid., vol. 1, pp. 146, 174, 283; Shurtleff, op. cit. note 38, vol. 5, p. 227; James N. Arnold, ed., "The Records of the Proprietors of the Narragansett, Otherwise Called The Fones Record," *Rhode Island Colonial Gleanings* (Providence, RI: Narragansett Historical Publishing Co., 1894), vol. 1, pp. 6-7, 101.

[130]E.g., Bartlett, op. cit. note 43, vol. 1, pp. 35-38, 45, 48.

[131]Cox, op. cit. note 40, vol. 1, p. 520. Deeds were also set aside for other reasons, such as coercion. Weeks, op. cit. note 48, vol. 1, p. 98; also Springer, op. cit. note 70.

[132]Cox, op. cit. note 40, vol. 2, pp. 341, 680; Bartlett, op. cit. note 43, vol. 1, p. 45.

[133]Shurtleff, op. cit. note 38, vol. 5, p. 328.

[134]E.g., Trumbull and Hoadley, op. cit. note 23, vol. 1, pp. 335, 344; vol. 2, p. 174; Shurtleff, ibid., vol. 3, pp. 76, 85, 246, 294, 301, 348, 406; vol. 5, p. 136; Bartlett, op. cit. note 43, vol. 4, p. 52; E. P. Walton, ed., *Records of the Governor and Council of the State of Vermont* (Montpelier, VT: J. & J. M. Poland, 1873-1880), vol. 2, pp. 128, 180; vol. 3, p. 200; Browne, et al., op. cit. note 78, vol. 1, pp. 329-330.

[135]Bartlett, op. cit. note 43, vol. 6, pp. 221, 357, 401, 564, 598.

[136]Beverley, op. cit. note 13, p. 318. The other side of this was the damage done by Indians' dogs. E.g., Rogers, et al., op. cit. note 47, vol. 3, p. 7; Weeks, op. cit. note 48, vol. 1, p. 127; Trumbull and Hoadley, op. cit. note 23, vol. 2, p. 56; Hoadley, op. cit. note 41, vol. 2, p. 362.

[137]E.g., Weeks, op. cit. note 48, vol. 1, p. 127; Shurtleff, op. cit. note 38, vol. 1, p. 294; Trumbull and Hoadley, op. cit. note 23, vol. 1, p. 226; vol. 2, p. 51; *Provincial Council of Pennsylvania*, op. cit. note 27, vol. 1, pp. 162, 180; Browne, et al., op. cit. note 78, vol. 49, p. 139.

[138]Hall, op. cit. note 10, p. 345.

[139]Bartlett, op. cit. note 43, vol. 1, pp. 81, 107, 113; vol. 3, p. 519.

[140]Beverley, op. cit. note 13, p. 233.

[141]E.g., Bartlett, op. cit. note 43, vol. 1, p. 465; vol. 2, p. 128; vol. 7, pp. 9-10, 18, 46, 214.

[142]Pownall, op. cit. note 33, vol. 2, pp. 186-188.

[143]Ibid.

[144]Cox, op. cit. note 40, vol. 1, pp. 267, 313. Also see Reid, *Law of Blood*, op. cit. note 8, pp. 68-70, on traditional Cherokee law relating to women's rights.

[145]Arber, op. cit. note 9, pp. 49, 67-68.

[146]Lechford, op. cit. note 10, p. 50; Boyd, op. cit. note 21, p. 116.

[147]Burke, op. cit. note 12, p. 186.

[148]Stanley Pargellis, "An Account of the Indians in Virginia," *William & Mary Quarterly* (3d ser.) 16: 2 (1959): 228-243 at 232-233. English ambivalence did not stop at the question of women's labor. Noting widespread rumors of Indian prostitution, Beverley accused his countrymen of "an aspersion cast upon those innocent Creatures, by reason of the freedom they take in Conversation, which uncharitable Christians interpret as Criminal, upon no other ground, than the guilt of their own Consciences." The truth, he supposed, was simply that "the Maidens are entirely at their own disposal, and may manage their persons as they think fit," a scandalous degree of sexual liberty. Beverley, op. cit. note 13, pp. 170-171. Compare Byrd's account of Indian women's sexual freedom in Boyd, op. cit. note 21, p. 116.

[149]*Congressional Record* 11 (January 31, 1881), p. 998. Compare Tacitus, *Germania*, chapter 8, on the superior policy of holding women as hostages, owing to their great influence in German tribal society.

[150]Beverley, op. cit. note 13, p. 9.

[151]Russel L. Barsh, "Native American Loyalists and Patriots: Reflections on the American Revolution in Native American History," *The Indian Historian* 10: 3 (Summer 1977): 9-19 at 15-16.

[152]Pownall, op. cit. note 33, vol. 2, pp. 59-60.

[153]On the democratization of American law, see Perry Miller, *The Life of the Mind in America, from the Revolution to the Civil War* (New York: Harcourt, Brace & World, 1965).

[154]E.g., Arthur Hippler and Stephen Conn, "The Village Council and its Offspring: A Reform for Bush Justice," *UCLA-Alaska Law Review* 5: 1 (Fall 1975): 22-57; Laura Nader, "Styles of Court Procedure: To Make the Bal-

ance," in Laura Nader, ed., *Law in Culture and Society* (Chicago: Aldine, 1969), pp. 69-91.

[155]Barsh and Henderson, op. cit. note 18; Russel L. Barsh, "Navajo Property and Probate Law, 1940-1972," *Law & Anthropology* 6 (1991).

[156]Rabindranath Tagore, *Nationalism* (London: MacMillan, 1917), p. 110.

[157]Morton Horwitz, *The Transformation of American Law, 1780-1860* (Cambridge, MA: Harvard University Press, 1977).

[158]Albert O. Hirschman, *The Passions and the Interests: Political Arguments for Capitalism Before its Triumph* (Princeton, NJ: Princeton University Press, 1977). But as William Appleman Williams observed, while free market capitalism may have been an intellectual ideal by the 1770s, early America was governed by men who believed in regulating markets. "The Age of Mercantilism: An Interpretation of the American Political Economy, 1763-1828," *William & Mary Quarterly* (3d ser.) 15: 4 (October 1958): 419-437.

[159]Roberto M. Unger, *Knowledge and Politics* (New York: Free Press, 1975), p. 153.

[160]Douglass, op. cit. note 16, p. 206.

[161]Sigmund Diamond, "From Organization to Society: Virginia in the Seventeenth Century," in Stanley N. Katz, ed., *Colonial America: Essays in Politics and Social Development* (Boston: Little, Brown, 1971), pp. 3-31.

[162]Shurtleff, op. cit. note 38, vol. 3, p. 252.

[163]Kennedy, op. cit. note 51, p. 29.

[164]Van Doren, op. cit. note 1, p. 78.

[165]"Journal of the Treaty Held at Albany, in August, 1775, with the Six Nations," *Collections of the Massachusetts Historical Society* (3rd ser.) 5 (1836): 75-100 at 83.

[166]Wallace, op. cit. note 8, pp. 162-168.

[167]Alexis de Tocqueville, ed. by J. P. Mayer and Max Lerner, *Democracy in America* (New York: Harper & Row, 1966), p. 312.

[168]Davenant, op. cit. note 31, p. 31.

[169]Boyd, op. cit. note 21, p. 10.

[170]Quoted in Barsh and Henderson, op. cit. note 5, p. 107.

[171]Menno Boldt and J. Anthony Long, "Tribal Traditions and European-Western Political Ideologies: The Dilemma of Canada's Native Indians," *Canadian Journal of Political Science* 17: 3 (September 1984): 537-553.

[172]Paula Gunn Allen, "Dear World," *Skins and Bones: Poems 1979-1987* (Albuquerque, NM: West End Press, © 1988), p. 56.

# THE CONCEPT OF SOVEREIGNTY: THE KEY TO INDIAN SOCIAL JUSTICE

Sharon O'Brien

*University of Notre Dame*

> We believe in the inherent right of all people to retain spiritual
> and cultural values, and that the free exercise of these values is
> necessary to the normal development of any people . . . .
>
> We believe that the history and development of America show
> that the Indian has been subjected to duress, undue influence, un-
> warranted pressures, and policies which have produced uncer-
> tainty, frustration, and despair. Only when the public under-
> stands these conditions and is moved to take action toward the
> formulation and adoption of sound and consistent policies and
> programs will these destroying factors be removed and the Indian
> resume his normal growth and make his maximum contribution
> to modern society.[1]

As the statement above from the 1961 American Indian Chicago Conference indicates, the American concept of social justice has not only
proven of little benefit to American Indians, but has actually operated
to destroy Indian cultures and identity. The attainment of social justice for American Indians has been and remains elusive. Why this is the
case — especially in a modern society which prides itself on a long history of freedom and justice — is the subject of this chapter.

John Rawls, in his renowned work on social justice, *A Theory of Justice,* offers some preliminary insights into this dilemma. Rawls contends that the manner in which a community assigns societal rights
and duties, and defines the appropriate distribution of rewards and
burdens, constitutes its concept of social justice.[2] For mainstream
America, individualism, competition and the acquisition of private
property are the operative societal values. Social justice is attained
through laws protecting the equality of individuals in their exercise of
basic political liberties, such as the right to vote, freedom of speech,
ownership of personal property and protection from arbitrary arrest.

Rawls further maintains that a well-ordered society is one where all
members hold a similar philosophy of social justice.[3] Americans Indi-

ans, however, possess a concept of social justice that differs fundamentally from that of the dominant population. According to many tribal traditions, social justice is defined as an equilateral relationship of respect and harmony with all things in nature.[4] Social justice is attained through laws promoting spiritualism, communalism, and cooperation within the community.

American society historically has proven reluctant to accept and integrate the Indian definition of social justice and culture into its mores. The United States, as an immigrant society, has worked towards the assimilation of diverse groups into a unified whole, arguing that a greater good is served when the population is integrated and cohesive. This assimilative process has produced a history of antagonism towards groups desiring to maintain differing philosophies, values and languages.[5]

Rawls, as have many other philosophers, questions this basically utilitarian contention — that justice is served if one group experiences a loss of freedom for the sake of the greater good. This is, however, exactly the rationale used by American society to deny tribes justice. The dominant society has sacrificed Indian rights to lands, resources, cultures and identities in the name of progress, development and social integration. The federal government has accomplished this divestment of Indian sovereignty and rights through a series of policy changes supported by changing legal interpretations.

Indian people have not willingly acquiesced to this denial of their rights. Realizing that their very existence depends upon the maintenance and expansion of their remaining sovereign rights, Indian people have protested, lobbied, gone to court and even war to protect their right to govern themselves according to the dictates of their own values and laws.[6]

This chapter examines the importance and the maintenance of tribal sovereignty in the quest of Indian people for social justice. It first defines sovereignty and chronicles the federal government's attempts through legal maneuvers and legislation to diminish tribal status from that of independent international sovereigns to individual wards in need of total government protection and control. It next reviews the federal government's current legal definition of tribal sovereignty and the impact of political, economic and cultural factors in the definition and attainment of sovereignty and therefore social justice. Its final section looks towards a new future realm of protection — at attempts by all indigenous peoples to secure from the international community recognition of and protection for their particular needs and rights.

## Evolution of Federal Recognition of Tribal Sovereignty

To appreciate the importance of sovereignty to the tribes in their quest for social justice, it is necessary to understand the history of federal-tribal relations: how the federal government has attempted to destroy tribal identities, cultures, governments, and the land base by divesting tribes of their inherent sovereign powers. What follows is an historical and legal analysis of the policies and judicial measures employed by the federal government to reverse the executive and legislative branches' initial recognition of the international sovereignty of the Indian nations and to turn them into wards of the government.

### Historical Recognition of Indian Sovereignty

Sovereignty is a legal concept denoting the existence of a unified authority in a political community; it is a claim by a community to be at liberty, to assert a collective will against all outsiders.[7] The intangible core of sovereignty, i.e., the desire of a people to be sovereign, can be truly extinguished only by the people themselves. The exercise of sovereignty, customarily termed independence or self-government, refers to the political powers exercised by a people pursuant to their willingness to act as a unit.

The theory of sovereignty is the creation of modern political philosophy.[8] Although elements of the concept existed in Roman and medieval thought, the French philosopher Jean Bodin introduced the term in his treatise, *De la République*, in 1576. Bodin argued that God had granted to the monarchs, and not to the Pope, the right to organize the secular relations of the state. In the seventeenth and eighteenth centuries, John Locke, Thomas Hobbes and Jacques Rousseau refuted the divine right of kings, arguing that the people were the source of sovereign authority.[9] Thomas Jefferson, among others, further refined the theory, postulating that sovereignty, rather than being absolute and unlimited, was separable into parts. Striving to match theory with the newly-created federal institutions, Jefferson argued that sovereignty was divisible between the legal, which was vested in the federal institution, and the political, which was ultimately vested in the citizenry.[10]

A traditional Indian view of sovereignty, by contrast, does not separate the secular from the religious, or the political from the legal. Rather, Indian philosophy unifies all aspects of life. The spiritual, secular, political and legal are indivisible; symbolized by a sacred circle representing the integration of the land, the people, and all animal and plant life into a whole.[11]

Although European colonizers had little comprehension of the Indian concept of sovereignty and social justice, they did recognize that Indian nations possessed the requisites of a sovereign state: territory, population, governing stucture, and the ability to govern.[12] International law at the time of early colonization defined states as

> political bodies, societies of men who have united and combined their forces, in order to procure their mutual safety and welfare. Every nation which governs itself, under whatever form and which does not depend on any other nation, is a sovereign state. . . . To . . . be truly sovereign and independent, it must govern itself by its own authority and its own laws.[13]

The European nations' recognition of Indian sovereignty is evidenced principally by their decision to conduct relations with the Indian nations through the treatymaking process. Francisco de Vitoria, the noted Spanish theologian, first suggested treating with the Indian nations for land cessions.[14] The Dutch concluded the first known treaty in 1613 with the Iroquois.[15] England adopted the practice, negotiating more than twelve hundred treaties with the eastern Indian nations.[16] The United States signed its first Indian treaty with the Delaware nation, thereby establishing a mutual defense alliance between the two nations. This treaty was followed by more than 370 treaties concluded by the United States with various tribes between 1778 and 1871.[17]

Indian treaties exhibited the same format and subject matter of other international treaties during this period — the fixing of boundaries, the promise of mutual assistance, the exchange of prisoners and hostages, and the establishment of garrisons and forts.[18] Other points of negotiation included provisions concerning passports, extradition, non-Indian immigration onto Indian lands, and the right to declare war and conclude treaties with third powers.[19]

A review of early congressional legislation further demonstrates that tribes were treated neither as conquered subjects nor as citizens, but as separate sovereigns. Laws governing citizens and states were clearly regarded as inapplicable to Indian nations. Even legislation involving the tribes, such as the Trade and Intercourse Acts, did not legislate over the tribes, but regulated only the manner in which United States citizens were allowed to relate to the tribes. Citizens and states, for example, were forbidden to negotiate with the Indian nations for land, passports were required for travel in Indian country, and strict licensing procedures were established for the conduct of commercial relations — restrictions placed on all citizens in their dealings with other foreign nations.[20]

Respect for tribal sovereignty continued for some years after the American Revolution, in part due to the Indian nations' skillful diplomatic alliances with competing European powers. By the 1820s, however, the withdrawal of the French, English and Spanish, combined with an enormous influx of new settlers desiring land, shifted the federal government's view of tribes from that of an external foreign problem to that of an internal domestic issue.

## The Diminishment of Tribal Sovereignty

In 1828, presidential candidate Andrew Jackson campaigned for office on a removal platform that advocated the relocation of eastern tribes to regions west of the Mississippi, and the opening of their former territory to white settlement. Tribal reactions to the proposed policy were uniformly negative. A number of Indian nations, especially those of the Southeast, had successfully adopted elements of non-Indian agriculture, education and political structures, partly to protect themselves from the pressures of removal. The Five Civilized Tribes, as the whites referred to them, became successful farmers, at times outproducing white farmers.[21] The Cherokees, using the invention of Sequoyah's syllabary, reportedly achieved a higher literacy rate than their frontier neighbors. These successes, however, in conjunction with the discovery of minerals on tribal lands, only intensified the states' greed for tribal lands and their determination to rid themselves of their Indian neighbors.

In 1827 the Cherokees adopted their own constitution and reemphasized their status as an independent nation with full title within their boundaries.[22] The Georgia legislature passed laws immediately to distribute Cherokee lands to various Georgian counties and voided all Indian laws and customs after June 1, 1830. In support of Georgia's actions, President Jackson introduced legislation in Congress to move the eastern tribes to lands set aside for their use west of the Mississippi River.[23] The tribes mounted an intense lobbying effort against the bill, arguing that it violated previous treaties and laws recognizing Indian sovereignty and Indian title. Nonetheless, the bill passed by five votes. The tribes could move west or stay in the South and submit as individuals to state authority.

The passage of laws in Mississippi and Alabama similar to those of Georgia and the threat of removal set the stage for the first legal determination by the American courts of the political status and rights of Indian nations. At the urging of Daniel Webster and several other well-known members of Congress, the Cherokees sought an injunction from the U.S. Supreme Court against the State of Georgia "from the execution of certain laws of that State, which . . . go directly to annihilate the Cherokees as a political society, and to seize, for the use of Georgia, the lands of the nation which have been assured to them by the United States in solemn treaties . . . ."[24] Former United States Attorney General William Wirt, the tribe's attorney, argued that the Cherokees were a foreign state. Georgia's laws, therefore, were inapplicable to the Cherokees. Wirt stressed that the Cherokees had been sovereign from time immemorial, "acknowledging no earthly superior."[25] Despite the Cherokee's formidable case, Chief Justice John Marshall ruled that the tribe had no standing as a foreign nation and denied their motion for an injunction. The Supreme Court's decision held that the Cherokees were neither a foreign state, a member state, nor conquered subjects. Rather, the Cherokees were "a domestic dependent nation . . . in a state of pupilage. Their relation to the United States resembles that of a ward to a guardian."[26]

To support his finding, Marshall referred to the Constitution and the wording of the commerce clause. Article 3, Marshall reasoned, granted Congress the power to "regulate commerce with foreign nations and among the several states, and with the Indian tribes." Marshall ruled that this separate listing of foreign nations and Indian tribes was evidence that the constitutional framers considered Indian tribes to occupy a position distinct from that of international sovereigns.[27] Undaunted, the Cherokees and their white supporters continued to press their case before the Court.

The following year, Samuel Worcester, Elizur Butler and several other missionaries deliberately disobeyed a Georgia law requiring state permission to live on Indian lands. The Georgia state court sentenced Worcester and Butler to four years of hard labor. William Wirt again appeared before the Supreme Court to argue the inapplicability of Georgia's laws over Cherokee lands.[28] Following a line of reasoning suggested in the earlier *Cherokee Nation* decision, Wirt contended that only the federal government had the authority through treaties and congressional acts to deal legally with the tribes. Any attempts by states to intrude upon this sovereign-to-sovereign relationship violated federal law.

Marshall agreed with the plaintiffs, finding Georgia's laws to be an unconstitutional interference with the treaties concluded between the United States and the Cherokees. Marshall also elaborated on his earlier description of the Cherokees as a "domestic dependent nation." Following the example of Great Britain, Marshall wrote, the United States had recognized the Indian nations as "distinct political communities, having territorial boundaries, within which their authority is exclusive, and having a right to all the lands within those boundaries."[29] The United States "considered the Cherokees as a nation."[30]

In *Cherokee Nation*, Marshall had characterized the relationship between the Indian nations and the United States as "resembling that of a ward to his guardian." In *Worcester*, Marshall stressed that the federal government's obligation to protect the tribes did not entail a loss of tribal sovereignty. Rather, the relationship between the United States and the Cherokees, according to Marshall, "was that of a nation claiming and receiving the protection of one more powerful: not that of individuals abandoning their national character, and submitting as subjects to the laws of a master. . . . Protection does not imply the destruction of the protected."[31] Marshall's words, written to protect the tribes in their relationship with the federal government, proved sadly prophetic, forecasting exactly the course the United States would pursue to divest tribes of their sovereignty, land, cultures and governments.

The *Cherokee Nation* and *Worcester* rulings became the foundational decisions in federal Indian law, setting the initial parameters of tribal sovereignty and outlining the federal and state relationship with the Indian nations. Given the context of these two decisions — that Marshall wrote them foremost to meet national needs and only secondarily to protect Indian interests — it is not surprising that these two decisions served to provide future courts with legal supports for two conflicting policies, assimilation and honored separatism, that characterized Indian-federal relations after removal. Decisions affirming the right of tribes to maintain their own communities free from encroachment by the non-Indian population cited *Worcester* as precedent. Rulings diminishing tribal sovereignty and supportive of federal efforts to assimilate tribes into the American mainstream referred to the guardian-ward analogy of *Cherokee Nation*.

As settlers poured westward in the 1800s, the federal government between 1832 and 1842 moved nineteen tribes across the Mississippi River to an area established as the Unorganized Indian Territory. The U.S. Army used physical force to move some tribes and thousands died along the way. The Cherokees alone lost four thousand of their people, one-fourth of those who journeyed west. Prior to removal, tribes had grudgingly agreed to relocate only after securing treaty guarantees that they would be allowed to retain a land base and maintain their way of life free from non-Indian control.[32] Within a decade, however, it became apparent that the tribes would not be secure in lands west of the Mississippi either.

By 1830 the American population in the old Northwest Territory had risen to three million. Settlers traveling to the fertile Pacific Northwest and to the gold fields in California flooded into Indian country. In 1854 Congress passed the Kansas-Nebraska Bill,[33] thereby opening lands to settlement that Congress had set aside twenty-five years earlier for the Indian nations. With the decision in the mid-1850s to open the West to homesteading, the federal government, frequently employing duress and fraud, continued to treat with tribes for the cession of their lands and their relocation to reservations. Over the next ten years the federal government negotiated fifty-three treaties with various tribes, thereby acquiring more than 174 million acres for settlement.[34]

As the first transcontinental railroad neared completion, bringing in more settlers, the tribes reacted fiercely to protect their lands and way of life. In 1867 Congress appointed a peace commission to examine the sources and solutions to the wars raging in the West. The commission's report blamed the hostilities on the federal government's failure to keep its treaty commitments and on its repeated demands for more tribal land cessions. Congress agreed with the commission that the root of the problem lay in the treaty process.[35] The solution, however, according to federal officials, lay not in improved adherence to the treaties, but in discontinuing treatymaking and solving the Indian problem by absorbing tribes into mainstream America.

To assimilate the tribes, the federal government had to convince or compel them to forego their communal societies and to adopt individualistic values; i.e., Indian people would have to accept the Western concept of social justice, destroying in the process their culture and identity. To accomplish this objective, the government needed legislation to diminish sovereignty and to alter the internal affairs of the tribes. The treaty process, with its emphasis on national identity and sovereignty, was particularly unsuited to assimilation. In 1871 the House of Representatives attached a rider onto an appropriations bill providing that thereafter no Indian nation or tribe would be recognized as an independent power with whom the government could treat.[36]

With the 1871 Appropriations Act, Congress signaled its intention to bring Indian policies completely under its authority as an internal matter. In the future, Indian affairs would be handled not through treaties, but through legislation. To legitimize this action, the courts would have to "domesticate" the principles which had previously governed the federal-tribal relationship. The courts had signaled their ability to effect this change in two previous decisions, the 1846 *Rogers* and 1870 *Cherokee Tobacco* cases.[37]

Rogers, a white man adopted by the Cherokee Nation, had killed another adopted white tribal member. Tried by federal officials, Rogers appealed his conviction on the grounds that the Cherokee courts were the proper judicial forum to examine the commission of crimes by

Cherokees on Cherokee land. Rogers based his argument on historical tradition and on the New Echota treaty which guaranteed to the Cherokees the right to pass laws deemed necessary for the protection of persons and property within their boundaries.

Ignoring the treaty's provision and the tribe's right to determine its own membership, the Supreme Court ruled that Rogers, adopted at a mature age, was not an Indian. More importantly, the Court stated that the federal government had never treated with the tribe as an independent sovereign, nor were they regarded as the owners of their lands. Congress, therefore, had the authority to punish any offense committed in Cherokee Territory. By doing so, the government was merely exercising "its power over this unfortunate race in the spirit of humanity and justice," and endeavoring "to enlighten their minds . . . and to save them if possible from the consequences of their own vices."[38]

Justice Roger Taney's decision considerably diluted the protections provided by Justice Marshall only fifteen years earlier. Both Marshall and the Removal Bill had acknowledged the tribes' right to control their own internal affairs. Taney ignored these important points and decreed that the federal government, as owners of the land, had ultimate territorial jurisdictional rights over the land. With this decision, the courts added federal ownership of Indian lands to the treatymaking and commerce clauses as sources of governmental authority over tribes.

Following the Civil War, the United States negotiated another treaty with the Cherokees. Article 10 of the 1866 treaty provided that Cherokee farm products would be exempt from all taxation.[39] Two years later, Congress passed an act imposing a tax on all liquor and tobacco sold "anywhere within the exterior boundaries of the United States."[40] Pursuant to this provision, federal officials assessed Cherokee tobacco manufacturers a tax on the tobacco sold within the Cherokee Nation. A Cherokee businessman, E. C. Boudinot, with the Cherokee Nation as an interested party, filed suit in the Supreme Court, arguing that the 1866 treaty specifically exempted the Cherokees from payment of such a tax.[41]

The Court, denying the Cherokees' claim, informed Boudinot and the nation that as their territory lay within the United States, Cherokee members fell under the act's provisions. The justices handled the abrogation of the Cherokees' treaty by holding that a domestic law which conflicted with a treaty and passed subsequent to it, took precedence — a domestic legal principle which clearly violated the international legal principle of *pacta sunt servanda*, that treaties must be upheld.

The 1871 law to terminate treatymaking with tribes and the *Cherokee Tobacco* decision permitting the abrogation of previous treaty commitments effectively ended the mechanism by which the federal government had related to the Indian tribes as nations. Without the requirement of making treaties, the government could begin the assimilation of individuals through legislation. Over the next thirty years, Congress passed a series of laws designed to accomplish this goal. In 1874, Congress passed a bill requiring tribal members to perform "service upon the reservation" in return for their annuities, even though the annuities were in payment for lands already ceded.[42] Five years later, Congress instituted the rudiments of an Indian educational system by establishing the Carlisle Indian School. In testimony before Congress, the school's director stated the school's ultimate objective: "We accept the watchword, let us by patient effort kill the Indian in him and save the man."[43] As late as the 1930s, reports detailed the forcible removal of Indian children from their homes — lassoed from horseback on the Navajo reservation — and sent to off-reservation boarding schools where school officials punished them for speaking their Indian languages and practicing their native religions and ceremonies.[44]

As traditional tribal society dissolved through the education of the young, the teaching of Christianity, and the rise in power of the Indian agent, the federal government increasingly supplanted native practices with non-Indian structures and procedures. Congress had authorized Indian police forces and Indian courts of appeals. In 1886, however, with the passage of the Seven Major Crimes Act, the federal government assumed jurisdiction over major crimes committed by Indians.[45] A year later Congress passed the most assimilative and destructive piece of legislation to date, the Land in Severalty Act or Dawes Act as it became known.[46] Far surpassing any previous infringement on tribal life, Theodore Roosevelt heralded the act as "a mighty pulverizing engine to break up the tribal mass."[47] The Dawes Act provided that reservation lands be allotted to individuals, with each tribal member receiving forty acres of farm land or 160 acres of grazing land. Land remaining after the allotment process was deemed surplus and sold to white settlers.

The federal government focused its determination to dissolve tribal lands and governments most concertedly on the Indian Territory. In what is now the state of Oklahoma, Congress relocated over fifty tribes with the promise that their property and powers of self-government would remain free from federal and state control. Under the terms of the 1898 Curtis Act,[48] however, Congress dissolved reservations and tribal governing bodies in the Indian Territory. The area guaranteed in numerous treaties always to remain in Indian hands was now opened to white settlement. Within fifty years, Congress had changed from treating with the tribes as sovereigns and acknowledging their rights to their lands and culture, to a policy of controlling Indians as individuals and attempting to engineer their integration into the dominant society.

By the turn of the century, the courts had completed the legal maneuverings necessary to support the federal government's decision to diminish tribal sovereignty and to encourage assimilation. In cases decided between 1876 and 1903, the Supreme Court broadened congressional authority under the commerce clause, allowed state jurisdiction in Indian country, further sanctioned the abrogation of Indian treaties, and provided for plenary or total congressional control over Indian affairs.[49] The judiciary effected these important changes by transforming Marshall's reference to a guardian-ward relationship in *Cherokee Nation* into a separate independent power over tribes.

In 1883, the Supreme Court handed down the *Ex Parte Crow Dog* decision, upholding the existence of tribal sovereignty.[50] In this case the Court ruled that the federal courts did not have jurisdiction under the Constitution to decide a case involving the murder of Spotted Tail by Crow Dog on the Lakota reservation. In answer to the government's claim that it had a treaty obligation to provide the Lakota with an orderly government, the Court responded that "[t]he pledge to secure to these people . . . an orderly government . . . necessarily implies . . . that among the arts of civilized life, which it was the very purpose of all these arrangements to introduce and naturalize among them, was the highest and best of all, that of self-government, the regulation by themselves of their own domestic affairs, the maintenance of order and peace among their own members by the administration of their own laws and customs."[51]

Congress reacted to the Court's ruling in *Crow Dog* with disbelief and anger. Two years later, as previously mentioned, Congress assumed partial criminal jurisdiction on reservations by tacking the Seven Major Crimes Act onto the 1885 appropriations bill. Under the provisions of this act, the federal courts assumed jurisdiction over Indians committing murder, manslaughter, rape, assault with intent to kill, arson, burglary and larceny. A year later in *U.S.* v. *Kagama*, the Supreme Court reviewed congressional authority to exercise criminal jurisdiction in Indian country.[52]

Heretofore, Congress's power under the Constitution to relate to Indians had emanated from the treatymaking, warmaking and commerce clauses. The attorney general argued in the *Kagama* case that the federal government possessed authority under the commerce clause to assume criminal jurisdiction over Indians. The Court (not surprisingly, given the lack of commerce involved in the murder) refused to support the government's analysis. But in a decision reminiscent of Marshall's ingenious ability to create new legal principles to fit the needs of the dominant society, the Court ruled that the government could assume jurisdiction under its authority as a guardian to the tribes. Justice Miller acknowledged the tribes as having a semi-independent position; that the government had recognized them "not as States, not as nations, . . . but as a separate people, with the power of regulating their internal social relations, and thus far not brought under the laws of the Union or of the State within whose limits they resided."[53]

Despite this recognition and the federal government's history of relating to tribes through the treaty process, the Court explained that Congress had decided upon a new approach — to govern the tribes by legislation. This change in procedure, according to the Court, was warranted by the tribes' dependent condition: "These tribes are the wards of the nation. . . . From their very weakness and helplessness, . . . and the treaties in which it has been promised, there arises the duty of protection, and with it the power."[54]

By admitting that the federal government had no clearly defined constitutional authority by which to assume criminal jurisdiction over tribes, but then inferring the power from the guardianship doctrine, the *Kagama* decision completely convoluted the previous understanding of the protectorate relationship. As Marshall had originally stressed in *Worcester*, the treaties represented the federal government's acknowledgement of and agreement to protect tribal self-government; they did not imply destruction of the protected.[55] The *Kagama* interpretation of the guardianship responsibility, which Marshall had viewed as protecting the Indian nations, was now overturned and interpreted to allow the destruction of the tribes.

With the *Lone Wolf* v. *Hitchcock* decision in 1903, the Supreme Court succeeded in placing tribes firmly and totally under the legal authority of the federal government.[56] Lone Wolf, on behalf of himself and other members of the Kiowa and Comanche tribes, charged the federal government with abrogating the Treaty of Medicine Lodge and disposing of tribal property in violation of the Fifth Amendment. Congress had taken lands from the tribes despite Article 12 of their treaty, which guaranteed that the federal government would take no property without the approval of three-fourths of the adult males. In more than one election, the tribes overwhelmingly refused to cede any of their lands. Ignoring the election results, the federal government extinguished the tribes' title to a large portion of their reservation.

The Court refused to enforce the treaty's guarantees, ruling that the tribes' dependent status and the government's role as their guardian took precedence. To hold Congress to the treaty, the Court wrote, would limit congressional authority to care for and to protect Indians. The Court conceded that previous decisions had described the tribes' right to their lands as fee simple. That characterization, the justices explained, protected the tribes only from the taking of their lands by states or private individuals. The tribes' title could not be protected against the federal government. Federal control over Indian lands was plenary by virtue of its guardianship duty. Citing an earlier case, *Beecher* v. *Wetherby*, the Court emphasized that the only limitations on federal authority to dispose of Indian lands were those "considerations of justice as would control a Christian people in their treatment of an ignorant and dependent race."[57]

The Court's elevation of the federal government's obligation to protect tribes to an independent power *over* tribes proved devastating to tribal sovereignty. Rather than regarding Indian treaties as a bar against all uninvited governmental incursion, the courts interpreted the treaties as protection against state regulation, but also as a license for federal control. The federal government's decision during this period to disregard tribal sovereignty and to assimilate the Indians by whatever means possible has remained one of American society's most blatant denials of social justice to any group. In the attainment of assimilation, the federal government attacked every aspect of Indian society — ruining the economic base through the individualization of tribal property; destroying the social base through the abridgement of religious rights, the extinction of language, and the forced acceptance of the white educational system; and dissolving the political base through the imposition of Bureau of Indian Affairs' agents and other white political structures.

These efforts to diminish Indian sovereignty and to destroy tribal traditions and authority, however, were not entirely successful. Indian cultures proved tenacious, adaptable and viable. And, as had occurred with the *Crow Dog* case, the judicial system periodically reported decisions which affirmed the continued existence of tribal sovereignty and rights. The 1896 *Talton* v. *Mayes* ruling was one example.[58] In this case, a Cherokee plaintiff convicted of murder by his tribal court requested that his conviction be overturned on the grounds that the Cherokee jury consisted of fewer members than required under the United States Constitution. At issue in the case was the source of powers exercised by the Cherokee government. Did the Cherokee Nation administer authority delegated to it by the United States Constitution, or were they implementing local powers not created by the Constitution?[59] The Court ruled that the Cherokees exercised powers which predated the federal Constitution; their governmental powers were, in essence, extraconstititutional.

This decision points to the confusing legal status of tribal sovereignty as the twentieth century unfolded. Two conflicting lines of cases existed. *Worcester, Crow Dog* and *Talton* stood for the viability of inherent tribal sovereignty. Tribes were distinct political communities protected by their treaties and sovereignty from federal and state intervention. These cases recognized tribal authority to regulate their own members and territory, thereby ensuring tribes the freedom to govern themselves according to their own religious and cultural imperatives.

The *Cherokee Nation, Kagama* and *Lone Wolf* line of cases, conversely, recast the protectorate relationship into a guardian-ward relationship which granted the United States plenary or total control over the tribes. The guardianship doctrine became the primary authority by which the federal government exerted administrative control over the tribes and their members. Tribal sovereignty was no longer safeguarded against federal and state incursions. And, as discussed, Congress passed, pursuant to the legal precepts established in these cases, numerous pieces of legislation designed to undermine tribal sovereignty and force the Indian population into mainstream America.

### The Reassertion of Tribal Sovereignty

By the 1930s, conditions in Indian country revealed that the federal government's attempts to assimilate Indians had failed miserably. As the often-cited Meriam Report of 1928 demonstrated, Indian people were living in desperate circumstances. This study reported that tribes had lost ninety million acres or almost two-thirds of their lands through the allotment process. The report also disclosed the dismal state of education and health care and lack of economic opportunity found on all reservations.[60]

To remedy these conditions, Congress passed the Indian Reorganization Act (IRA) in 1934.[61] The act prohibited the further allotment and alienation of reservation lands, provided for the establishment of a revolving loan fund for economic development, instituted procedures whereby tribes could incorporate for business purposes, and supported Indian culture for the first time with the establishment of the Indian Arts and Crafts Board. Moreover, the act provided to tribes accepting the provisions of the law the opportunity to establish tribal councils and courts. Defenders hailed the IRA as important legislation which affirmed and strengthened Indian sovereignty. Critics labeled the act as but one more effort in a lengthy process designed to destroy traditional Indian governing systems. Traditionalists argued that the Bureau of Indian Affairs had reestablished tribal governments and court systems, but had done so using non-Indian frameworks and practices. Tribes exercised increased autonomy and control, but authority was administered using Anglo practices, rather than traditional Indian ones.

The pendulum again swung towards the renouncement of tribal rights in the 1950s and 1960s. Neither the federal government nor the general population had fully supported the IRA. Three years after the act's passage, John Collier, the Commissioner of Indian Affairs, wrote in the *New York Times* that the two largest interests lobbying against the bureau's work were companies hoping to acquire Indian lands, and Indian welfare groups, including religious groups, who believed the Indians' communal values and cultural practices to be un-American and uncivilized.[62] This view of Indian culture as backward and slightly suspicious gained prominence after World War II as the nation experienced a frenzy of economic prosperity and ideological purity. By 1953, congressional members had again become convinced that the solution to the Indian problem lay essentially in "getting rid of the Indian," i.e., ending tribal status by terminating the federal-Indian trust relationship.[63]

House Concurrent Resolution 108 provided that Congress, "as rapidly as possible," move to free those tribes listed "from Federal supervision and control and from all disabilities and the limitations specially applicable to Indians."[64] For those tribes falling under the resolution, termination meant the end of the trust relationship and their recognition by the federal government as distinct legal entitites. For the most part, reservation lands were sold with proceeds going to tribal members. For those tribes who had their lands placed in a private trust, federal protection and aid were no longer available. Termination also meant the end to all special tribal programs, the removal of individual state tax exemptions, and the imposition of state civil and criminal authority. Tribes were free to retain their cultural identity, but their legal identity and rights to inherent sovereignty were no longer recognized.

The federal government's repudiation of tribal sovereignty through the termination process created enormous problems for those tribes directly affected by the process and disquiet throughout Indian country for those whose turn was yet to come. In response to the termination legislation and the serious problems brought about by tribal disenfranchisement, tribes and urban Indians across the country organized, lobbied, sued and protested. Out of numerous meetings, fish-ins, sit-ins, takeovers and confrontations, such as Wounded Knee and the

Longest Walk, came statements defining the Indian concept of social justice. From the American Indian Chicago Conference in 1961 mentioned previously, 460 Indians representing ninety tribes urged: "We, the Indian People, must be governed by principles in a democratic manner with a right to choose our way of life. Since our Indian culture is threatened by presumption of being absorbed by the American society, we believe we have the responsibility of preserving our precious heritage."[65]

In 1974, the National Congress of American Indians (NCAI) adopted an American Indian Declaration of Sovereignty which stated, in part, "that the Government of the United States of America, in performance and recognition of its treaty obligations and responsibilities, has Failed and Neglected: To fully recognize inherent Aboriginal American Indian sovereignty and the rights and powers of self-government and self-determination. . . ."[66] In these and other public statements, Indian people demanded justice from the dominant society through the affirmation of tribal sovereignty, the recognition of treaty commitments, and the extinguishment of BIA paternalism.

The federal government, in another reversal of policy, responded positively to these demands. In 1970, President Richard Nixon, in a special address to Congress, repudiated the termination policies of the previous decade and the Bureau of Indian Affairs' paternalistic orientation. In response to Nixon's pledge to embark on a new federal policy oriented toward Indian self-determination, Congress passed the Indian Self-Determination and Education Assistance Act of 1975.[67] The main thrust of the act provided tribes with the opportunity to assume control of programs and services currently provided by the bureau, such as housing, education and economic development. The act proved to be one of the most significant pieces of Indian legislation ever passed by Congress. It has allowed tribes to manage their own programs, administered by their own people. In several instances, tribes have assumed the administration of all federal programs previously operated by BIA personnel.

## Current Status of Tribal Sovereignty

Several truths emerge from the preceding historical review of tribal-federal relations. Without a commitment to tribal sovereignty, social justice for Indians is nonexistent. It is clear that Indians have suffered most severely at those points in history when the United States has sought to reduce or destroy tribal sovereignty. And as history has also shown, despite the federal government's stated commitment in recent years to respecting and to protecting tribal sovereignty, its existence remains precarious.

As the following section discusses, the courts' current assessment of tribal sovereignty is a product of the judiciary's pronouncements over the last 150 years. Elements of the original status and relationship as defined by Marshall remain, but are tempered and limited by judicial legacies of the federal government's recurring efforts to assimilate the tribes. Tribal authority over reservation lands and inhabitants is no longer exclusive but a shared responsibility of tribal, federal and state governments.

*Federal Powers*

The Indian nations occupy a unique and, for the most part, illogical position within the federal structure. Tribes retain aspects of their inherent sovereignty, yet are subject to the plenary control of Congress. Tribal governments are extraconstitutional, yet the courts have only once overturned a congressional law applicable to Indians. This anomalous situation is the consequence of a conflict between policies affirming inherent tribal sovereignty and legislative and administrative measures devised to assimilate tribal individuals.

Today the federal government refers to the federal-tribal relationship as a government-to-government and trust relationship. Congress maintains a unique and separate relationship with each of the 309 recognized tribes in the United States. This relationship arises from the inherent sovereignty of each party and the acknowledgement that the United States, in exchange for millions of acres of land, pledged to protect Indian property and existence.

In the mid-1930s, the courts began to refashion the guardianship doctrine into the trust relationship. For example, in *Creek Nation* the Supreme Court ruled that the federal government's control over tribal property was not absolute.[68] Rather, tribes possessed judiciable rights and the federal government possessed fiduciary responsibilities within the relationship. Successive courts have found the trust relationship to extend to the protection of tribal lands, resources, funds, and certain aspects of tribal existence. Specific promises of protection are contained within the more than 370 treaties and agreements still legally binding on the United States, within scattered pieces of legislative provisions such as the Indian Health Care Improvement Act, and within judicial decisions.

Over the last few decades, the courts have relocated the once independent guardianship or plenary doctrine in the Constitution. Federal authority over tribes, according to recent court decisions, is derived from the congressional power to regulate commerce with the Indian tribes, the power to conclude treaties and, to a lesser extent, congressional authority to make regulations governing the territory belonging to the United States.[69]

No matter the precise location or source of the federal government's relationship with tribes, it is a relationship that is political, not racial, in nature. This was clearly stated by the Court in *Morton* v. *Mancari*.[70] At issue in the *Mancari* case was whether the Bureau of Indian Affairs' preferential hiring of Indians constituted invidious discrimination against non-Indians. According to the decision, the constitutionality of the hiring statute turned "on the unique legal status of Indian tribes under federal law and upon the plenary power of Congress, based on a history of treaties and the assumption of a 'guardian-ward' status to legislate on behalf of federally recognized Indian tribes."[71] The authority of Congress to deal with the special problems of Indians was derived from the treatymaking clause and the commerce clause, which singled Indians out as a proper subject for special legislation. Therefore, the Court stressed, the hiring was of a political and not of a racial nature. As long as the government's special treatment of the tribes could be "tied rationally to the fulfillment of Congress' unique obligation toward the Indians," the Court would not interfere with the actions of Congress.[72]

The *Mancari* decision initially instilled hope in Indian people and lawyers that successive courts would use the "tied rationally" test to limit the plenary doctrine and to protect tribal sovereignty against unwarranted federal and state encroachments. This has not occurred, however. While the courts have trimmed the excesses of the guardianship doctrine by finding that the tribes have enforceable rights against the executive branch, the plenary authority of Congress remains intact. As the judiciary stated in a relatively recent decision, tribal sovereignty exists "only at the sufferance of Congress" which has the "plenary authority to limit, modify or eliminate the powers of local self-government."[73] One important way Congress and the courts have limited tribal powers is allowing increased state authority over reservation lands.

*State Powers*

For almost fifty years, Marshall's ruling in *Worcester* that states were barred from exercising control over tribes protected the Indian nations from state interference. Federal authority and tribal sovereignty,

Marshall stressed, preempted state authority from assuming jurisdiction over tribal lands and Indian people. The United States Constitution did not grant authority to the states to exercise jurisdiction over tribes, and states did not possess the requisite sovereignty to conclude treaties with the Indian nations. As the Tenth Circuit court wrote many years later, tribes possess a status higher than states.[74]

The first serious divergence from the *Worcester* analysis came in the 1881 *McBratney* decision.[75] In this case, the Supreme Court found that the trial of a non-Indian charged with the murder of another non-Indian on the Ute reservation properly lay within the jurisdiction of the state courts. The Court ruled that Congress had not expressly preempted state jurisdiction over such offenses when Colorado was admitted to the Union. The decision, which neglected to consider tribal jurisdictional interests and to weigh tribal political independence as a bar to state incursion, seriously impaired tribal authority to assert jurisdiction over events within their boundaries and narrowed the federal preemption doctrine.

*McBratney* was but one of several attempts by states to claim jurisdiction over tribal affairs. In the following years, states successfully asserted control over the person or property of nontribal members and won the right to levy some taxes within reservation boundaries.[76] By the twentieth century, the state had replaced the federal government as the more formidable threat to tribal sovereignty. Ignorance of Indian rights and traditions, jealousies over Indian exemptions, greed for Indian lands and resources, economic competition and racial prejudice merged to create a troubled and adverse relationship between states and tribes.

Congress exacerbated the tensions between tribes and states with the passage of Public Law 93-280 in 1953.[77] This legislation, which was part of the termination momentum, enabled five states — California, Minnesota, Nebraska, Oregon and Wisconsin — to assume complete civil and criminal jurisdiction over most tribes within their borders. In addition to granting jurisdiction to those states, the bill contained procedures which allowed the remaining states to assume jurisdiction. As with the termination policy, tribes were given no opportunity to decide whether they wished to fall under state control. Finally, after intense lobbying, tribes obtained in 1968, as part of the Indian Civil Rights Act, passage of a provision allowing for retrocession of jurisdiction to the tribes and a provision requiring tribal consent before states could claim future jurisdiction under P.L. 93-280.[78]

As congressional policy concerning state jurisdiction over reservations vacillated, the judicial branch entered the controversy with two decisions which were to have a major impact on tribal-state jurisdictional disputes. In *Williams* v. *Lee,* the Supreme Court held that a non-Indian trader on the Navajo reservation could not sue a Navajo tribal member in state court for collection of a debt incurred within reservation boundaries. "[T]he basic policy of *Worcester* has remained," the Court stated. "Essentially, absent governing Acts of Congress, the question has always been whether the state action infringed on the right of reservation Indians to make their own laws and be ruled by them."[79]

The infringement test, as it became known, consisted of two parts. Courts first had to decide if Congress had preempted the field either for itself or for state action. Previously, if the answer was negative, jurisdiction remained with the tribe. Now the second part of the test provided that if the jurisdiction did not interfere with the tribes' right to self-government, state authority would be allowed. The extent to which tribal sovereignty remained free of state incursions thus depended upon the courts' willingness to broadly interpret tribal actions as necessary components of self-government.

In 1973, the Supreme Court in *McClanahan* v. *Arizona State Tax Commission* expanded upon its explanation of the infringment test.[80] In ruling that Arizona could not tax the income of an Indian earned on the reservation, the Court emphasized that state law would be allowed to intrude on the reservation only if it did not interfere with tribal self-government and if non-Indians were involved.

In reaching his decision, Justice Thurgood Marshall noted that the trend was away from the idea of inherent Indian sovereignty and towards federal preemption as a bar to state jurisdiction. Furthermore, "[t]he modern cases thus tend to avoid reliance on platonic notions of Indian sovereignty. . . . The Indian sovereignty doctrine is relevant . . . [as] a backdrop against which applicable treaties and relevant statutes must be read."[81] Although the *McClanahan* case was a victory for tribes, the infringement test combined with Thurgood Marshall's analysis of tribal status have left tribes open to the vagaries of the courts' interpretation of the viability of "a platonic notion" and a "backdrop" and of what constitutes "self-government."

Recent court decisions have shown a marked orientation toward interpreting self-government on the basis of individual as opposed to territorial jurisdictional rights. Tribal self-government, according to the federal judiciary, refers basically to the tribes' relationship with its own members or citizens. The non-Indians living on the reservation, according to the courts, are the proper concern of the state.

This reasoning has proven to be a serious blow to tribal sovereignty and to the practical administration of tribal government. For example, hunting and fishing, until recently, were considered to be under the total purview of the tribes.[82] Even during the termination period, Congress had carefully excluded hunting and fishing rights from state control under the terms of P.L. 93-280. In 1981, however, the Supreme Court diminished the tribes' right to regulate hunting and fishing by finding that states possessed the authority to regulate hunting and fishing by nonmembers on non-Indian lands within the reservation.[83] Given that game is transitory, the ruling has impeded tribal efforts to implement comprehensive fish and game programs.

The courts have used a similar rationale when faced with the issue of state taxing authority within reservation boundaries. In general, the courts have held that the state may not tax the reservation-generated income of tribal members, but may tax the reservation-generated income of nontribal members.[84] In the late 1970s, the state of Washington argued that it had a right to collect cigarette taxes from non-Indians on the Colville reservation. The Colvilles countered the state's assertion with the argument that they levied their own tribal cigarette tax. The resulting revenue was used to fund a variety of tribal programs. If forced to collect the state tax, the competitiveness of the cigarettes, and hence their taxing scheme, would generate little revenue for tribal programs. Pushing aside the tribe's claims, the Court ruled that requiring a tribe to collect a state cigarette tax from nonmembers did not interfere with the Colvilles' right of self-government.[85]

## Tribal Powers

Despite the legal and practical curtailments that tribal sovereignty has suffered, the most basic premise of tribal sovereignty has remained. The powers of Indian tribes are "inherent powers of a limited sovereignty which has never been extinguished."[86] Inherent sovereignty is what distinguishes tribal governments from municipalities, which also possess self-government. While closely related, the terms sovereignty and self-government are not synonomous. Sovereignty refers to the intangible and spiritually derived feeling of oneness. Sovereignty is not something that one government can delegate to another. Powers of self-government, on the other hand, can be delegated from one governmental body to another. Municipalities, for example, are not inherently sovereign, but operate using powers of self-government delegated by the states. The powers which Indian nations choose to exercise, however, are not delegated to tribes by the federal government or by the states. Tribal powers of self-government are derived from inherent tribal sovereignty. Hence, the appropriate question in determining whether a tribe possesses governmental powers is not to ask if the power has been delegated to the tribes, but whether the authority has been removed.

Initially, the United States acknowledged the tribes' exclusive authority to expand or limit their own sovereign powers. Indian nations, like all international sovereigns, periodically relinquished aspects of their sovereignty through the treaty process. For example, some tribes found it advantageous to cede jurisdiction over crimes committed by non-Indians to the United States. Others concluded exclusive trade arrangements with the United States or other sovereign powers.[87] Unrestricted governing jurisdiction continued for the most part until the latter 1800s and the advent of the federal government's assimilation policy. Supported by the courts, Congress enacted a host of legislative measures designed to assimilate the Indian into the white mainstream. Tribal authority, the courts concluded, could now be extinguished or limited by treaties and express congressional legislation.

In 1978, the Supreme Court in *Oliphant* v. *Suquamish Indian Tribe* added a third limitation on the exercise of tribal powers, holding that tribes may not exercise authority which is inconsistent with their status as a domestic dependent nation.[88] In this case, two non-Indians sentenced by the Suquamish tribal court for disturbing the peace on the reservation appealed their convictions to the federal courts, arguing that the Suquamish did not possess jurisdiction over non-Indians. After reviewing congressional legislation from 1834 to the present, the Court held that although the federal government had never extinguished the tribal exercise of criminal jurisdiction over non-Indians, Congress had intended to preempt the field. The Court ruled that the Suquamish's exercise of criminal jurisdiction over non-Indians was inconsistent with their status as a domestic dependent nation and conflicted with the United States' overriding interest as the superior sovereign.

By stressing congressional intent rather than express legislation, the Court revised the traditional principle that tribal powers remained unless specifically removed by Congress. The new judicial test now stated that tribes could not exercise powers limited by treaties or congressional statute (the old test), or in areas which conflicted with their status as a domestic dependent nation. Exactly what was considered to be "in conflict with a domestic dependent nation status" and in the "interest of the overriding sovereign," the Court did not define. And in light of history, the obvious danger of the new test is that if Congress should decide to embark once again upon a policy of termination and assimilation, the Court's test is sufficiently vague to support virtually any federal action.

The above limitations notwithstanding, tribes have retained impressive powers of self-government. The most basic authority within the constellation of tribal powers is the right to define and structure government. Tribal governing structures vary considerably from the traditional democracies of California bands, Alaskan natives, and member nations of the Iroquois Confederacy, to the pueblo theocracies and the anglo-oriented Indian Reorganization Act-governments possessed by approximately one-half of the tribes in the United States. Like all government, tribal governments are basically responsible for governing their citizens and territory. The governing of one's citizens begins with the right to determine membership. Citizenship specifies who shall be eligible to share in the benefits that accrue to the polity. Tribes determine membership according to one or a combination of the following four methods: blood quantum, descendancy, or according to the patrilineal or matrilineal traditions of the tribe.

The Supreme Court upheld tribal authority to determine membership in *Santa Clara Pueblo* v. *Martinez*.[89] Under Santa Clara Pueblo law, children of women who married non-Pueblo men could not enroll as tribal members, inherit their mother's portion of tribal property, or claim the right to reside on the reservation after their mother's death. Children of Pueblo men who married outside the reservation were allowed to participate in all tribal benefits. Mrs. Martinez, on behalf of herself and her children, sued the tribal council for violation of the equal protection of the laws under the Indian Civil Rights Act.

In this important case upholding tribal sovereignty, Justice Thurgood Marshall stressed that the federal government recognized the tribes as quasi-sovereign nations, which "by government structure, culture, and source of sovereignty are in many ways foreign . . . ."[90] Congress, as a means of furthering tribal self-government, had recognized the tribal courts as the most appropriate forum for adjudicating tribal disputes. Mrs. Martinez's dispute with the tribe over its membership criteria, the Court reasoned, properly lay with the tribal and not the federal courts.

Approximately 146 tribal court systems operate throughout Indian country. These court systems range from the complex Navajo Tribal Court system, which is headed by an attorney general and governed by more than fifteen tribal codes, to the traditional laws of the pueblo theocracies. These courts exercise limited criminal and full civil and regulatory authority over members, as well as civil and regulatory authority over nonmembers.

In 1978, the Supreme Court clearly affirmed in the *Wheeler* case the inherent right of tribes to exercise criminal jurisdiction over members.[91] The Navajo Tribal Court had convicted Anthony Wheeler of disorderly conduct. More than a year later, the District Court for the State of Arizona convicted him of statutory rape. As both the tribal and federal convictions resulted from the same incident, the defendant appealed, arguing his conviction in federal court had violated his right against double jeopardy.

At issue was whether the Navajo Nation was an independent sovereign, or was in some manner an extension of the federal government. The Court denied Wheeler's motion. Although within the United States and subject to the plenary control of the United States, the Navajos were a separate sovereign with powers of regulating their internal and social relations.

The *Wheeler* decision, while vigorously supportive of tribal sovereignty, illustrates one of the difficulties experienced by tribes in providing law and order on the reservation. Had the Navajos tried Wheeler for statutory rape, this case in all likelihood would not have arisen. The provisions of the Major Crimes Act,[92] which allows the federal government to assume jurisdiction over felonies committed by Indians, and of the Indian Civil Rights Act,[93] which prevents tribes from levying penalties over one year in jail and $5000 in fines, effectively prevent tribes from handling major crimes which occur on the reservation. This limitation, combined with the extinguishment of criminal jurisdiction over non-Indians, has severely hampered tribes from being able to provide reservation inhabitants with proper law and order. Tribal police are prevented from adequately responding to the commission of a crime if a non-Indian is involved, and Indians who may have committed serious crimes might escape prosecution due to overworked or uncaring federal authorities.

Civil jurisdiction over members and nonmembers presents fewer complexities. Tribes have clear and recognized authority to determine membership and to regulate domestic affairs such as marriage, divorce, inheritance and child custody. Regulatory powers include taxation and zoning, and the right to regulate commerce, property and on- and off-reservation fishing rights.[94]

As discussed previously, the Court ruled in the *Williams* case that in situations involving non-Indians and "essential tribal relations," tribes possess clear authority. Accordingly, the courts have consistently upheld the right of tribes to license and to tax nonmembers. This right was mostly recently affirmed in *Merrion* v. *Jicarilla Apache Tribe*.[95] The Court ruled that the power to tax was an essential attribute of Indian sovereignty because it is a necessary instrument of self-government and territorial management.[96]

The management of hunting and fishing, like taxation, is another important regulatory power exercised by tribes. Particularly in the

Northwest and Midwest, fishing is an important tribal enterprise for several tribes. For many other Indian people, hunting and fishing provide an important supplement to other economic endeavors. The judiciary has affirmed that hunting and fishing, like water and resource rights, are part of the reserved rights doctrine, which affirms that tribes retain all property rights to their land unless ceded to the federal government. Also implicit within this principle is the right to regulate the use of these resources by members and nonmembers. Tribes possess full authority to regulate hunting and fishing by members on- and off-reservation and by nonmembers on tribal lands. The states can regulate non-Indian hunting and fishing on non-Indian-owned lands located within the boundaries of the reservation.

### Sovereignty: The Political, Economic and Cultural Dimensions

The preceding discussion has examined the historical and current legal definition and parameters of Indian sovereignty. The vitality of tribal sovereignty, however, is not measured solely by legal determinants. Political, economic and cultural considerations may also prove to be of major importance in assessing the degree of tribal sovereignty possessed by any particular tribe.

While the courts are responsible for interpreting the broad outlines of the tribal-federal and tribal-state relationships, each tribe maintains its own separate and unique government-to-government relationship with Congress. The content of each tribe's relationship with the federal government is defined by general legislation and court cases and by the specific treaties, legislation and legal decisions which apply to each tribe. State laws may also be of importance, such as for those tribes in P.L. 93-280 states.

Given that Congress possesses plenary authority over tribes and with it the ability to enhance or extinguish tribal rights, it is essential that tribes maintain good relations with their congressional representatives and correctly interpret the political climate. Especially in recent years, tribal lobbying campaigns have proven that tribes can be effective in protecting themselves against negative legislation as well as in obtaining the passage of important specific and general legislation which enhances their inherent sovereign powers. For example, the Seneca Nation of New York and the Colvilles of Washington prevented the termination of their relationship with Congress because of successful lobbying efforts with their congressional representatives. Other tribes, including the Menominee of Wisconsin and the Klamath and

Silitz of Oregon, successfully obtained congressional restoration of their tribal status and land bases several years after termination.

To date, individual congressional bills have proven to be the only vehicle by which tribes have obtained the return of land. Until the mid-1940s, Congress had barred Indian nations from filing suit to collect compensation for the unlawful extinguishment of their property title. In 1946, Congress passed the Indian Claims Commission Act to provide tribes with judicial redress for the illegal taking of tribal lands. Three hundred and seventy petitions were filed and $818 million in awards money distributed.[97] The Claims Commission Act, however, only provides for monetary compensation. The legislation does not allow for the return of lands — a demand many Indians see as basic to tribal sovereignty and justice. The few tribes which have been successful, such as the Yakima Nation of Washington and the Taos Pueblo of New Mexico, have had to mount extensive lobbying campaigns to obtain legislation providing for the return of tribal property. The Lakota people are the most recent group seeking to regain sacred lands. Following the 1980 Supreme Court decision which found that the United States had illegally taken the Black Hills,[98] Senator Bill Bradley of New Jersey introduced legislation to return 1.3 million acres of the sacred area to the Lakota people.

Significant legislation of a general nature passed pursuant to tribal political efforts includes the 1975 Indian Self-Determination Act and the 1978 Indian Child Welfare Act.[99] Future tribal lobbying efforts may focus on legislation to return to tribes the criminal jurisdiction over major crimes committed by members and over crimes committed by nonmembers. Such legislation would greatly assist tribes in the maintenance of peace and order on reservations. Another frequently mentioned piece of proposed legislation is the substitution of block grants for individual line items in the budget. Tribal leaders have frequently complained that under the present system, they are required to operate programs dictated by the federal government rather than programs which the tribe considers of greater economic and cultural priority.

If the 1970s were an era of political gains and losses, the 1980s and early 1990s have become a quest for economic self-sufficiency. Many Indian leaders today agree that true self-determination must include, in addition to political and cultural progress, the development of reservation economies. Economic conditions on many, if not most, reservations remain dismal and stagnant.

Tribal energies to strengthen their economies are proceeding on two fronts, public and private. Unfortunately, legislative attempts to increase or even to maintain federal spending levels have not proven successful. Budget cuts under the Reagan administration plunged several reservations into unemployment rates approaching 90 percent. Reduced appropriations combined with an ineffective administrative record of Bureau of Indian Affairs' funds have left tribes frequently unable to provide basic services.[100]

All tribes, in an effort to lessen their dependence on federal monies, are striving to develop their reservation economies through the exploitation of mineral resources, the establishment of enterprises, and the delivery of services. The Mississippi Choctaws, for example, have established a prosperous industrial park, housing more than five enterprises. Several of the northwestern tribes own and operate major fishing concerns complete with vessels, fish hatcheries and processing plants, which employ skilled biologists and fishery experts. Numerous other tribes, such as the Cherokee of North Carolina, the Warm Springs of Oregon and the Oneida of Wisconsin, have constructed tribal hotels and recreational facilities. One of the more lucrative endeavors now undertaken by over one hundred tribes is high-stakes bingo operations. The revenues collected from gaming have enabled tribal governments to infuse social programs with much-needed funds to maintain adequate levels of service.

Successful bingo operations, however, have again engendered state jealousies and attempts to limit tribal powers. Congressional representatives have introduced legislation to place bingo under state control, to limit proceeds, and to tax winnings. While the federal government may well pass legislation which will limit bingo operations, the Supreme Court has upheld the right of tribes to manage bingo operations free of state control. In *California, et al.* v. *Cabazon Band of Mission Indians*, Justice Byron White stressed that "Indian tribes retain attributes of sovereignty over both their members and their territory . . . ."[101] Bingo enterprises are a proper exercise of Indian sovereignty and of federal objectives to promote tribal self-sufficiency and economic development.

The *Cabazon* and other decisions notwithstanding, the failure of Congress to constitutionally protect tribal existence has created concern for many Indian people as they exercise increased powers of self-determination and attain greater economic self-sufficiency. This apprehension arises from a fear that the federal government's current self-determination policy may become "termination in disguise." The termination policies of the 1950s were predicated on the belief that American Indians would only attain true self-determination when the federal government's trust relationship with the tribes ended. Therefore, tribes chosen for termination were those that in the federal government's view, possessed some degree of stability, advancement and economic self-sufficiency. Many tribes fear that as Congress provides the vehicle for greater autonomy and as tribes progress in handling their own affairs, Congress will again decide to terminate its relationship with "its Indian wards."[102]

A related concern for many tribes is the impact of political and economic development on the maintenance of cultural identity. Culture is the soul of sovereignty and a necessary component of self-determination. For most Indian people, to sacrifice culture knowingly in the effort to attain increased powers of self-government and economic self-sufficiency is unacceptable.

Blatant federal attempts to destroy Indian languages, religions and cultures have ceased. Government policies of the last twenty years have recognized, and in some instances offered concrete support, for the maintenance of tribal culture. The Indian Child Welfare Act, for example, acknowledging that "there is no measure that is more vital to the continued existence and integrity of Indian tribes than their children and that the United States has a direct interest, as trustee, in protecting Indian children,"[103] provides tribes with the primary legal jurisdiction over the custody of their children.

The American Indian Religious Freedom Act of 1978 (AIRFA) recognized an official federal commitment to protect and preserve Indian religions, and mandated federal agencies to review procedures which could interfere with the free exercise of Indian religions.[104] While the Indian Child Welfare Act has been moderately successful in fulfilling its objectives, AIRFA has proven to be a dismal failure. To date, Indian plaintiffs have invoked AIRFA in approximately two dozen suits seeking the protection of First Amendment rights. The courts have denied their claims in all but four cases. The failure of tribes to win legal protection of their religious and cultural rights points to the continuing discrimination and ignorance of non-Indian society.


**Tribal Sovereignty at the International Level**

The Indian nations in the United States have expanded their efforts to attain social justice to the international level. Working in cooperation with Canadian Indians, people of the circumpolar region, tribes of Latin America, aborigines, Maoris and native peoples the world over, indigenous populations have carried their efforts beyond their own lands.

After World War II, human rights became a major focus of a number of international organizations, including the United Nations and the International Labor Organization. The human rights work of these bodies, however, generally has not reflected the needs and rights of indigenous peoples. Human rights, as defined by the United Nations Declaration on Human Rights and two international covenants, are individual-oriented principles emphasizing political and economic rights. Influenced primarily by the United States, much of the United Nations' human rights studies have centered on issues relating to discrimination.

Recognizing that the current UN orientation towards human rights was inadequate to the needs of indigenous populations, native peoples, specialists and concerned individuals initiated lobbying campaigns for the recognition and protection of aboriginal rights. Several new organizations, such as the World Council of Indigenous Peoples, the Indian Council of South America, the Inuit Circumpolar Conference, the Indian Law Resource Center, the International Indian Treaty Council, Four Circles Directions and the National Indian Youth Council, have joined with longer-established organizations such as Survival International to work towards the publication and promotion of indigenous needs.[105]

Their efforts culminated in a number of international conferences convened in the 1970s and 1980s to call attention to the plight of indigenous peoples. In 1977, the Non-Governmental Organization (NGO) Sub-Committee on Racism, Racial Discrimination, Apartheid and Decolonization of the Special NGO Committee on Human Rights sponsored the International NGO Conference on Discrimination Against Indigenous Populations in the Americas. Barbados II, a conference held the same year in the West Indies, evolved from an earlier conference of anthropologists sponsored by the University of Berne, Switzerland, and the World Council of Churches. In 1978, the World Conference to Combat Racism and Racial Discrimination endorsed the right of indigenous peoples to retain their traditional cultures and economies. In September 1979, the International Commission of Jurists and the Latin American Council for Law and Development, headquartered in Bogota, Colombia, sponsored a seminar which considered the economic, social and cultural rights of Indians of the Andean region. A year later, the Work Group Indian Project of the Netherlands hosted the Fourth Russell Tribunal on the Indians of the Americas. The tribunal considered and decided fourteen cases of violations of the rights of American Indians and produced a set of recommendations, a final statement, and a proclamation issued by indigenous participants.

In 1981, the aforementioned Special NGO Committee on Human Rights and the NGO Sub-Committee on Racism, Racial Discrimination, Apartheid and Decolonization sponsored an International NGO Conference on Indigenous Peoples and Land in Geneva, Switzerland.

The same year, UNESCO, in cooperation with the Latin American School of Social Sciences, convened a conference of specialists on ethnocide and ethnodevelopment in Latin America.[106]

Until the mid-1970s, the International Labour Organisation (ILO) was the only international governmental organization to have studied and reported in any detail on the plight of indigenous populations. In 1957, the ILO adopted Convention No. 107, Indigenous and Tribal Populations,[107] a document aimed at the eventual integration of indigenous peoples into the dominant populations. With the exception of the convention's provisions recognizing the traditional property and legal rights of indigenous populations, the document has received less than their full support. Responding to statements by indigenous groups about the convention's misdirected focus on assimilation, the secretariat has undertaken a revision of the convention, one that will promote indigenous definitions of social justice.

In the early decades of the United Nations' existence, the promotion of individual rights and protections against discrimination lent little assistance to Indians and other indigenous peoples in their struggle to obtain recognition of their right to self-determination and the protection of their land, resources and culture. The UN's human rights orientation broadened slightly in the late 1960s, however, laying the groundwork for a greater understanding of the special needs of indigenous peoples.

In 1971, the UN's Economic and Social Council (ECOSOC) passed resolution 1580(L) authorizing the Sub-Commission on the Prevention of Discrimination and Protection of Minorities to undertake a comprehensive study of discrimination against indigenous peoples and to suggest necessary national and international measures for eliminating such discrimination. The resulting "Study of the Problem of Discrimination Against Indigenous Populations," completed in 1983, is a voluminous compendium of information on indigenous populations in thirty-seven different countries.[108] As originally stated, the special rapporteur's mandate was to analyze the existence of discrimination against indigenous populations. After twelve years of study, the special rapporteur, reflecting the concerns of indigenous peoples the world over, correctly emphasized that the more important and vital concern was not the problem of discrimination, but was the attainment of self-determination: "[S]elf-determination [which includes economic, social, cultural and political factors and which exists in many forms] . . . must be recognized as the basic precondition for the enjoyment by indigenous peoples of their fundamental rights and the determination of their own future."[109]

This recommendation, and the more than 330 others contained in the final report, have formed the basis of discussion for the Working Group on Indigenous Populations, a body created in 1982 pursuant to one of the study's preliminary proposals.[110] The working group's mandate is to: (1) review recent developments in regard to the rights of indigenous peoples; and (2) give special attention to the evolution of standards for the promotion and protection of human rights and fundamental freedoms of indigenous peoples.[111]

In comparison with other UN bodies, the working group has proven to be relatively progressive and responsive to indigenous concerns. From the beginning, the working group adopted the policy of allowing all groups, not just those with formal consultative status, to speak before the body. More importantly, the working group has begun serious work on the drafting of a set of principles on indigenous rights. Working towards the goal of completing a draft by the time of the 1992 "cinquecentennial" of the "discovery" of the Americas, the working group has identified a number of principles for possible inclusion. Specified thus far for incorporation are principles concerning the rights to: life and freedom from torture; maintain one's own culture, language and way of life; land and mineral rights; self-government or self-determination; and freedom of religion and traditional practices.

### Conclusion

Social justice for American Indians can be defined as the acknowledgement and maintenance of their tribal sovereignty and, by extension, the retention of the tribal land base, the right to self-government, and the protection of tribal cultures. These are, however, social justice objectives which are group-oriented and, therefore, not goals inherent in the dominant population's definition of social justice. Rather, in general, the latter focuses on the protection of individual rights in the pursuit of civil and economic rights. This dissimilarity in philosophy, as revealed by the preceding historical review of tribal-federal relations, has resulted in Indians suffering most severely at those points in history when the United States has sought to reduce or to destroy tribal sovereignty.

The federal government's present policy is to acknowledge and support tribal sovereignty. Tribes are recognized as possessing the authority to define their own governments, determine their own membership, regulate their property and economic endeavors, levy taxes, and administer most criminal and civil matters. The existence of Indian sovereignty, however, remains precarious. The federal government still possesses plenary authority over tribes, including the unfettered ability to dispose of Indian lands and to withdraw recognition of Indian identity and services. Recently developed and vaguely worded legal tests — that the states may exercise jurisdiction that does not "infringe on tribal self-government"; that the government's role must be "tied rationally" to its commitment to Indians; that tribes may not exercise power "inconsistent with their status" — may well provide future courts with the mechanisms by which to divest tribes of a portion or all of their remaining sovereign powers. Economic self-sufficiency continues to be out of reach for most tribes, and the dominant population, due to ignorance and prejudice, continues to infringe upon tribal cultural identity and rights.

Respect for Indian sovereignty and their attainment of social justice ultimately depends upon two factors. The dominant population must be educated about the needs and rights of America's indigenous peoples and about America's moral and legal commitments to the fulfillment of those rights. And finally, there is the element which has been the best guarantor of tribal existence for the last five hundred years — the tenacious will of Indian people to retain their identities and cultures.

## NOTES

[1] American Indian Chicago Conference, "Creed," in *Declaration of Indian Purpose: The Voice of the American Indian*, held at the University of Chicago, June 13-20, 1961 (Chicago: University of Chicago Press, 1961), p. 5.

[2] John Rawls, *A Theory of Justice* (Cambridge, MA: Harvard University Press, 1971), pp. 3-4.

[3] Despite this viewpoint, Rawls does not advocate a society in which group rights would be recognized and respected. See, for example, the works of Vernon Van Dyke, "The Cultural Rights of Peoples," *Universal Human Rights* 2: 2 (April-June 1980): 1-21; "The Individual, the State and Ethnic Communities in Political Theory," *World Politics* 29: 3 (April 1977): 343-369; and "Human Rights and the Rights of Groups," *American Journal of Political Science* 18: 4 (November 1974): 725-741.

[4] See, for example, Howard L. Harrod, *Renewing the World: Plains Indian Religion and Morality* (Tucson, AZ: University of Arizona Press, 1987); Sam D. Gill, *Native American Religions: An Introduction* (Belmont, CA: Wadsworth Publishing, 1982); Ake Hultkrantz, *The Religion of the American Indians* (Berkeley, CA: University of California Press, 1979); and Peter J. Powell, *Sweet Medicine: The Continuing Role of the Sacred Arrows, the Sun Dance, and the Sacred Buffalo Hat in Northern Cheyenne History* (Norman, OK: University of Oklahoma Press, 1969).

[5]See Sharon O'Brien, "Cultural Rights in the United States: A Conflict of Values," *Law and Inequality* 5: 2 (July 1987): 267-358.

[6]See, for example, Felix S. Cohen, *Handbook of Federal Indian Law* (Washington, D.C.: U.S. Government Printing Office, 1942); David Getches, Daniel Rosenfelt and Charles F. Wilkinson, *Cases and Material on Federal Indian Law* (St. Paul, MN: West Publishing, 1978); Charles F. Wilkinson, *American Indians, Time and the Law: Native Societies in a Modern Constitutional Democracy* (New Haven, CT: Yale University Press, 1987); Vine Deloria, Jr., and Clifford M. Lytle, *The Nations Within: The Past and Future of American Indian Sovereignty* (New York: Pantheon Books, 1984); Russel Lawrence Barsh and James Youngblood Henderson, *The Road: Indian Tribes and Political Liberty* (Berkeley, CA: University of California Press, 1980); and Rennard Strickland and Charles F. Wilkinson, eds., *Felix Cohen's Handbook of Federal Indian Law* (Charlottesville, VA: Michie: Bobbs-Merrill, © 1982).

[7]See, for example, Francis Harry Hinsley, *Sovereignty*, 2d ed. (Cambridge, England, and New York: Cambridge University Press, 1986); Harold J. Laski, *The Foundations of Sovereignty, and Other Essays* (New York: Harcourt, Brace & Co., 1921); Charles E. Merriam, *History of the Theory of Sovereignty Since Rousseau* (New York: Columbia University Press, 1900); and Roscoe Pound, *Jurisprudence*, Vol. II, "The Nature of Law" (St. Paul, MN: West Publishing, 1959).

[8]Sir Robert Warrand Carlyle and Alexander James Carlyle, *History of Mediaeval Political Theory in the West* (Edinburgh: W. Blackwood, 1950-1962), Vol. V, "The Political Theory of the Thirteenth Century," pp. 45-85, 457-474.

[9]For a partial collection and discussion of the works of Locke, Hobbes and Rousseau, among others, see Alan Gerwith, *Political Philosophy* (New York: The MacMillan Company, 1965).

[10]Wilkinson, *American Indians, Time and the Law*, op. cit. note 6, p. 54.

[11]See sources cited in note 4.

[12]For a discussion of the impact of Indian political theories on the development of American democracy, see Bruce E. Johansen, *Forgotten Founders: Benjamin Franklin, the Iroquois, and the Rationale for the American Revolution* (Ipswich, MA: Gambit, 1982).

[13]Emer de Vattel, trans. Charles G. Fenwick, *The Law of Nations, or, Principles of the Law of Nature, Applied to the Conduct and Affairs of Nations and Sovereigns*, number 4 in James B. Scott, ed., *The Classics of International Law* (Washington, D.C.: Carnegie Institute of Washington, 1916), p. 11.
    Sovereignty, then, in western legal terms, refers to the state's ability or capacity to act as a sovereign, that is, to assume the rights and meet the responsibilities of an independent power. Among the chief rights and obligations of sovereign states are the conduct of war, peace, and commerce, the cession of territory, and the conclusion of treaties with other nations.

[14]Francisco de Vitoria, *De Jure Belli Relectiones* (New York: Oceana Publications, 1964), sec. 2, titles 6 and 7.

[15]See L. G. Van Loon, "Tawagonshi: The Beginning of the Treaty Era," *Indian Historian*, New Series, 1: 3 (Summer 1968): 22-26.

[16]See, for example, Henry De Puys, *A Bibliography of the English Colonial Treaties with the American Indians, including a Synopsis of Each Treaty* (New York: Lenox Club, 1917); and Julian P. Boyd, ed., *Indian Treaties Printed by Benjamin Franklin, 1736-1762* (Philadelphia: Historical Society of Pennsylvania, 1938).

[17]Charles Kappler, *Laws and Treaties* (Washington, D.C.: U.S. Government Printing Office, 1903).

[18]Hugo Grotius, trans. Francis W. Kelsey, *De Jure Belli ac Pacis Libri Tres*, number 3 in James B. Scott, ed., *The Classics of International Law* (Oxford: Clarendon Press, 1925), pp. 390-392. By 1739, Jean Barbeyrac had listed sixty subjects of treaties. See Denys P. Myers, "The Names and Scopes of Treaties, *American Journal of International Law* 51: 3 (July 1957): 574-605 at 579. See also Vattel, op. cit. note 13, p. 160.

[19]See, for example, treaties of: January 21, 1785, 7 U.S. Statutes at Large 16-18 [with Wyandots]; November 28, 1785, 7 U.S. Statutes at Large 18-21 [with Cherokees]; August 7, 1790, 7 U.S. Statutes at Large 35-38 [with Creeks]; July 2, 1791, 7 U.S. Statutes at Large 39-42 [with Cherokees]; June 16, 1802, 7 U.S. Statutes at Large 68-70 [with Creeks]; May 24, 1834, 7 U.S. Statutes at Large 450-457 [with Chickasaws]; and August 24, 1835, 7 U.S. Statutes at Large 474-477 [with Comanches and Witchetaws].

[20]Trade and Intercourse Act of 1790, 1 Stat. 137, July 22, 1790 (1st Congress, 2nd Session).

[21]The Cherokees, Choctaws, Chickasaws, Creeks and Seminoles comprise the Five Civilized Tribes.

[22]See Rennard Strickland, *Fire and the Spirits: Cherokee Law from Clan to Court* (Norman, OK: University of Oklahoma Press, 1975), pp. 227-228.

[23]S. Doc. No. 61, 1830 (21st Congress, 1st Session). For an excellent account of the political circumstances of the *Cherokee Nation* and *Worcester* cases, see Joseph C. Burke, "The Cherokee Cases: A Study in Law, Politics and Morality," *Stanford Law Review* 21: 3 (February 1969): 500-531.

[24]*Cherokee Nation* v. *Georgia*, 30 U.S.(5 Peters) 15 (1831).

[25]"The Cherokee Case," *Niles Weekly Register* (Baltimore, MD: September 25, 1830), p. 81.

[26]*Cherokee Nation*, op. cit. note 24, 30 U.S.(5 Pet.) at 17.

[27]The question facing Marshall was one of international law, i.e., whether the Cherokee Nation constituted an international sovereign. Chief Justice Marshall did not apply international legal principles to the issue, however, but rather looked at the question under domestic law. See Sharon O'Brien, "The Application of International Law to the Legal Status of American Indians" (Ph.D. Dissertation, University of Oregon, 1978).

[28]*Worcester* v. *Georgia*, 31 U.S.(6 Pet.) 515 (1832).

[29]Ibid., 31 U.S.(6 Pet.) at 557.

[30]Ibid., 31 U.S.(6 Pet.) at 553.

[31]Ibid., 31 U.S.(6 Pet.) at 552, 555.

[32]Contained within the Removal Bill was the promise that "the United States will secure and guaranty to them, their heirs or successors, the country so exchanged with them . . . ." Act of May 28, 1830, 4 Stat. 411-412 (21st Congress, 1st Session). President Jackson, speaking to an agent charged with negotiating with the tribes for removal, reportedly said, "Say to them, their father, the President, will lay off a country of equal extent. . . . He will establish landmarks for them never to be moved, and give them a fee simple title to their lands. You must be prepared to give assurances of permanency of title and dwell upon the idea that they will never be asked to surrender an acre more." Quoted in D'Arcy McNickle, *They Came Here First: The Epic of the American Indian*, rev. ed. (New York: Harper & Row, 1975), p. 195.

[33]Kansas-Nebraska Bill, 10 Stat. 277-290, May 30, 1854 (33rd Congress, 1st Session).

[34]"From the very beginnings of this nation, the chief issues around which federal Indian policy has revolved has been, not how to assimilate the Indian nations whose lands we usurped, but how to transfer Indian lands and resources to non-Indians." *U.S.* v. *Ahtanum Irrigation District*, 236 F.2d 321 (9th Cir. 1956), at 337, quoting Dorothy Van de Mark, "The Raid on the Reservations," *Harper's Magazine* 212: 1270 (March 1956).

[35]"The Indian tribes of the United States are not sovereign nations, capable of making treaties, as none of them have an organized government of such inherent strength as would secure a faithful obedience of its people in the observance of compacts in this character. . . . As civilization advances and their possession of land are required for settlements, such legislation should be granted to them as a wise, liberal, and just government ought to extend to subjects holding their dependent relations." Cohen, op. cit. note 6, pp. 17-18.

[36]Appropriations Act, 16 Stat. 544-571, March 3, 1871 (41st Congress, 3rd Session).

[37]*U.S.* v. *Rogers*, 4 How. 567 (1846) and *Cherokee Tobacco*, 11 Wall 616 (1870).

[38]*Rogers*, ibid., 4 How. at 572.

[39]"Every Cherokee Indian and freed person resident in the Cherokee nation shall have the right to sell any products of his farm . . . and to ship and drive the same to market without restraint, paying any tax thereon which is now or may be levied by the United States on the quantity sold outside of the Indian territory." Treaty with the Cherokees, 14 Stat. 799-809, July 19, 1866, Article 10.

[40]An Act Imposing Taxes, 15 Stat. 125-168, July 20, 1868 (40th Congress, 2nd Session), Section 107.

[41]*Cherokee Tobacco*, op. cit. note 37, 11 Wall 616 (1870).

[42]18 Stat. 146-178, Part 3, June 22, 1874 (43rd Congress, 1st Session), Section 3.

[43]Quoted in Edward J. Ward, "Minority Rights and American Indians," *North Dakota Law Review* 51: 1 (Fall 1974): 137-190 at 157.

[44]The government's efforts were effective. By the 1900s, one-half of all Indian languages in the United States had disappeared.

[45]Appropriations Act, 23 Stat. 362-385, March 3, 1885 (48th Congress, 2nd Session), Section 9.

[46]Dawes Act, 24 Stat. 388-391, February 8, 1887 (49th Congress, 2nd Session). For a discussion of the allotment period, see Delos S. Otis, *The Dawes Act and the Allotment of Indian Lands*, 2nd ed. (Norman, OK: University of Oklahoma Press, 1973).

[47]Theodore Roosevelt, *Messages and Papers of the Presidents*, Vol. XIV (New York: Bureau of National Literature, [no date]), p. 6674.

[48]Curtis Act, 30 Stat. 495-517, June 28, 1898 (55th Congress, 2nd Session).

[49]*U.S.* v. *43 Gallons of Whiskey*, 108 U.S. 491 (1883); *U.S.* v. *McBratney*, 104 U.S. 621 (1881); *Ward* v. *Race Horse*, 163 U.S. 504 (1896); *Thomas* v. *Gay*, 169 U.S. 264 (1898); and *Lone Wolf* v. *Hitchcock*, 187 U.S. 553 (1903).

[50]*Ex Parte Crow Dog*, 109 U.S. 556 (1883).

[51]Ibid., 109 U.S. at 568.

[52]*U.S.* v. *Kagama*, 118 U.S. 375 (1886).

[53]Ibid., 118 U.S. at 381-382.

[54]Ibid., 118 U.S. at 383-384.

[55]*Worcester*, op. cit. note 28, 31 U.S.(6 Pet.) at 552.

[56]*Lone Wolf* v. *Hitchcock*, op. cit. note 49, 187 U.S. 553 (1903).

[57]Ibid., 187 U.S. at 565, citing *Beecher* v. *Wetherby*, 95 U.S. 517, 525 (1877).

[58]*Talton* v. *Mayes*, 163 U.S. 376 (1896).

[59]Ibid., 163 U.S. at 384.

[60]Lewis Meriam, technical director, et al., *The Problem of Indian Administration*, the Meriam Report (Baltimore, MD: Johns Hopkins Press, published for the Brookings Institution, 1928).

[61]Wheeler-Howard Act (Indian Reorganization Act), 48 Stat. 984-988, June 18, 1934 (73rd Congress, 2nd Session).

[62]"Conflicting Opinions between Commissioner J. Collier and Senator B. K. Wheeler over Indian Reorganization Act of 1934," *New York Times* (March 14, 1937), p. 16.

[63]See Donald L. Fixico, *Termination and Relocation: Federal Indian Policy, 1945-1960* (Albuquerque, NM: University of New Mexico Press, 1986).

[64]House Concurrent Resolution 108, 67 Stat. B132, August 1, 1953 (83rd Congress, 1st Session).

[65]American Indian Chicago Conference, "Statement of Purpose," in *Declaration of Indian Purpose,* op. cit. note 1, p. 4.

[66]National Congress of American Indians, *American Indian Declaration of Sovereignty,* 31st annual convention, San Diego, California, October 21-25, 1974.

[67]Indian Self-Determination and Education Assistance Act, P.L. 93-638, 88 Stat. 2203-2217, January 4, 1975 (93rd Congress, 2nd Session).

[68]*Creek Nation* v. *U.S.,* 295 U.S. 103 (1935).

[69]See, for example, *Warren Trading Post Co.* v. *Arizona Tax Commission,* 380 U.S. 685, 691, n. 18 (1965); *Poafpybitty* v. *Skelly Oil Co.,* 390 U.S. 365, 368-369 (1968); *U.S.* v. *John,* 437 U.S. 634, 652-653 (1978); *McClanahan* v. *Arizona Tax Commission,* 411 U.S. 164, 172, n. 7 (1973); and *Morton* v. *Mancari,* 417 U.S. 535, 551-552 (1974).

[70]*Mancari,* ibid., 417 U.S. at 535.

[71]Ibid., 417 U.S. at 551.

[72]Ibid., 417 U.S. at 555.

[73]*U.S.* v. *Wheeler,* 435 U.S. 313, 323 (1978) and *Santa Clara Pueblo* v. *Martinez,* 436 U.S. 49, 56 (1978).

[74]*Native American Church* v. *Navajo Tribal Council,* 272 F.2d 131 (10th Cir. 1959).

[75]*U.S.* v. *McBratney,* 104 U.S. 621 (1881).

[76]*Thomas* v. *Gay,* 169 U.S. 264 (1898); *Utah & N. Ry.* v. *Fisher,* 116 U.S. 28 (1885); and *Langford* v. *Monteith,* 102 U.S. 145 (1880).

[77][Act conferring criminal jurisdiction . . .], P.L. 93-280, 67 Stat. 588-590, August 15, 1953 (83rd Congress, 1st Session).

[78]Indian Civil Rights Act, Titles II-VII, U.S. Civil Rights Act, P.L. 90-284, 82 Stat. 77-81, April 11, 1964 (90th Congress, 2nd Session).

[79]*Williams* v. *Lee,* 358 U.S. 217, 219-220 (1959).

[80]*McClanahan,* op. cit. note 69, 411 U.S. 164 (1973).

[81]Ibid., 411 U.S. at 172.

[82]Congress has the authority to regulate hunting and fishing under the plenary doctrine, but has rarely chosen to do so.

[83]*Montana* v. *U.S.,* 450 U.S. 544 (1981).

[84]See, for example, *Bryan* v. *Itasca County,* 426 U.S. 373 (1976); *McClanahan,* op. cit. note 69; and *Kahn* v. *Arizona State Tax Commission,* 16 (Ariz.App. 17), 490 P.2d 846 (Ariz.App. 1971), *appeal dismissed* 411 U.S. 941 (1973).

[85]*Washington* v. *Confederated Tribe of Colville,* 447 U.S. 134 (1980).

[86]*Wheeler*, op. cit. note 73, 435 U.S. 313 (1978).

[87]See, for example, Article 3 of the January 9, 1789 Treaty with the Wyandotts, et al., and the November 10, 1808 Treaty with the Osage, in Kappler, op. cit., note 17.

[88]*Oliphant* v. *Suquamish Indian Tribe*, 435 U.S. 191 (1978).

[89]*Santa Clara Pueblo* v. *Martinez*, 436 U.S. 49 (1978). See also *Roff* v. *Burney*, 168 U.S. 218 (1897), upholding the right of tribes to confer or withdraw tribal citizenship privileges.

[90]*Santa Clara Pueblo*, ibid., 436 U.S. at 71.

[91]*Wheeler*, op. cit. note 73, 435 U.S. 313 (1978).

[92]Indian Major Crimes Act, 62 Stat. 757-760, June 25, 1948 (80th Congress, 2nd Session).

[93]Indian Civil Rights Act, op. cit. note 78.

[94]Another important right held by tribes is that of sovereign immunity. See, for example, *Santa Clara Pueblo*, op. cit. note 89, 436 U.S. at 58; and *Morgan* v. *Colorado River Indian Tribe*, 103 Ariz. 425, 443 P.2d 421 (1968).

[95]*Merrion* v. *Jicarilla Apache Tribe*, 455 U.S. 130 (1982).

[96]Ibid., 455 U.S. at 137.

[97]Francis Paul Prucha, *The Great Father: The United States Government and the American Indians*, Vol. II (Lincoln, NE: University of Nebraska Press, 1984), pp. 1023-1024.

[98]*U.S.* v. *Sioux Nation of Indians*, 448 U.S. 371 (1980).

[99]Indian Self-Determination and Education Assistance Act, op. cit. note 67; and Indian Child Welfare Act, P.L. 95-608, 92 Stat. 3069-3078, November 8, 1978 (95th Congress, 2nd Session).

[100]Recent reports have indicated that approximately 90 percent of the Bureau of Indian Affairs' one-billion-dollar annual budget goes for administration.

[101]*California, et al.* v. *Cabazon Band of Mission Indians*, 480 U.S. 202, 207 (1987), citing *U.S.* v. *Mazurie*, 419 U.S. 544, 557 (1975).

[102]Fixico, op. cit. note 63, p. 203.

[103]Prucha, op. cit. note 97, p. 1156.

[104]American Indian Religious Freedom Joint Resolution, P.L. 95-341, 92 U.S. Statutes at Large 469-470, August 11, 1978 (95th Congress, 2nd Session).

[105]Several of these organizations, including the World Council of Indigenous Peoples, the Indian Council of South America (CISA), the Inuit Circumpolar Conference, the Indian Law Resource Center, the International Indian Treaty Council, Four Circles Directions and the National Indian Youth Council have been granted consultative status by the United Nations Economic and Social Council (UNESCO).

[106]For a summary of ad hoc international conferences relating to indigenous peoples, see UN Doc. E/CN4/Sub.2/476/Add.5 of the "Study of the Problem of Discrimination against Indigenous Populations." For a review of the United Nations' work on indigenous peoples, see Russel L. Barsh, "Indigenous Peoples: An Emerging Object of International Law," *American Journal of International Law* 80: 2 (April 1986): 369-385.

[107]International Labour Organisation, "Convention 107: Indigenous and Tribal Populations Convention," passed by the 40th Session, General Conference of the ILO, June 26, 1957, in ILO, *International Labour Conventions and Recommendations, 1919-1981* (Geneva: International Labour Office, © 1982), pp. 858-864.

[108]UN Doc. E/CN.4/Sub.2/1983/21/Add.8.

[109]Ibid.

[110]Ibid. On May 7, 1982, the Economic and Social Council authorized the establishment of a working group on indigenous populations. UN ECOSOC Resolution No. 1982/34.

[111]UN ECOSOC Resolution No. 1982/34.

# ORGANIZING FOR SELF-DETERMINATION: FEDERAL AND TRIBAL BUREAUCRACIES IN AN ERA OF SOCIAL AND POLICY CHANGE

## Paul H. Stuart

*University of Alabama*

In this chapter, the concept of self-determination and its use in recent United States Indian policy will be examined. Both the development of the policy and the organizational development of the Bureau of Indian Affairs are discussed. Among a number of impediments to the full realization of the potential of self-determination, particularly problematic is the organizational structure of the federal agencies responsible for implementing the policy, especially the Bureau of Indian Affairs. It seems likely that current and proposed federal policy will fall short of achieving the promise of full self-determination for American Indians.

### The Concept of Self-Determination

"Self-determination" has been the official Indian policy of the United States since the administration of President Richard Nixon. Originally promulgated to signal a departure from the discredited policy of termination, Congress and the executive branch institutionalized the policy during the 1970s in a series of acts and administrative guidelines.[1] Today, the self-determination policy seems firmly established.

Self-determination is an ambiguous term. Most tribal leaders would probably prefer "sovereignty" as a description of the status of contemporary tribal governments. Self-determination, however, appears to be the term preferred by Congress and by federal administrators. But what does the term mean? And more important, does the way in which the self-determination policy has been implemented in the last two decades conform with that meaning?

In international law, self-determination refers to the right of a people to self-rule, as opposed to political domination by outsiders. According to the political philosopher Dov Ronen, there have been five manifestations of self-determination since the nineteenth century: national self-determination; Marxist, working-class self-determination; Wilsonian self-determination of minorities; anti-colonialism; and ethnic self-determination.[2] If the term has been ambiguous, the power of the concept has been undeniable in recent times.

According to Ronen, the presence of an oppressor is an essential element in the quest for self-determination, which he considers to be a manifestation of humankind's pursuit of freedom and self-fulfillment. European history is replete with examples of national identity formed in opposition to perceived oppression on the part of an outsider. Thus, the modern states of Germany and Italy were formed as the result of self-determination movements organized in response to the Napoleonic occupation of central and southern Europe in the early nineteenth century. The conditions for the initiation of a quest for self-determination, according to Ronen, include, most importantly, domination by an outsider, who is seen to be blocking the people's genuine aspirations for the good life.[3]

Self-determination is seldom granted; instead, it is won. While examples of the various forms of self-determination can be identified, Ronen considers the contemporary era to be dominated by ethnic self-determination as a result of the success of earlier quests for national self-determination, a sympathetic world opinion, and the influence of the United Nations.

The right of self-determination is recognized in the United Nations Charter, as well as in a number of covenants adopted by the United Nations and other international organizations. The application of the principle, however, is not always clear. While a number of recent declarations suggest that the principle should be applied to indigenous people living within established nation-states, the United Nations General Assembly has limited the application of the principle in situations which "would dismember or impair . . . the territorial integrity or political unity of sovereign and independent states."[4] While the ultimate outcome of a quest for self-determination may be difficult to achieve, the principle, at a minimum, means the right to maintain traditional culture and to use land and natural resources.[5] The principles of the United Nations Covenant on Civil and Political Rights of 1966, and of the Helsinki Accords of 1975, for example, have been held by the Norwegian Supreme Court to apply to the rights of the Sami people (Lapps) in Norway.[6] Similarly, Canada's participation in a number of international agreements has been held to require its adherence to the principle of self-determination in its relations with Canadian Indian peoples, although attempts to implement this principle have been less than satisfactory.[7]

The self-determination of subnational groups has been held by some to exert unacceptably centrifugal pressure on nation-states. This argument is particularly salient for Canada and many African nations. In Canada, demands by Québecois and the Western provinces for autonomy, in addition to Indian, Inuit and Métis demands, have been perceived as potentially disintegrative.[8] In postcolonial Africa, fragile state systems have been confronted with ethnoregional demands for self-determination which "threaten the very existence of the state itself."[9] Meaningful self-determination for subnational ethnic groups is thus seen by some as incompatible with the modern nation-state.

Congressman Lloyd Meeds' dissent to the final report of the American Indian Policy Review Commission, issued in 1977, seems consistent with this line of thinking. The commission concluded that "Indian tribes are sovereign political bodies," although their sovereignty is limited as a result of their political relationship with the United States.[10] Meeds disagreed: "In our Federal system . . . there are but two sovereign entities: the United States and the States," he wrote. "American Indian tribes lost their sovereignty through discovery, conquest, cession, treaties, statutes, and history. . . . The Congress of the United States has permitted them to be self-governing entities" to allow them "to preserve the uniqueness of their own cultures."[11]

While Meeds' dissent is based on the assumption that the modern nation-state is the ultimate, terminal entity in political evolution, Ronen views self-determination efforts as one manifestation of an ongoing quest for freedom. According to Ronen, then, if the nation is seen as alterable, it may be changed to "accommodate quests for ethnic self-determination."[12] In fact, he predicts the proliferation of such small political entities because of an aspiration towards more ethnically homogenous entities and growing international support for human rights, including the right of self-determination.[13] Nor would Ronen concur that ethnic self-determination is necessarily a disintegrative force. While demands for ethnic self-determination are salient in the social and political realms, Ronen predicts increasing economic and normative integration as a result of the internationalization of the world economy and the rise of mass communications. Increasing integration in economic and normative terms may be accompanied by a multiplication of small sociopolitical units.[14]

In conclusion, as numerous authors have noted, self-determination is a concept that has vacillating meanings and applications, depending upon the situation. In the context of subnational ethnic groups, self-determination often means something less than complete independence. However, true self-determination must mean something more than permission from the nation-state to engage in self-government. Meeds appropriately avoided using the term to describe his conception of the legal relationship between the United States and the Indian tribes. Self-determination involves, minimally, the right of a people to determine its internal political structure, to enjoy religious and cultural freedom, and to protect their land and natural resources. Judged against this standard, however, the past record of United States-Indian relations has not been a positive one.

## United States Indian Policy

Some scholars date the Indian New Deal as the beginning of a self-determination period in American Indian affairs.[15] The Bureau of Indian Affairs had exercised nearly autocratic control over American Indians for a century by the 1920s, when John Collier became the leader of an Indian reform movement. Established during the early years of the republic to supervise trade with the Indian tribes, the agency proved to be highly adaptable to changing conditions. Policy objectives of removal, concentration and containment gave way to "civilization" or the acculturation of the Indians as the agency's *raison d'être* in the late nineteenth century. This objective implied a centralized administration, a formalization of administrative procedures, and an emphasis on education as the central tool of the organization.[16] The goals of civilization and progress were used to justify opening Indian resources to exploitation by the white population. Aboriginal economies were held to be inefficient, supporting only small numbers of people on large tracts of land. Civilizing the Indian, it was expected, would result in opening vast expanses of the national estate to settlement by non-Indians, who could presumably make more productive use of it. The acquisition of new farming techniques and habits of industry would, at the same time, make it possible for the Indians to do better with less. Thus, the expropriation of the Indians' estate could be justified as being in their ultimate interest.[17]

By the 1920s this theory, like so many other Victorian notions, had lost much of its appeal. Self-confident Euro-Americans had good reason to question the assumptions of nineteenth-century Indian policy. Dispossessed of much of their land, American Indians were among the poorest of Americans, in income, in educational status and in health status. John Collier railed against the Indian Office, which he said exercised an autocratic rule comparable to that of Czarist Russia or the Belgian Congo. The failure of the "movement for Indian assimilation" was everywhere apparent. Scandals and exposure of its complicity in attempted land grabs of the 1920s left the Indian Service weakened and demoralized.[18]

While the movement to protect Indian rights can be seen as one more in a series of efforts by non-Indians to reform Indians, this was a reform movement with a difference: Indigenous Indian social organization and culture were more respected, and the pressure for rapid assimilation, so common a goal of non-Indian reformers, was less evident. Indeed, Collier acknowledged the importance of maintaining some aspects of Indian culture in future policy decisions.

Collier's criticisms of the Indian Service's administrative style were central to his attack on the Indian policy of the 1920s. Like European imperialist administrators, also under attack in the 1920s, the Indian Office ran roughshod over its aboriginal charges, with little regard for elementary human rights or for the value of indigenous social institutions. For models to reform Indian administration, Collier turned to English liberal colonial reformers, particularly the advocates of "indirect rule."[19]

Indirect rule, or "indirect administration" as Collier preferred to call it, was developed by colonial administrators in Africa as a way to preserve some aspects of indigenous social organization while simultaneously preparing the colonized society for eventual independence on a European model. Rather than concentrating all operating authority in the colonial administration, native political structures could be induced to carry out some of the activities of government, albeit under the supervision of colonial administrators. By encouraging an appreciation for African culture and indigenous forms of social organization, colonialism theoretically could become more sensitive to the needs of decultured African tribesmen. And by enlisting African traditional leaders in the business of government, colonial administrators could aspire to legitimacy in the eyes of the colonized. Their allies in this endeavor were social scientists, particularly the anthropologists who studied African social organization.

## The Indian New Deal

Indirect administration provided the rationale for the Indian New Deal when Collier became Commissioner of Indian Affairs in 1933. The cornerstone of Collier's program was the Indian Reorganization Act, which provided the legislative basis for the modern tribal government. Collier, like the proponents of reform in African colonial administrations, looked toward the day when the formerly dependent charges of the Indian Bureau would be self-governing; in the meantime, a transformed Indian Service would guide Indians toward eventual self-rule.

In the American context, indirect administration was probably more beneficial than not for American Indians. While the Indian Reorganization Act gave the federal government veto power over the decisions of Indian tribes, and while some federal administrators dominated local tribal councils, the Indian New Deal did end the process of allotment, encouraged the formation of tribal governments, brought Indians into the Indian Service in larger numbers and in positions of increased responsibility, and increased the attention paid to community development and social organization by the agency.[20]

The Indian New Deal, however, did not change the fundamental relationship between the Indian Service and American Indians. Indirect administration required central direction; while a change in the goals for the Indians was implicit in the Indian New Deal, a change in the administrative relationship was deemed to be premature. Preparation for independence, like preparation for "civilization," required tutelage. As had been the case under earlier administrations, Indian affairs remained centralized during the New Deal and federal powers over Indian tribes actually increased during the 1930s.

Centralization of the Indian Service also resulted from Collier's ability to attract funds from New Deal emergency relief agencies to finance Indian programs. In 1934, for example, Indian Service expenditures totaled over $23 million, 55 percent more than 1928 appropriations. Most of the increase, 82 percent, resulted from emergency appropriations provided to the Indian Service by New Deal agencies which had been created to provide work relief and other programs to deal with the consequences of the depression.[21] Since these funds were allocated to the agencies by the Washington office, the effect was to increase the power of the central administration and the federal government.

More important than new funding for Indian programs were the new powers given to the Indian Office by the Indian Reorganization Act. The act required federal approval of tribal constitutions and of the decisions made by tribal governments. This resulted in a standardization of tribal governments which, if not complete, evidenced considerable uniformity. It is probably true, as Wilcomb Washburn asserts, that Collier achieved as much autonomy for the tribes as could reasonably have been expected. Whether intended or not, however, the Indian New Deal resulted in a consolidation of power within the Bureau of Indian Affairs.[22]

Much of the Indian Service staff, particularly the field personnel who were in direct contact with Indian people, was inherited from an earlier era. As a career office, the Indian Service was composed primarily of people who had started their positions when policy goals for the Indians were very different from those of the New Deal era. Some Indian Service employees testified against the Indian Reorganization Act, leading to a controversial "gag order" issued by Secretary of the Interior Harold Ickes. Others, in spite of the intent of the law, continued to relate to Indians in an authoritarian manner. Some Indian Service employees probably genuinely did not understand the law's purpose. For many reservation Indians, the Indian New Deal affected their dealings with federal officials only slightly.[23]

As World War II progressed, the Indian Office headquarters was moved from Washington, D.C., to Chicago to make room for the expanding war-related agencies in the nation's capital. During this period, Collier's relations with Congress, never excellent, deteriorated. Congress reduced appropriations for tribal development purposes, while increasing appropriations for such individually-oriented programs as education and health care.[24] Clearly, these developments would portend changes in Indian administration in the years ahead.

## The Termination Era

If active resistance to external control epitomizes the struggle for self-determination, then the origins of modern Indian self-determination surely date to the post-World War II era. A number of events coincided to open up the organizational environment of American Indians, while threats to Indian autonomy and their control of natural resources increased.

The United States emerged from World War II in a nationalistic frame of mind. Liberal patriotism combined with jingoistic flag-waving to celebrate the values of Americanism and the virtues of American society. For liberals as well as conservatives, the persistence of an unassimilated aboriginal group within the United States seemed anomalous. The unusually severe winter of 1947-48, which wreaked much suffering on Indian communities in the Southwest, underlined this paradox. The exclusion of Indians from federally subsidized public assistance programs in Arizona and New Mexico, the continuing domination of Indians by the Bureau of Indian Affairs, and the extreme poverty of Indian people all seemed to contradict the ideals of democracy and equal treatment which had informed the allied struggle in World War II.

The postwar era was also a post-New Deal era. In the late 1940s many questioned the size and complexity of the federal government. Congress established a Commission on the Organization of the Executive Branch of the Government, headed by former President Herbert Hoover, to recommend ways of streamlining federal administration. The Hoover Commission recommended the termination of special services and protection provided to American Indians. Rather than maintaining separate programs, the commission felt that the service functions of the Bureau of Indian Affairs should be distributed to federal and state agencies serving the general population. This approach would allow the bureau to be dismantled, and Indians would be integrated into the general population.[25]

These sentiments led to a policy embracing the decentralization of the Indian Service, settlement of longstanding Indian claims against the United States, and the termination of federal protection and supervision of Indian people. Congress created the area office system in 1946 to decentralize Indian administration. In the same year, Congress established the Indian Claims Commission to extinguish Indian claims against the United States.

Eventual termination of federal supervision over Indian people was an implicit goal of all federal Indian policy, including the Indian New Deal. However, never before had there been such urgency to get Uncle Sam out of the Indian business. While Collier had thought it would take generations to free the Indians from federal supervision, Senator Arthur V. Watkins of Utah, a leading congressional proponent of termination, estimated in 1957 that "for most tribes it can be numbered in a few years."[26]

Some specific aspects of post-World War II Indian policy were welcomed by many Indians as well as by non-Indian public opinion. Many Indians approved of the repeal of Indian prohibition in 1953, particularly veterans of World War II and the Korean conflict, who could fight for their country but not legally drink alcoholic beverages. The creation of the Indian Claims Commission promised to expedite what had been a difficult process of pursuing tribal claims in the U.S. Court of Claims. Providing public assistance to individual Indian people, however grudgingly it was done, did much to alleviate the suffering of many who were poverty-stricken.[27]

While Indians might have found much to applaud in Indian policy developments of the 1940s and 1950s, Indian opinion was largely irrelevant to policymakers. During the New Deal years, tribes voted on whether or not to accept the Indian Reorganization Act and expressed their dissatisfaction with federal administrators by electing tribal leaders who opposed aspects of the New Deal. In contrast, Indians had little opportunity for input as the proposals of the terminationists were debated. The "Indian problem," when viewed as a symptom of an overpowerful bureaucracy, had created problem people, it seemed, who were doomed to suffer from dependency, the twentieth-century name for what had been called pauperism a century earlier. In an early form of "blaming the victim," Indian opposition to termination was attributed to this government-created dependency.

Congress proceeded to trim the powers of the Indian tribes, redistribute some functions of the Bureau of Indian Affairs to other agencies, and terminate the special services and protection extended to specific tribes. While the overall threat of termination was a significant force affecting tribal actions, more specific changes in tribal powers and in the functions of the bureau were equally significant.

Law enforcement jurisdiction was both a troubling problem and a symbol of Indian exceptionalism. Public Law 280, passed by Congress in 1953, provided for the automatic assumption of civil and criminal jurisdiction over Indian reservations by five states, and, in other states, for state assumption of jurisdiction by state action, without consultation with the tribes affected.[28] Assimilating Indians to the states' legal systems, it was believed, would go a long way towards incorporating American Indians into American society.

The threats of losing criminal jurisdiction and of termination acted as a catalyst for Indian groups to organize to oppose these initiatives. Peter Iverson describes the 1940s and 1950s as an era of "building toward self-determination," since it was during this period that the intertribal organizational structures were created which made the "Indian renaissance" of the 1960s and 1970s possible.[29] Groups like the National Conference of American Indians and the United Sioux Tribes of South Dakota provided national and state-level forums for tribal leaders. Later, the National Indian Youth Council, organized in 1961, provided a basis for political action by the young.

In 1954, Congress transferred responsibility for Indian health care from the Bureau of Indian Affairs to the Public Health Service in the Department of Health, Education, and Welfare. This was part of the effort to dismantle the Indian Service and to allocate its functions to agencies serving the general population, as recommended by the Hoover Commission.[30] Introducing another agency, and another cabinet department, into Indian affairs diluted the power of the Bureau of Indian Affairs by providing a second agency with service responsibilities for American Indians. If the Department of Health, Education, and Welfare was never successful in its efforts to achieve the transfer of more branches of the bureau to HEW, the alternative was available to tribal leaders through legal action.

Pursuing claims in the Indian Claims Commission involved tribes with attorneys to a greater extent than ever before. While the tribal attorney had never been absent from Indian affairs, lawyers became more prominent in the years after World War II. In addition to claims work, lawyers took on a variety of Indian causes, including access to state welfare benefits, the legality of state assertions of jurisdiction under Public Law 280, and the management of Indian assets by the BIA. Increased availability of legal representation resulted in significant changes in the legal status of Indian tribes. In 1959, the Supreme Court decided *Williams* v. *Lee*, a crucial case in the evolution of Indian tribal sovereignty, inaugurating the modern era in Indian law. The decision prevented a non-Indian plaintiff from using state courts to sue a reservation Indian defendant.[31]

Legal representation, a more complex administrative environment, and the perception of an increasingly hostile political climate provided the basis for an Indian movement for self-determination during the 1960s and 1970s. The relocation of large numbers of Indian people to urban areas, an explicit policy of the overall termination program, also had unexpected results. As Kenneth Philp suggests, relocation provided Indians with alternatives to reservation life, as well as increased incomes and educational levels. Less anticipated was an increase in Indian identity, albeit a pan-Indian one, and an increase in militancy, all of which were associated with relocation in many instances.[32] This was often true even for those who had not identified themselves strongly as Indians when living in reservation areas. Confrontations with genuine curiosity, indifference and hostility on the part of non-Indians led some Indian relocatees to reexamine their tribal identities. An anthropologist studying relocated Indians in the San Francisco Bay area in the 1960s found increases in Indian identity, particularly among Indians for whom Indian identification had not been important prior to relocation.[33]

## The New Frontier and the Great Society

Events of the 1960s resulted in increased sophistication on the part of tribal governments as the choices available to them expanded. Programs of the Office of Economic Opportunity and the Area Redevelopment Administration (later the Economic Development Administration) became available to the tribes, which designated themselves community action agencies to take advantage of poverty program grants. Both federal agencies set up "Indian desks," and Office of Economic Opportunity representatives, in particular, were vocal in criticizing the Bureau of Indian Affairs.

Despite the rhetoric, the amount of real tribal input in OEO and EDA programming was questionable. Tribes competed for program grants for specific purposes which were developed by the OEO and EDA bureaucrats. Adherence to the terms of the grants was enforced by the "memorandum writers" who occupied the "Indian desks" in Washington. Consultants and subcontractors, many of them academics, advised tribes and Washington officials on program design and implementation. Consequently, reservation programs, while ostensibly tribally operated, exhibited a striking degree of similarity. As in the case of Collier's "indirect administration," plans hatched originally in Washington were being carried out by tribal governments.

This is not to dismiss the real effects of the programs of the 1960s on tribal governments, however. In operating the programs designed for them, tribes gained valuable experience in grant administration, negotiation and, as alternatives to the programs packaged in Washington were increasingly proposed, program design. Incipient tribal bureaucracies were created to administer the new programs, and the minimal indirect costs that the grants allowed did permit some development of tribal administrative structures. Under pressure from the tribes, the BIA and the Indian Health Service began to contract with the tribes according to the provisions of the Buy Indian Act of 1910, a Progressive Era effort to improve tribal economies and Indian work habits by contracting for Indian labor.[34] Other federal grant-in-aid programs became available in such areas as housing, law enforcement and education. The *Catalog of Federal Domestic Assistance Programs*, similar in size and format to a department store catalog, became a fixture in the library of every tribal headquarters.

### The Self-Determination Policy

In 1970, President Nixon called for a new policy of self-determination for American Indians. Rejecting both termination and paternalism, Nixon proposed that "Indians . . . become independent of Federal control without being cut off from Federal concern and Federal support." To this end, he asked Congress for legislation to enable the tribes to assume responsibility for service programs administered by federal agencies. The decision whether to take responsibility for program administration was to be the tribe's alone. The tribe would also have a "right of retrocession," enabling it to return administrative responsibility to the federal agency at its own option. Funding for the program would be secure under either arrangement — federal or tribal administration — and tribes would be free to determine how the federal services would be delivered and by whom.[35]

Tribal assumption of federal program administration seemed a logical next step in Indian policy, since by 1970 nearly all tribes had had several years of experience administering programs of the Office of Economic Opportunity and the Economic Development Administration, as Nixon noted in his message to Congress. As a result of the Nixon administration's promotion of tribal contracting of federal programs under the provisions of the Buy Indian Act of 1910, two tribes, the Salt River and Zuni, negotiated Buy Indian contracts covering virtually all BIA functions. In the Indian Self-Determination Act of 1975, Congress provided the authority Nixon had requested in his message.[36]

Title I of the act provided that tribes could at their option elect to contract for services provided to tribal members by the Bureau of Indian Affairs or the Indian Health Service. The amount of the contract was to be equivalent to the amount of federal funds expended for the activity. The tribe had the right of retrocession, but the federal agency could not revoke the contract except in cases where there was danger to life.

The Indian Self-Determination Act represented a significant conceptual advance in Indian self-government. Particularly important was the initiative given to the tribe, rather than the federal agency involved, to determine the timing of contracting. This was a significant change, one which broke ground with previous practice. Contracting under the act has continued to expand in the years since its enactment. In addition, other legislation, such as the Indian Child Welfare Act of 1978, has strengthened tribal governments and promoted self-determination.[37]

The Indian Child Welfare Act of 1978 gave tribes exclusive jurisdictional rights in child custody proceedings involving Indian children. The act provided for the reestablishment of tribal jurisdiction in states affected by Public Law 280. Tribes were given jurisdiction in cases involving tribal children residing away from reservations, and the act provided funding for tribal courts and child care programs. In another area, the Tribally Controlled Community College Assistance Act of 1978 provided operating grants to support tribal institutions of higher education.[38]

By the 1980s, self-determination seemed established as a bipartisan policy supported by a broad consensus. The policy seemed to imply an expanded recognition of the self-governing powers of the tribes. In 1983, President Ronald Reagan transferred the White House management of Indian affairs from the Office of Liaison to the Office of Intergovernmental Affairs, explicitly defining the relationship between the tribes and the federal government as a "government-to-government" relationship.[39]

The decades of the 1970s and 1980s have seen significant advances in the status of Indian tribal self-government. The question remains, though, whether the legal and administrative arrangements which have evolved constitute actual self-determination. While perhaps administrative arrangements can help meet demands for self-determination, a mere administrative response alone cannot be satisfactory. As Dov Ronen suggests, the quest for self-determination is "sentimental, emotional, patriotic, [and] national."[40]

### Limitations of the Self-Determination Policy

A central criticism of the self-determination policy is that it involves contracting with tribes, rather than actually transferring power to them. In a self-determination contract, called a 638 contract after the public law number of the Indian Self-Determination Act, the tribe agrees only to carry out a program designed by a federal agency, the Bureau of Indian Affairs or the Indian Health Service. The power to define problems and devise solutions is not transferred from the federal agency to the tribe.[41]

When problems, the methods for their solution, and the standards to evaluate success are defined from the outside, the meaningfulness of the self-determination policy must be questioned. The Indian Health Service views the activities of tribal 638 contractors as "extensions of IHS itself, and therefore [believes] IHS should retain responsibility and control."[42] Rather than a reduction in the size of area office staff and the scope of its oversight responsibility, 638 contracting has resulted in their expansion, at least in the IHS.

Other complaints center around the tribe's access to information to facilitate planning and around the financing of tribal programs. Both the BIA and the IHS have difficulty determining the costs of specific programs. Since the tribe is supposed to receive the level of funding which would be expended by the operating agency under a 638 contract, such information is crucial in tribal planning for self-determination. Tribes have had difficulty gaining access to other kinds of information necessary for planning contracts, such as the incidence of criminal activity on reservations. Indirect costs are also an issue in financing self-determination. The indirect costs of a program may be higher for a tribe than for the federal government, because the tribe lacks the support services built into federal administration.[43]

The Indian Health Service has been accused of not aggressively pursuing the implementation of the self-determination policy. By IHS policy, 638 contracts are neither encouraged nor discouraged. Tribes are neither rewarded nor punished for contracting to provide health services. While this approach is consistent with that outlined in Nixon's self-determination message, some tribal leaders have criticized the agency's approach to promoting tribal self-determination as too passive.[44]

Francis Paul Prucha has called attention to the continuing economic dependency of the tribes as a central problem in the drive for increased tribal autonomy. As long as the tribes are economically dependent on the federal government, he suggests, paternalism, and something less than self-determination, will persist.[45] Certainly, the tribes' lack of control over appropriations is a central problem for them.

An example of this lack of authority is that the Indian Self-Determination Act provides no protection against cuts in the budget for Indian services.[46] During the 1980s, with reductions in the overall budget allocations for domestic programs, Indian tribes experienced static funding or budget cuts in the face of increasing needs and a growing number of eligible Indians and tribes. Even apparent budget increases can be illusory. Funding for programs for elderly Indians under the Older Americans Act, for example, increased 20 per cent, from $6 million in 1980, the first year of the program's operation, to $7.2 million in 1986. Yet the number of older American Indians increased during this period, and the number of tribal grantees rose 45 percent, from 85 to 124. The result was a decline in the available funds per tribal grantee and a reduction in services on those reservations which had participated in the program from its inception.[47]

The budget problem has been severe during the 1980s, underlining the importance of economic development efforts. The consequence of the absence of successful economic development on most reservations has been the continued dependence of tribes and Indian people on federal appropriations. It is questionable how much self-determination can actually occur in a context of limited funding. In the fall of 1987, the *Arizona Republic* characterized the Reagan administration's Indian policy as one of dumping "the responsibility for operating Indian programs onto states and tribes."[48]

It is clear that the legislation of the 1970s and its implementation in the 1970s and 1980s have fallen short of the promise of self-determination. This was recognized by the leadership of the Bureau of Indian Affairs during the Reagan administration. In 1987, Ross Swimmer, then Assistant Secretary of the Interior for Indian Affairs, proposed separating the trust responsibilities of the BIA from its service responsibilities. The funding for services not required as part of the bureau's trust responsibilities would be designated "self-determination funds."

These funds would be distributed to the tribes based on a formula. The tribes would have complete discretion in determining how the self-determination funds would be used. Tribes, if they wished, could contract with the bureau or another federal agency to provide services, paying for them with the self-determination funds.[49]

Adoption of Swimmer's proposal would have resulted in an expansion in tribal autonomy. Problem definition and program design would have been initiated at the tribal level, and the proposal contemplated considerable programmatic diversity among tribes. However, while the proposal implied great decentralization in Indian affairs and might have increased the real powers of tribes, questions still remained.

The past record of policy changes did not support an overly optimistic view of the probable results of the Swimmer proposal. The level of funding for Indian programs was a serious concern. The proposal bore a striking resemblance to the revenue sharing and block grant programs which had been a significant element of intergovernmental fund transfers since the 1970s. While these latter programs increased the amount of discretion possessed by states, the effectiveness of the programs depended upon the maintenance of federal funding levels and on the administrative capacity of the states. The adequacy and stability of funding for self-determination would have been crucial in determining the success of the Swimmer idea.

How the trust responsibilities of the federal government were defined would also have been important. The federal trust responsibility was used to justify intensive supervision of 638 contracts; an expansive definition of the trust responsibility could justify continued close supervision of self-determination funds, frustrating the goals of the program.

Even with a limited definition of the trust responsibility, which was implicit in Swimmer's proposal, habits built up in over a century of Indian-government relations can be expected to persist. Implicit in the Swimmer proposal was a continued relationship between the Bureau of Indian Affairs and the tribes. The BIA would serve as trustee and, at a tribes's option, as contractor and provider of services. The nature of the tribal and governmental organizations involved will continue to be significant in determining the success of any new self-determination program.

### Organizations

Formal organization provides a way to achieve immortality. While human lives are finite, formal organizations have the potential to transcend the lifespans of their individual members. For example, a number of the federal agencies included in Donald Whitnah's reference book, *Government Agencies*, are over one hundred years old.[50] The Bureau of Indian Affairs, established in 1824, has survived for over 165 years, more than double the average human life expectancy. While organizations frequently do cease to exist, the concept of organizational death presents difficult problems of definition. When, for example, an organization changes its membership, its goals and its methods of operation, can we way that the old organization has perished and a new organization has begun? Or, are such transformations a sign of adaptability? Of the many characteristics of formal organizations, their persistence seems to be the most striking.

Continuity in an organization's existence is achieved through a variety of formal and informal mechanisms. Organizational change is difficult to achieve. Stability and security are perceived as beneficial by members of most organizations; mental blinders, calculated opposition, and lack of resources to retool all make achieving organizational change difficult, perhaps more so than individual change.[51] Indeed, organizations may employ a different standard of morality than individuals. Self-sacrifice is the highest morality, Reinhold Niebuhr suggests, but "it is obvious that fewer risks can be taken with community interests than with individual interests." If it is not quite true that "no one has a right to be unselfish with other people's interests," the capacity for unselfishness is limited in most collective enterprises, including formal organizations.[52]

The voluminous literature on organizations provides a variety of approaches to define them, as well as understand their importance for society. Moreover, it is certainly a mistake to view organizations as passive tools, mere instrumentalities created to accomplish a task. One can focus on several dimensions in trying to understand the operation of organizations.

*Formal Structure*

Organizations can be considered to be collections of positions, roles and statuses, together with the rules which govern the relationships between the occupants of the positions. This conception calls attention to the formal structure of the organization, the pyramid of authority or chain of command which might be illustrated on an organizational chart. Problems of organizational structure have been significant in the history of the Bureau of Indian Affairs.

Finding a structure which permits both a modicum of central direction and sufficient autonomy for local officials has been a persistent problem. The Bureau of Indian Affairs has a relatively small central office that operates a large number of geographically dispersed field offices or agencies. The work carried out at the agency level is highly nonroutine in character, demanding a relatively large amount of discretion from local officials. During the late nineteenth century, the bureau developed an organizational structure that was highly centralized and that exhibited a high degree of formalization. The organization's chief administrative problem during the early twentieth century was finding a way to decentralize, to delegate authority and responsibility to the field units. The Meriam Report of 1928 recommended the decentralization of operations, thus granting increased powers to the agency's field units. The creation of regional offices, another plausible solution to the problem of overcentralization, was rejected by the authors of the Meriam Report, who reasoned that such intermediate centers of authority would tend to reduce the powers of the local units.[53]

As we have seen, the New Deal hardly signaled a decentralization of the Bureau of Indian Affairs. Rather, a number of factors including the personality of the commissioner, the new approach to Indian-white relations, and the expansion of financial resources flowing through the central office, resulted in the increased centralization of the Indian Service during the 1930s. This was perhaps all the more surprising given Commissioner Collier's expressed commitment to decentralization.

The 1946 reorganization of the Bureau of Indian Affairs resulted in the creation of a group of area offices intermediate between the Washington office and the field agencies. The bureau adopted a line-and-staff form of organization, in which area office directors had direct authority over reservation superintendents. Operating branches at the field agency level were reflected in staff positions at the area and central office levels. As part of the reorganization, Congress permitted the delegation of authority from the Commissioner of Indian Affairs to the area director, and from that official to the reservation superintendent.[54]

The intent was to bring Indian administration "closer to the Indian people," in the words of Dillion S. Myer, Commissioner of Indian Affairs during the early 1950s and a strong proponent of termination.[55] Despite the goal of decentralization, the result of the creation of the area office system was to decrease local autonomy, just as the authors of the Meriam Report had predicted. Decentralization, a major objective of the reorganization, was not achieved, due to a tendency on the part of central office officials to check area office decisions. The Bimson Report, a 1954 administrative study of the Bureau of Indian Affairs completed for the House Committee on Interior and Insular Affairs, concluded that the failure to delegate authority to the agencies was the result of the assumption of line responsibility by specialist staff members in the area offices.[56]

The area office system evidenced centralizing tendencies for another reason. Authority was not delegated to the operating level because the area offices became sources of negative authority within the Bureau of Indian Affairs. They could say no, but area office personnel had difficulty initiating new programs. The area office system did result in a great deal of regional variation within the Bureau of Indian Affairs and in the Indian Health Service, which also adopted the area office system when it was created in 1955. *Indian Health Care*, a study completed by the Office of Technology Assessment in 1986, found significant differences between IHS areas in allocations to budget categories, the extent of tribal self-determination contracting, and even in the data systems utilized.[57]

The structure of an organization is significant when attempting to determine its organizational performance. The area office organizational structure adopted by the Bureau of Indian Affairs in 1946 was designed to reduce the number of field units reporting directly to the Commissioner of Indian Affairs. Yet, by reducing the autonomy of the local units, the structure probably made the achievement of the goals of the self-determination policy more difficult. Advocates of Indian self-determination have viewed the area office system as an impediment to tribal control of BIA programs, since as tribes assume more responsibility for local programming, the role of the area office in contract monitoring and administration becomes more significant. The Indian Health Service has resisted efforts by the tribes to reduce the size of area offices and reallocate the resulting savings into program efforts. IHS officials have argued that the responsibility of administering 638 contracts and the availability of retrocession to the tribes make a strong area office essential to their administration.

The Bureau of Indian Affairs has both a line-and-staff and a regionalized area office administrative structure. Despite periodic efforts to decentralize the organization, centralization has increased as a result of the interaction of the two structural forms. The line-and-staff structure, which duplicates the administrative functions carried out at the local level with staff members (who technically lack line authority but frequently exercise it effectively) at the area and central office levels, makes each local employee of the bureau a "cosmopolitan," to borrow Robert Merton's term.[58] The exercise of line authority by administrative staff members results in an organization which is fragmented along functional lines.

The area office system results in an organization which exhibits considerable internal variation. Area directors have evolved methods of operating in the absence of, or sometimes in spite of, central office directives. The area office system shelters the Washington office from direct complaints from the reservation level, which may explain partially its long-term survival.

## Informal Structure

Understanding organizational structure is essential for understanding how organizations work. However, a focus on structure alone yields an incomplete picture of the organization, since its members participate as whole people, not merely as owners of formal statuses and roles. They bring individual characteristics, likes and dislikes, with them to the organization. Thus, many investigators have probed deeper by examining the informal structure of organizations.

Institutionalization, the transformation of an organization from a rational tool to an entity invested with emotional meaning, results from the exercise of leadership in an organization. According to Philip Selznick, when an institutional leader can successfully identify an organization's goals and purposes, define the organization's boundaries, manage relations with the external environment, and structure the organization to embody its purpose, members of the organization will invest organizational activities with meaning and significance.[59]

Such organizational transformation can have lasting effects on the way the organization is perceived by its members. An institutional mission can infuse one's participation in an organization with significance and meaning, and can result in an intensified commitment to the organization's goals. More than twenty years after John Collier resigned as Commissioner of Indian Affairs, some career employees still spoke of the bureau's mission of "bringing democracy to the Indian people," in terms reminiscent of 1930s rhetoric.

Infusing organizational purpose with significance can, of course, be self-serving. An organization seeking to fulfill a vital mission may be justified in seeking more resources, in promoting itself, and in denigrating its opponents. Thus, Washburn argues that John Collier's use of persuasion was justified by the importance of his ultimate goal.[60] In addition, participants in an organization may derive satisfaction from their adherence to organizational norms by identifying them with a transcendent goal.

*Other Views*

A popular recent view of organizations, exemplified in many descriptions of the Bureau of Indian Affairs, is of the organization as an interest group.[61] All organizations may be assumed to have an interest in their own survival. Thus, organizations allocate resources to maintenance, to monitoring their environment and to influencing relevant elements in that environment. Manufacturing concerns may invest in advertising or other marketing devices; government organizations may lobby legislators, prepare glittering evaluation reports, or emphasize their competence. Perpetuating the organization's *raison d'être* or discovering a new mission for the organization are two ways in which an organization may function as an interest group.

Alternatively, organizations can be viewed as polities, as political arenas within which interest groups composed of differing factions of members compete with each other for dominance.[62] Such a view of organizations seems to be implicit in much of the literature on organizational renewal. By bringing new blood into an organization, the organization's presumed tendency toward rigidity and the routine can be shifted. While most of the old guard can be expected to resist innovation, a large enough cadre of newcomers can "turn the organization around," thereby securing innovative change. The successful attempt to increase Indian employment within the Bureau of Indian Affairs reflects such a situation. A BIA dominated by Indians in policymaking positions would be more empathetic and consequently more effective, many Indians and non-Indians believe.[63]

While introducing new elements into the decisionmaking structure of an organization can produce change, the reverse is often found to be true. Organizations exert a powerful pull on their members to conform, in spite of interest group conflicts which may occur. In part, this is because, other things being equal, power within organizations is based on length of tenure within the organization.[64] In addition, while innovation may be required to address organizational interests (when an organization is performing poorly, for example), the organization's long-range interests may not be changed by the introduction of new talent. Therefore, even the vigorous application of Indian preference rules will not necessarily change the BIA's definition of purpose, its method of operating, or the meaning it holds for its employees. While the players may change, the nature of the game likely will remain the same if the structure of the organization and its definition of purpose remain unchanged.

In addition to Indian preference, Congress and the executive branch should emphasize restructuring the BIA and redefining its mission in the 1990s. Unfortunately, the Swimmer proposals for reform in Indian policy devoted too little attention to the administration of the organization responsible for implementing Indian policy. Indeed, the proposal neglected the organization of the bureau, seemingly hoping it would go away. Such an approach is unlikely to result in organizational renewal. The proposal, though, did focus attention on the organization of the tribes, which would be the central actors if the reforms were accomplished.

The literature on tribal government organization is not extensive as of yet, but scattered evidence suggests that tribes have responded to the changing political and economic environment by increasing their administrative capacity. On the Fond du Lac Reservation in Minnesota, Joyce Kramer reports that the self-determination policy resulted in the development of "a local bureaucracy," which delivers an increasing array of services to tribal members. Tribal members correspondingly report a high degree of satisfaction with the services.[65] While tribal bureaucracies have not met with approval on all reservations, tribes have responded to the availability of contracts and grants by expanding the services provided directly to members by a tribal civil service.

Because the funds available to tribes have been tied to programmatic areas established outside of the reservation context, the tribal organizations tend to mirror the organization of the BIA and the IHS. Two examples of such areas where grant programs for Indian tribes have been established are aging services and manpower training. Organizations of tribal contractors, often funded by the federal agency which supplies grants-in-aid to the tribes, have emerged and function as lobbying groups in the national arena, while they support the aspirations of local members for recognition on the tribal level.[66]

To the extent that tribes successfully have replicated non-Indian priorities and definitions in their administrative structures or have developed "administrative capacity," it might be expected that few problems would be encountered in implementing a real transfer of power from the federal government to the tribes. However, tribal administrations, no less than federal agencies, are formal organizations too, with their own internal interest groups, statements of mission, and needs for survival and growth. Only in a situation where tribal government structures do not mirror federal government agencies and functions will the effects of a transfer of decisionmaking authority to the tribes prove to be more favorable from the standpoint of self-determination.

A study of the Pine Ridge Indian Reservation published in 1980 concluded that a rapid expansion of the Oglala Sioux tribal bureaucracy between 1968 and 1972 contributed to a political crisis on the reservation. Tribal expenditures increased from $100,000 to over $3 million per year, reflecting the tribe's success in securing a variety of federal grants. New tribal employees were oriented toward traditional Oglala values. But the programs which they administered were not developed on the reservation. Both "mixed blood" and "cultural nationalist" factions were alienated from tribal government, since the resulting programs represented the aspirations of neither group.[67] A lesson on the proper place for the genesis of Indian programs can be learned from this experience.

### Conclusion

The past performance of the federal government in Indian affairs is unsatisfactory when measured against the standard of the right to self-determination. While recent policy changes, implemented and proposed, represent real increases in the amount of Indian tribal autonomy, they fall short of achieving true self-determination. The government's record in the near future is unlikely to be much better, primarily because of a lack of attention to the organization of the agencies that implement federal policy. Tribal organization, as well as the organization of federal agencies, is important to consider in any evaluation of the probable success of a self-determination policy. The control and direction of tribal government has proved to be a divisive issue on some reservations; such tensions would be expected to continue as tribal autonomy increases.

As discussed earlier, Dov Ronen sees the quest for self-determination as a part of an ongoing quest for human freedom, and he considers it unlikely that any administrative arrangement will satisfy that desire. Such would seem to be the case with Indian self-determination, particularly in the absence of improvements in the economic, health and educational status of American Indian people.

### NOTES

[1]Richard M. Nixon, "Message to Congress on Indian Affairs," July 8, 1970, in *Public Papers of the Presidents of the United States, Richard Nixon, 1970* (Washington, D.C.: U.S. Government Printing Office, 1971), pp. 564-576.

[2]Dov Ronen, *The Quest for Self-Determination* (New Haven, CT: Yale University Press, 1979), pp. 27-51.

[3]Ibid., p. 6.

[4]Aureliu Cristescu, *The Right to Self-Determination: Historical and Current Development on the Basis of United Nations Instruments* (New York: United Nations, 1981), p. 41.

[5]Judith L. Andress and James E. Falkowski, "Self-Determination: Indians and the United Nations — the Anomalous Status of America's 'Domestic Dependent Nations,' " *American Indian Law Review* 8: 1 (1980): 97-116; Sharon O'Brien, "Federal Indian Policies and the International Protection of Human Rights," in Vine Deloria, ed., *American Indian Policy in the Twentieth Century* (Norman, OK: University of Oklahoma Press, 1985), pp. 35-61.

[6]Norwegian Sami Rights Committee, *Summary of the First Report from the Norwegian Sami Rights Committee* (Oslo: n.p., n.d.).

[7]Michael Asch, *Home and Native Land: Aboriginal Rights and the Canadian Constitution* (Toronto: Methuen, 1984); Russel Lawrence Barsh and James Youngblood Henderson, "Aboriginal Rights, Treaty Rights, and Human Rights: Indian Tribes and 'Constitutional Renewal,' " *Journal of Canadian Studies* 17: 2 (Summer 1982): 55-81.

[8]Alan C. Cairns, "The Politics of Constitutional Renewal in Canada," in Keith J. Banting and Richard Simeon, eds., *Redesigning the State: The Politics of Constitutional Change* (Toronto: University of Toronto Press, 1985), pp. 95-145.

[9]Donald Rothchild and Victor A. Olorunsola, "Managing Competing State and Ethnic Claims," in Donald Rothchild and Victor A. Olorunsola, eds., *State Versus Ethnic Claims: African Policy Dilemmas* (Boulder, CO: Westview Press, 1983), pp. 1-24 at 10.

[10]U.S. Congress, American Indian Policy Review Commission, *Final Report*, May 17, 1977, vol. 1 (Washington, D.C.: U.S. Government Printing Office, 1977), p. 101.

[11]Lloyd Meeds, "Separate Dissenting Views," in U.S. Congress, ibid., pp. 567-612.

[12]Ronen, op. cit. note 2, p. 18.

[13]Ibid., p. 21.

[14]Ibid., pp. 99-101.

[15]See, for example, O'Brien, op. cit. note 5, p. 43; and Michael G. Lacy, "The United States and American Indians: Political Relations," in Deloria, op. cit. note 5, p. 92.

[16]Paul Stuart, *The Indian Office: Growth and Development of an American Institution, 1865-1900* (Ann Arbor, MI: UMI Research Press, 1979).

[17]Robert F. Berkhofer, Jr., *The White Man's Indian: Images of the American Indian from Columbus to the Present* (New York: Alfred A. Knopf, 1978), pp. 166-175.

[18]Randolph C. Downes, "A Crusade for Indian Reform, 1922-1934," *Mississippi Valley Historical Review* 32: 3 (December 1945): 331-354.

[19]Laurence M. Hauptman, "Africa View: John Collier, The British Colonial Service and American Indian Policy, 1933-1945," *The Historian* 48: 3 (May 1986): 359-374.

[20]Wilcomb E. Washburn, "A Fifty-Year Perspective on the Indian Reorganization Act," *American Anthropologist* 86: 2 (June 1984): 279-289.

[21]Paul Stuart, *Nations within a Nation: Historical Statistics of American Indians* (Westport, CT: Greenwood Press, 1987), pp. 136-138.

[22]Hauptman, op. cit. note 19; Washburn, op. cit. note 20.

[23]Paul Stuart, "United States Indian Policy: From the Dawes Act to the American Indian Policy Review Commission," *Social Service Review* 51: 3 (September 1977): 451-463.

[24]Ibid.

[25]Paul Stuart, "Administrative Reform in Indian Affairs," *Western Historical Quarterly* 16: 2 (April 1985): 133-146.

[26]Arthur V. Watkins, "Termination of Federal Supervision: The Removal of Restrictions Over Indian Property and Person," *The Annals of the American Academy of Political and Social Science* 311 (May 1957): 47-55.

[27]Tom Holm, "Fighting a White Man's War: The Extent and Legacy of Indian Participation in World War II," *Journal of Ethnic Studies* 9: 2 (Summer 1981): 69-81; Jerry R. Cates, "Administrative Justice, Social Security, and the American Indians," in Peter T. Simbi and Jacob N. Ngwa, eds., *Administrative Justice in Public Services: American and African Perspectives* (Stevens Point, WI: Worzalla Publishing, 1988), pp. 34-50.

[28]Criminal and civil jurisdiction were transferred to the states of California, Minnesota (except the Red Lake Reservation), Nebraska, Oregon (except the Warm Springs Reservation), and Wisconsin (except the Menominee Reservation). P.L. 280, 67 Stat. 588-590, August 15, 1953 (83rd Congress, 2nd Session).

[29]Peter Iverson, "Building toward Self-Determination: Plains and Southwestern Indians in the 1940s and 1950s," *Western Historical Quarterly* 16: 2 (April 1985): 163-173.

[30]Transfer Act, 68 Stat. 674-675, August 5, 1954 (83rd Congress, 2nd Session). The transfer took effect on July 1, 1955.

[31]Charles F. Wilkinson, *American Indians, Time, and the Law: Native Societies in a Modern Constitutional Democracy* (New Haven, CT: Yale University Press, 1987), pp. 1-4.

[32]Kenneth R. Philp, "Stride toward Freedom: The Relocation of Indians to Cities, 1952-1960," *Western Historical Quarterly* 16: 2 (April 1985): 175-190.

[33]Joan Ablon, "Relocated American Indians in the San Francisco Bay Area: Social Interaction and Indian Identity," *Human Organization* 23: 4 (Winter 1964): 296-304.

[34]The Buy Indian Act, 36 Stat. 861, June 25, 1910 (61st Congress, 2nd Session), was a proviso in an amendment to the General Allotment Act of 1887.

[35]Nixon, op. cit. note 1.

[36]Indian Self-Determination and Education Assistance Act, P.L. 93-638, 88 Stat. 2203-2217, January 4, 1975 (93rd Congress, 2nd Session).

[37]Indian Child Welfare Act, P.L. 95-608, 92 Stat. 3069-3078, November 8, 1978 (95th Congress, 2nd Session).

[38]Tribally Controlled Community College Assistance Act, P.L. 95-471, 92 Stat. 1325-1331, October 17, 1978 (95th Congress, 2nd Session).

[39]Ronald Reagan, "Statement on Indian Policy," January 24, 1983, *Public Papers of the Presidents of the United States, Ronald Reagan, 1983*, Book I (Washington, D.C.: U.S. Government Printing Office, 1984), pp. 96-100.

[40]Ronen, op. cit. note 2, p. 23.

[41]Russel Lawrence Barsh and Ronald L. Trosper, "Title I of the Indian Self-Determination Act," *American Indian Law Review* 3: 2 (1975): 361-395 at 361.

[42]U.S. Congress, Office of Technology Assessment, *Indian Health Care*, OTA-H-290 (Washington, D.C.: U.S. Government Printing Office, 1986), p. 216.

[43]Ibid., pp. 224-225; Robert A. Nelson and Joseph F. Sheley, "Bureau of Indian Affairs Influence on Indian Self-Determination," in Deloria, op. cit. note 5, pp. 177-196.

[44]U.S. Congress, Office of Technology Assessment, op. cit. note 42, p. 221.

[45]Francis Paul Prucha, *The Indians in American Society: From the Revolutionary War to the Present* (Berkeley, CA: University of California Press, 1985), p. 97.

[46]Barsh and Trosper, op. cit. note 41.

[47]Paul Stuart, "American Indian Policy and American Indian Elders: Adequacy, Accessibility, and Acceptability," paper presented at the Annual Program Meeting, Council on Social Work Education (Atlanta, GA: March 1988).

[48]*Arizona Republic* (October 4, 1987), p. A21.

[49]Ross Swimmer, "Statement of the Assistant Secretary for Indian Affairs before the Subcommittee on Interior and Related Agencies, Committee on Appropriations, United States House of Representatives, October 27, 1987," in *Hearings before a Subcommittee of the Committee on Appropriations, House of Representatives, Subcommittee on the Department of the Interior and Related Agencies*, Part 12, Bureau of Indian Affairs, 100th Congress, 1st Session (Washington, D.C.: U.S. Government Printing Office, 1988), pp. 5-9.

[50]Donald R. Whitnah, ed., *Government Agencies*, Greenwood Encyclopedia of American Institutions, no. 7 (Westport, CT: Greenwood Press, 1983), pp. 645-655.

[51]Herbert Kaufman, *The Limits of Organizational Change* (University, AL: University of Alabama Press, 1971).

[52]Reinhold Niebuhr, *Moral Man and Immoral Society: A Study in Ethics and Politics* (New York: Scribner, 1932), p. 267.

[53]Lewis Meriam, technical director, et al., *The Problem of Indian Administration*, the Meriam Report (Baltimore: Johns Hopkins Press, published for the Brookings Institution, 1928), pp. 140-148.

[54]Paul Stuart, "The Washington Staff of the Indian Office, 1834-1984," paper presented at the Northern Great Plains History Conference (Sioux Falls, SD: October 1987).

[55]Dillion S. Myer, quoted in Patricia K. Ourada, "Dillion Seymour Myer, 1950-1953," in Robert M. Kvasnicka and Herman J. Viola, eds., *The Commissioners of Indian Affairs, 1824-1977* (Lincoln, NE: University of Nebraska Press, 1979), pp. 293-299 at 294.

[56]U.S. Congress, House of Representatives, Committee on Interior and Insular Affairs, *Survey Report on the Bureau of Indian Affairs* [*Bimson Report*], Committee Print (Washington, D.C.: U.S. Government Printing Office, 1954), p. 9.

[57]U.S. Congress, Office of Technology Assessment, op. cit. note 42, pp. 223-225.

[58]Robert K. Merton, "Patterns of Influence: Local and Cosmopolitan Influentials," in *Social Theory and Social Structure*, 1968 enlarged ed. (New York: Free Press, 1968), pp. 441-474.

[59]Philip Selznick, *Leadership in Administration: A Sociological Interpretation* (New York: Harper and Row, 1957).

[60]Wilcomb E. Washburn, "Response to Biolsi," *American Anthropologist* 87: 3 (September 1985): 659.

[61]Russel Lawrence Barsh, "The BIA Reorganization Follies of 1978: A Lesson in Bureaucratic Self-Defense," *American Indian Law Review* 7: 1 (1979): 1-50.

[62]Burton Gummer, "A Power-Politics Approach to Social Welfare Organizations," *Social Service Review* 52: 3 (September 1978): 349-361.

[63]John Gamino, "Bureau of Indian Affairs: Should Indians Be Preferentially Employed?" *American Indian Law Review* 2: 1 (Summer 1974): 111-118.

[64]David Mechanic, "Sources of Power of Lower Participants in Complex Organizations," *Administrative Science Quarterly* 7: 3 (December 1962): 349-364.

[65]Joyce M. Kramer, "The Policy of American Self-Determination and its Relevance to Administrative Justice in Africa," in Simbi and Ngwa, eds., op. cit. note 27, pp. 91-102.

[66]See, for example, Stuart, op. cit. note 47.

[67]Philip D. Roos, Dowell H. Smith, Stephen Langley, and James McDonald, "The Impact of the American Indian Movement on the Pine Ridge Indian Reservation," *Phylon* 41: 1 (March 1980): 89-99.

# THE PERSISTENCE OF IDENTITY IN INDIAN COMMUNITIES OF THE WESTERN GREAT LAKES*

Donald L. Fixico

*Western Michigan University*

Since the initial contact between Indian nations and the United States, the federal government has instituted harmful policies with devastating effects on American Indians. The consequences of such policies have ranged from paternalistic control to the total destruction of some tribal communities. In its efforts to forcibly assimilate the native peoples of the Western Great Lakes as well as the remaining Indian population into American society, the federal government has committed a grave social injustice. In order to survive, Indian people have resisted in numerous ways, including war. Although aspects of their original identity have endured, it has become vulnerable to change. Today, many communities on reservations and in urban areas are fragmented and in danger of losing their group identities.

In spite of constant policy bombardment, however, Indian identity persists in the twentieth century. Why do Indians still identify as native peoples, especially when their various cultures and communities have faced centuries of contact with white America? How have Indians managed to retain their identity? To what extent have federal government policies served to mistreat, socially and politically, both reservation and urban Indian communities?

Many of the answers to these questions rest in the internal composition of Indian communities. For example, fundamental values and traditional practices have sustained Indian people. Indian communities have continued to exist because these internal elements have been perpetuated through specific roles that dictate individual behavior. Perhaps somewhat surprisingly, external factors which have threatened the naturally developing relationship between Indian communities and their native environment also have brought about more cohesive tribal communities. These external factors include the actions of historical figures, governmental policies, legislative activities, treaties and war. In other words, both internal and external factors have contributed to a native identity essential to community existence historically as well as in more recent times. Today, the basic tenets of reservation and urban Indian life perpetuate and maintain a quasi-traditional identity which might be referred to as a protomodern traditionalism, a type of hybridization compromising the past and the present. More specifically, several factors have affected life for the tribal nations within the Western Great Lakes area, including the internal strengths of the communities, external threats, the interaction of these, and the environment. All of these factors working together have produced change in the life of the region.

This chapter first addresses the ethnohistorical backgrounds of Indian communities on reservations and in urban areas in the Western Great Lakes region. Following the ethnographic discussion, federal policies which affect Indian identity are discussed, especially in their role as external forces provoking the communities to preserve and solidify group identity. More emphasis is placed initially on tribal communities leading to the reservation period in order to help explain the developing identities of urban Indian communities, especially following World War II when federal policies and programs heavily affected Indian people. Important legislation, policies and historical events are used both to portray pre-1945 conditions and to explain the endurance and progress of Western Great Lakes Indian communities in the twentieth century. Examples of tribal groups and Indian urban communities are employed for general illustration, but are not used as specific models. Observations and general analysis are designed to bring attention to the fact that tribal communities and urban Indian communities of the Western Great Lakes have retained a native identity, although it may seem more appropriate to focus on a single Indian community. The objective of this chapter is to demonstrate how and why reservation and urban Indian identities have survived the social injustice of federal policies.

**Native Locations and Environment**

Geographically, the Western Great Lakes area covers western Michigan, the northwest corner of Illinois, the northeast corner of Iowa, eastern Minnesota, and Wisconsin. Tribal communities of the region include the Menominee, Brotherton, Stockbridge-Munsee, Oneida, Potawatomi, Sauk, Fox, Winnebago, Ottawa, Santee (Dakota) and Chippewa (originally called the Ojibwa, of which the southwestern Chippewas will be stressed). These groups represent two types, indigenous and migrant tribal communities, and each set of tribal communities established homelands in the Western Great Lakes area.

The homeland is relevant for stabilizing a community and providing identity for a tribespeople. Simultaneously, it is a part of the environment, as the migrant tribal communities — Oneida, Stockbridge-Munsee and Brotherton—proved in adjusting to the Western Great Lakes area and establishing identities within their new homelands. Basically, these identities resembled their original ones in the East, although the removal to the Western Great Lakes region fragmented the tribes and their leadership. The survival of their tribal communities in a new environment demonstrated the strength of group identity for perpetuating Indian societies.

Typically, a concentration of people living in an area establish a pattern of settlement. Many American Indian patterns of settlement historically utilized a large area for agriculture and an even larger area for hunting to support its members. For example, in the Western Great Lakes, Chippewa communities exhibited a similar pattern of settlement, with hunting parties not only providing necessary resources but alerting the community to potential danger from external factors such as the advancement of white settlers in the area.[1] Even though reservations in Indian America today appear sparsely populated, the land remains committed to the residence of the community's members. While outsiders might argue that there is no visible claim to the reservation lands, tribal communities (whether they are matrilocal or patrilocal) understand the pattern of families occupying certain areas.

In sum, the homeland provided a sense of place for the community. Furthermore, tribal communities mutually recognized the homeland of other tribal communities as their lives interacted. Continuity through history reinforced each community's identity until the intervention of external forces (e.g., the French and British) more powerful than the internal elements of the community interrupted or threatened that identity, thus causing an abnormal change.


**Internal Social Structure**


Since the beginning of tribal history in the Western Great Lakes area, certain internal elements have bonded people together to form communities. Today, these same elements hold communities together on reservations and in urban Indian communities. Interacting in unison, these elements are actually components of larger, interrelated social systems. This social infrastructure includes kinship networks (consisting of individuals and extended families), clans, societies, moieties, and leadership.

The individual and, as a unit, the tribe, represent the basic component of the community. Social interaction on a daily basis establishes community membership and produces group solidarity as the people congregate in friendship, in ceremonies, in singing or in laughter. As the primary component, the people represent the inner core of the tribal community, and kinship networks represent another element interacting with that inner core.[2]

The interaction of people through kinship networks involves controlled intratribal politics. For example, factions and interest groups interact on reservations and can serve either to unite or divide the community. The same observation currently holds for reservation and urban communities in the Western Great Lakes area when, for example, the governing body of members entertains an external issue that will affect the entire group. Among the Chippewas, this striving for native identity represents a strong legacy nurtured through the ages — what anthropologist Harold Hickerson has described as a "collective life."[3] Collective life provides group identity. In addition, life in a collective or community sense exists to defend against the difficulty of surviving in harsh conditions; one person alone would likely live for only a short time before the dangers of the environment would consume him.

In the Western Great Lakes area, a community of people maintained mutual relationships with other tribal communities, animals and plants within a larger relationship of nature. Philosophically, everything belonged within one established order. For instance, the Menominees believe that no dichotomy exists between people and animals, so that a mutual respect prevails.[4] Everything has a spirit. Similarly, the Chippewa had a holistic world view and "their belief system centered in establishing and maintaining close and friendly relations with spirits investing and giving form to the animals and plants upon which they subsisted and even to such nonanimate things as stars, stones, storms, hills, and lakes."[5] This philosophical relationship represented a part of the community's sociopolitical system in the same way that kinship networks and political relations interacted. Like the Chippewas, the other tribes of the area had kinship networks interlocked with other networks.

*Chippewa Individuality and Youth*

The roles played by individuals in a community are vital for perpetuating community existence. The emphasis on group solidarity meant that individual members of a tribal society acted interdependently within the group for survival. In order for the group to function successfully, the tribal community required cooperation among individuals, thereby creating the need for cultural norms and, especially, tribal laws.

The Chippewas were an exception to the emphasis on the group that was present among the tribal nations of the Western Great Lakes. Despite this tendency towards individualism, the Chippewas managed to hold a large northern portion of the Western Great Lakes as a tribal nation. Ruth Landes, also an anthropologist, concluded similarly that the northern Chippewas in Ontario stressed the private ownership of territory.[6] In support of the individual theory, Harold Hickerson surmised that the "individualistic" and "atomistic" nature of the southwestern Chippewas made them "intuitive and impressionistic,"[7] a quality that perhaps contributed to their rationalizing the need for cooperation with other Chippewas, especially during the numerous military campaigns against the Sioux.

The atomism theory also helps explain the Chippewa resistance to cultural change.[8] The Chippewas exemplified a tribespeople steeped in traditions, who experienced generations of contact with other tribal nations, as well as the French, the British, and then the Americans. In this process of cultural, political and social contact with other nations, the Chippewas did well to retain their tribal identity and cultural ways. It is likely that this identity was maintained via the atomism of the Chippewas, who proudly demonstrated their tribal nationhood.

Until approximately the last twenty-five years on the tribal reservations, or the beginning of the last generation, Chippewas had individually adopted a significant amount of the mainstream material culture. Since a correlation exists between the personality of an individual and one's culture, it is conceivable that Chippewa identity will become vulnerable as each tribal member decides to change his or her present lifestyle. Furthermore, Chippewa individuality remains congruent with tribal sociocultural conditions, and as the social and cultural conditions change with time and progress, individuals may change themselves as a result of exogenous variables, e.g., off-reservation experiences.[9]

Atomism among the Chippewa began with the youth.[10] Elders taught their youth to be extroverted in dealing with an unfriendly environment, so the youth learned individualism and survival behavior at an early age. Chippewa families have been described as loose and warm, as the youth become integrated with the kinship structure. From this extroverted perspective, the Chippewa children neither exhibited nor saw any difference between their human environment and their natural environment. Everything was integrated into the same sphere of life or world view.

In summary, the Chippewas are a rare example of the importance of individualism in a collective group — the tribal community. Other tribal nations of the Western Great Lakes are less individualistic, with more emphasis on family unity. The Chippewas also exemplify how tribal members can be individuals, yet work together along kinship lines in order for the tribal community to progress and accept change.

Within the sphere of tribal culture, the inner core of the community is defined by the people themselves. If they want to change and do, then the community changes; but if they are reluctant to change and do not, then the chance for their community to continue traditionally is enhanced. Because major changes might threaten the community, they are limited according to cultural norms, and perhaps tribal law.

For this reason, isolation from alien influences, such as during the pre-European contact years, was vital to the development of the traditional community. Chippewa communities exemplified this point best as they sought isolation and preferred atomistic individualism, even within their own communities.

*The Role of Men*

In recent years, the traditional role of men on Western Great Lakes reservations and urban communities has changed considerably. For example, within the last generation, men of the Western Great Lakes tribes have practiced few traditions and have adopted many of the mainstream ways. Prior to this generation, men held to their traditional roles steadfastly in spite of continual contact with other nations and their cultures.

One example of external influences from another tribe effecting changes occurred during the summer of 1832 when Henry Schoolcraft, an Indian agent, reported that factionalism was developing among the Chippewas at Leech Lake and at Cass Lake. The young men's warrior role conflicted with the civic leaders who sought peace in spite of unpredictable battles with the Dakota. Choosing between war and peace would have divided the village communities, but the external threat of attacks from the Dakota reinforced tribal identity by uniting the Chippewa communities.[11] Eventually the two factions resolved the issue, thereby preserving the community. In sum, an external factor acted simultaneously as a threat and a catalyst, thereby bonding the internal elements of the community. In social relations specifically among the Chippewas, "social norms over the historic period related directly to the imposition of outside socioeconomic and ideological systems that everywhere gained momentum," and which were "exploitative."[12] Changes in social organization were adaptations to local environmental conditions.

With their roles defined according to tribal norms, Chippewa males and men of the Western Great Lakes tribes in general faced a second possibility of change when external influences from the Europeans induced the male roles to be redefined. In this case, change occurred from the dynamics of external influences interacting with the men's roles; for example, the introduction of guns or alcohol overwhelmed the internal influences for maintaining the male role. In particular, new technology or a dependence on nonnative goods contributed to the decline of traditionalism among men and women.

As contact continued with other cultures, especially the Europeans and Americans, the preservation of the traditional male roles became more difficult. From the position of the traditionalists, men of the Western Great Lakes tribes became increasingly attracted to non-Indian cultural ways and increasingly dependent upon non-Indian cultural goods.

### The Role of Women

While men performed war and civic functions, women performed pertinent roles as the true holders of power and culture. Although the role of women has been underestimated, their roles were more likely to remain traditional than were those of men. While the men were away at war or hunting, the women generally stayed home to tend to the families and continue daily tribal activities. Their presence provided security for the children, and their performing responsibilities in familiar surroundings made them less apt to change. Women of the Western Great Lakes tribes were less exposed than men to other communities and their cultures until French, British and American traders encouraged the tribespeople, including the women, to adopt the goods of their cultures.

In a study of Menominee women and cultural change, Louise Spindler concluded that the Menominees were an ideal group for investigating sociocultural adaptation and the retention of identity.[13] In spite of the acculturation process, the Menominee community on the reservation has remained basically the same. In the acculturative transformation, some changes have occurred in value orientation, social self, and the pattern of self-perception of Menominee women. However, Menominee women continue to strongly identify as Menominees.

In her role as mother and as "keeper of the culture," the Menominee woman teaches social and cultural behavior to both her male and female children. Her responsibility to the male child ends at age fourteen or fifteen when the son's education becomes the responsibility of the father.[14] Moreover, it has been argued that since the role of Menominee women carries more responsibilities than men's roles, women are more likely to be conservative.[15] As keepers of the culture, the women's responsibilities are viewed by the community as imperative for maintaining its internal elements.

The Menominee maintain interpersonal relationships through the kinship system. This kinship system is carried forth by teaching members to instill passive reactions to conflict, thereby decreasing the chances for friction and helping to preserve peace in the community.[16] This behavior is inconsistent with the dominant white society's value on aggressive behavior, thereby causing the mainstream to perceive the Menominee as passive and unambitious.

Perception of one's self is also important to the Menominee. Louise Spindler employed the Rorschach personality test, which uses inkblot interpretation, to assess how contemporary Menominees perceive themselves.[17] She found that women viewed themselves as Menominees who were adaptive to cultural ways. Cultural values and socioeconomic backgrounds were also relevant to perpetuating this perspective, and thus for explaining the continuation of the Menominee community. Self-perception was more important than where the community physically resided.

Today's women of Western Great Lakes tribal communities continue to fulfill important roles as keepers of the family and culture. At the same time, many women have found it necessary to work outside of the home to contribute to the family's income. Although this might be considered as succumbing to the assimilation process, the women undoubtedly view themselves as tribal members.

*Family Types*

The families of Western Great Lakes tribes consisted of two extended types — adopted and bloodline. Individual members had specific roles enabling the family to perform as a working kinship unit within the large context of the community. In relationship with other families via the kinship network, the community was a working system of families. Large by today's American standards, the southwestern Chippewas, for example, had an estimated 8.2 persons per family, a high number of persons to feed and clothe.[18] Providing food for a family was a time-consuming task calling for hunting skills and good fortune in locating wild game, fish and wild rice. During crises, family members could depend on each other for moral support and assistance. In addition, as members of a kinship system of relatives and clans, they could also obtain assistance from the larger tribal community.

Traditionally, the tribal community included extended families so that grandfathers, grandmothers and other close relatives customarily conjoined the bloodline family. Extended families were prevalent among the tribal communities of the Western Great Lakes, except for the Oneida who emphasized the nuclear family structure as their primary economic unit.[19] During the eighteenth century the southwestern Chippewas functioned at three different levels, the village, the hunting band, and the household or family.[20] Among the Chippewas, extended families on average consisted of two or three generations who resided in a long wigwam.[21] The Chippewas' large families called for organization to maintain order in spite of the atomistic nature of the people.

Among the Fox, the bloodline family and the adopted family were important elements of the tribal community. In war or other crises, blood relatives could be depended upon without question for assistance. In fact, the bloodline family held more social importance than a marriage until the married couple produced a new bloodline family.[22]

The adopted family acted in the same manner. Families adopted new members for various reasons. The Fox, for instance, adopted individuals to maintain their population after losing members in war against other tribal nations and non-Indians.[23] Orphans frequently became favorites in a family, and were often raised as if they were true members of the bloodline family.

A higher order of kinship was represented by clan systems, which in some tribes were divided into complementary units called moieties. Clan systems played a strategic role in the community as the second largest kinship unit after the family. Represented by totemic animals or plants, families held membership in clan societies ranked according to their importance under tribal laws. As previously mentioned, because animals and plants were so important to the people and their world view, their respect by the Western Great Lakes tribal communities led to the establishment of a kinship relationship with them. In some situations, societies developed from clans and were also referred to as "councils," each with certain responsibilities. For instance, some councils within Western Great Lakes tribal communities were comprised of warriors of certain types according to age, or women of particular interests, or wise elders. Acting as guardian groups, the societies' elders advised the people about their spiritual life and administered cultural activities to insure their well-being. Finally, the highest order was achieved by the sociopolitical system of bands or villages, and then the tribal nation.

Except for the individual person, however, the family unit represented the most important segment of the tribal community. Because of the biological relationship, the family was the strongest kinship unit. Today in Western Great Lakes tribal communities, the extended family is common, as with the Menominees, whose average family consists of a man, wife and children, and frequently one or more grandparents.[24]

### Intertribal Wars

Warfare, especially in instances where the group felt threatened and war was supported, increased patriotism and loyalty to the community. Feelings of "we" versus "they" heightened and underscored this identity. This process was evident in all Western Great Lakes groups, from the more peaceful Menominee to the more individualistic Chippewa.

Despite the Chippewas' overall individualism, external threats could bring about a unification of the *do daim* (Chippewa) village or community, as well as discourage individualism and isolation.[25] As evidence of this, the Chippewas' wars with the Dakota (Sioux) during the late 1700s and early 1800s provoked periodic nationalism and unity within the villages.

Schoolcraft, the Chippewa agent, reported for 1831-32 that the villages between Lac Vieux Desert and Red Lake varied in population. Ranging from small to large, these villages or communities accounted for an estimated three-fourths of the Chippewa population of four thousand persons who resided in the seven largest villages or population centers. The population estimates ranged from nearly three hundred persons at Red Lake to over eight hundred at Leech Lake.[26] Interestingly, reports indicate that the Chippewa villages had undergone a deliberate fragmentation and forming of permanent communities while fighting the Dakota and their frequent Fox allies during the 1700s.[27] In this way, internal elements of the Chippewa communities were able to withstand the external threat of war from the Santee Sioux. Military cooperation proved essential to community survival; securing all villages in the immediate area fostered retribalization and community identification. Economically and politically autonomous, their sporadic associations with other villages were probably based on alliances of intercommunity marriages and clan relations.[28] Among the Lake Superior Chippewa, for example, bilateral cross-cousin marriages allied the villages through kinship.[29] Cross-cousin marriages established multiple bonds of alliances, creating a system of isolated, yet loyal, relationships among the village communities.[30]

Although the Menominee were not as warlike a people as the Fox, Sauk, Chippewa or Dakota, they did defend their hunting areas and trade interests. In addition to protecting their territorial interests, smaller confrontations resulted from feuds or raids by young men to earn prestige as warriors. Frequently, tribal communities agreed to fight as mercenaries or as allies with a particular European side or with another Indian group. Victory in war served to sustain the identity of the tribal community and maintain community relations among the people. (Interestingly, the Menominee takeover of the Alexian Brothers monastery in the 1970s underscored tribal community identity, and their restoration in 1974 as a federally recognized tribe, after termination in 1961, made them recognizable to the public.)

War as an external experience unites the community within, bringing together all internal elements of the society. Especially in an effort to defend one's homeland and nation, nationalism, manifested in emotional feelings of survival, emerges and is identified as patriotism and pride. Hence heritage, a source of a community's native identity, is also at stake.

### U.S. Policy of Indian Removal

Indigenous tribal communities who lived in the Western Great Lakes included the Santee Sioux, Chippewa, Winnebago, Menominee, Sauk, Fox, Potawatomi and Mascouten. (After 1800, the Mascouten merged with the Kickapoo and disappeared as a separate community.[31]) These tribes were among the numerous groups affected indirectly by Andrew Jackson's removal act.[32] Passed in 1830, the law forced eastern tribes to surrender their aboriginal territory for western lands. This created a domino effect as the indigenous Western Great Lakes and other western tribes had to make room for the displaced eastern tribes.

During the nineteenth century, leaders of tribal communities throughout the Western Great Lakes negotiated land agreements with the United States, thereby assigning reservations to tribal communities. These agreements reduced the land of the indigenous people and created surplus areas for white settlers and incoming tribal groups removed from the East, such as the Oneida of New York and the Stockbridge and Munsee from the Massachusetts area.

In 1831 the federal government established reservations in Wisconsin for New York Indians. These tribes had negotiated with the Menominees for land ten years earlier and had already started farms along the Fox River and Duck Creek flowing into Green Bay.[33] During the ensuing years, parties of Stockbridge, Munsee and Brotherton arrived, making their homes on lands set aside for their use along the eastern shore of Lake Winnebago. In 1833 the Brotherton sold their reservation, and the federal government dismissed them from its jurisdiction. The Oneida from New York, which had begun migrating in 1823, did not complete their move to the new reservation until the final group of 638 tribal members settled in 1838.[34] The Stockbridge and Munsee from Moraviantown in southern Ontario, who joined them in 1837, agreed to move to the southwestern part of the Menominee Reservation in 1856.[35]

In 1832 the federal government established the Sauk and Fox (Mesquakie) reservation in Iowa as a result of the Black Hawk War. At this time, the government also removed the Winnebago of Fox River to a reservation on the Minnesota-Iowa border, a part of the "neutral ground."[36] Five years earlier, the Winnebago had attacked mining settlements in southwestern Wisconsin, and with their defeat and that of Chief Black Hawk, the southern half of Wisconsin was free from war.

The Indian land experience in Wisconsin involved the dislocation of indigenous tribal communities and the relocation of certain eastern native groups to Wisconsin. Under federal pressures from treaty negotiations and the removal policy, both indigenous and new tribes faced considerable challenges regarding community survival. Even at this stage of Indian-white contact, the indigenous communities retained strong internal networks, and thus differed from the removed eastern groups whose communities had already experienced a generation of Indian-white cultural exchange and political contact. The Oneida, a member nation of the League of the Iroquois, consisted of two political divisions when they relocated to Wisconsin. One party consisted of those who were pro-American warriors during the American Revolution. These people were Christians and favored white society. The opposing party consisted of traditional political and religious supporters who criticized Anglo-American society and aided the British during the Revolution.[37] Political factionalism tested the internal composition of the Oneidas, yet their fundamental elements of community cohesion and native identity helped the community to survive despite the forced relocation to the Western Great Lakes.

As Indian-white contact increased via land negotiations and land reassignments, surrounding territories like Minnesota encountered a similar indigenous-migrant Indian experience. Feelings grew tense. Locating new reservation homes in the Western Great Lakes region for the removed eastern groups became the responsibility of the federal government, and this presented problems for both the United States and the indigenous Indian communities. The indigenous communities faced two types of newcomers intruding into their home areas — eastern tribal groups and white settlers. The federal government's treaty policy was based on the mistaken view that enough land existed for everyone, but this created problems for all three cultural exchanges occurring in the vicinity — indigenous-white settler, eastern Indian-white settler, and indigenous-eastern Indian. To compound the situation, fundamental racial and cultural differences between the eastern and indigenous tribes and between both and the white settlers produced friction. In order to maintain peace, policies involving land cessions were enforced, but these took advantage of the two Indian populations.

In Minnesota, the treaties signed in 1851 at Traverse des Sioux and Mendota forced the Dakota to cede their remaining lands in the area. In exchange, they were to receive a reservation twenty miles wide between the Minnesota River adjoining Lake Traverse and the mouth of the Yellow Medicine River. However, following the 1862 uprising of the Dakotas (Santees) in Minnesota, the federal government used military force to defeat and exile the Dakota. Next, the United States forced the Winnebago onto the Crow Creek Reservation in present-day South Dakota. Further removal of the Dakota in 1866 to the Santee Reservation on the Niobrara River in Nebraska promised a better future. The Winnebago at Crow Creek ultimately sought sanctuary among the Omaha in northwestern Nebraska. The federal government attempted some semblance of justice in an 1867 treaty, when it granted a reservation in Dakota Territory to the Dakotas identified as "friendlies" during the 1862 uprising, but the Santee Sioux War overshadowed any fair treatment of the defeated Indians. Soon thereafter, government officials received criticism for the mass execution of thirty-eight Santees found guilty of carrying out the war. The external events of war and removal due to government policy and Indian-white interactions tested the endurance of both the Winnebago and Dakota communities. A similar test confronted the Ojibwa.

Most Ojibwa reservations in northern Wisconsin and Minnesota date from treaties negotiated in 1854 and 1855. Before the creation of the first reservations there, President Zachary Taylor attempted to remove Wisconsin Indian bands to the headwaters of the Mississippi River in 1850. Unfortunately, the La Pointe agency had been closed, compelling the government to direct the Wisconsin bands to receive annuities at Sandy Lake in Minnesota. A conniving agent planned to withhold the 1850 annuity distribution until difficult weather conditions convinced the Indians to remain for the winter. Reports indicated that as many as four hundred perished near Sandy Lake or died trying to walk home. In late 1851, the government rescinded the removal order. Later, new treaties in 1863 and 1867 aimed to consolidate the Minnesota Ojibwa upon two large reservations, at Leech Lake and at White Earth, located directly west of Leech Lake. Years later the federal government established the last reservation in Minnesota at Red Lake in 1889.[38]

The federal policy of settling all three populations within the Western Great Lakes had worked in theory, but the human consequences yielded an unfortunate reality. Both the indigenous and eastern tribal groups suffered from the greed and pressure of the white population to settle, farm and mine the area. In its efforts to maintain peace, the federal government favored the white settlers at a terrible cost to the Indians, especially the indigenous groups who viewed themselves as the original occupiers of the region and who had to now accept the unjust situation of two foreign groups in their homeland.


### The Policy of Land Allotment

In the late nineteenth century, the federal government introduced policy changes which drastically altered the organization of Indian communities in the twentieth century. The Dawes Land Allotment Act of 1887,[39] the most severe measure, caused devastating cultural changes for all Indian people whose reservations were surveyed for allotments. Basically, the allotment of land to tribal members sought to individualize Indian society. By allotting 80-160 acre parcels to tribal members, the government expected the Indians to adapt to farming, learn to live as white men, and thus become "civilized." This did not happen, although many Indians began to adapt to agrarianism. Overall, forced agrarianism and the allotment of poor quality land fostered adverse farming conditions, thus causing frustration and the Indian rejection of white ways.

In a different light, environment played, and continues to play, a crucial role in perpetuating quasi-traditional communities on reservations and in urban areas. In discussing reservations and urban areas, it is important to define the environment of the community as it is affected by surrounding elements. A community's relationships with nature and other human communities, and the mutual dynamics between community and environment, are critical to the permanent existence of the Indian community. The community and environment must be in sync with everything in that the environment functions to maintain the community at the subsistence, kinship and interaction levels. Of course, weather is also a contributing factor, as well as such physical features as water, mountains, vegetation and other natural creations. How the community views itself among its environmental surroundings shapes its world view of universal equilibrium. The Chippewa, for example, view human and nature relationships to be of equal value. The Fox hold a similar world view, and also believe that all Fox have direct relations with the Manitou (supreme creator) power.[40] Obviously, an ingrained philosophy of evolved Indian cultures and belief systems could not be undone within two score of years, even by a forced policy of allotment.

### The National Policy of Assimilation

The distribution of land allotments and the granting of U.S. citizenship produced numerous sad examples concerning Indian land ownership. Indians were often soon exploited, with their allotted land being lost, stolen, sold or purchased for profits by non-Indians. A well-meaning Congress attempted to halt such debauchery when it passed the Burke Act in 1906.[41] This protective measure delayed American citizenship and placed allotted lands into "trust" status under the jurisdiction of the Secretary of the Interior. Unfortunately, this action failed to stem further exploitation of many Indians as their lands continued to fall into the hands of opportunists.

World War I interrupted the flow of Indian life. Though they were ineligible for the draft, this minor technicality did not stop more than six thousand young Indian men from volunteering to fight for the United States during its brief involvement in the global conflict known then as the Great War. For their patriotic service, Congress passed an act in 1919 stating "[t]hat every American Indian who served . . . against the Imperial German Government, [with] an honorable discharge, . . . be granted full citizenship."[42] Upon returning home, many Indian veterans chose to leave their communities, bringing disruption to community life. Following World War I, life remained generally difficult for Indian people as the allotment program offered little reprieve and much grief.

For the next two decades, Indians experienced continual exploitation as court-appointed guardians of the trust lands, many of whom were corrupt themselves, failed to stop the graft and corruption. In 1924 Congress enacted the General Citizenship Act, granting U.S. citizenship to the remaining Indian population. This landmark legislation allowed Indians to assume and enjoy the privileges and responsibilities guaranteed under the Constitution. The act stated: "That all non-citizen Indians born within the territorial limits of the United States be, and they are hereby, declared to be citizens of the United States: Provided, That the granting of such citizenship shall not in any manner impair or otherwise affect the right of any Indian to tribal or other property."[43] Whether they were ready or not, the U.S. government deemed all Indian people as fit to be U.S. citizens, which included all of the responsibilities. This effort was a part of the overall policy to mainstream American Indians.

The period from the turn of the century through the 1920s proved to be the darkest in Indian-white relations in this century. In spite of the exploitation and murdering of Indians for their allotments, tribal communities continued to exist, but advanced very little in improving their living conditions. Tribal community presence, however, did not coincide with the American mainstream standards. If tribal communities had been allowed to evolve in a normal state, perhaps hybrid examples of traditionalism would also have evolved over time. Instead, tribal communities began to change rapidly because of frequent interruptions from the dominant culture and federal policies. Tribal communities faced two polarized sets of cultural values. Unable to advance under normal cultural conditions, the communities strove to survive the influences of the dominant society.

During this hardship, the tribes endured in spite of two influential and competing cultural systems — that of native traditionalism and that of the white man's culture. Continuity was hindered by unnatural development, as the tribal communities became increasingly vulnerable to a powerful, influential dominant culture. This period can be construed as resulting in negative cultural change, but it nevertheless represented evolutionary change. Ideally, cultures develop via positive changes as their own people dictate it, but this was not the case for Indians during the allotment era.

### The Retention of Traditionalism and Leadership

One aspect of the Western Great Lakes native cultures that allowed members to maintain their native identity was the willingness to explore new ideas. For example, the Menominee culture had always been open to change. Their culture was in the process of developmental change before European arrival, and it continued to change afterwards at an accelerated rate. Menominee culture was of "great sophistication, with a strong cosmological and philosophical orientation . . . . It was never understood by whites, including those, such as agents, priests, and teachers who were trying to 'civilize' the Menominee."[44]

Thus, there was a general notion of change in indigenous Indian communities, but that change occurred gradually. Nevertheless, this element of the Menominee culture helps us to understand the opposition to, and perhaps inability of, Indian communities to accommodate drastic social changes in a short period of time.

The Fox tribe yields some insight into the importance of leadership roles in traditional tribal government for the maintenance of tribal identity. The Fox held tribal councils when a "head chief" announced the council. An "old chief" of no authority provided his wisdom and stated the council procedure according to law. The "quiet chief" spoke periodically to keep the discussion going, while the "war chief" spoke out when the discussion turned hostile. Usually, a council man seated near the council chief supported the chief's arguments and periodically substituted for him. An individual acted as a recorder of the council's actions, and the attending members of the tribe listened as they had no official voice.[45] This form of tribal government resulted in a general opposition to vertical authority and a negative reaction toward outsiders. This leadership structure also enabled the Fox to retain their native identity for over two hundred years of contact amidst violence and intervening pressures by reinforcing identity within the context of traditional tribal government.[46]

While certain individuals possessed influence over their peers and served as ceremonial and political leaders, leadership generally began to wane in tribal communities when external forces such as a greater sovereign power exerted control. When chiefs, or the preferred term "leaders," had their authority seized by military and territorial officials of the United States, their tribal authority was usurped. The Fox, Sauk and Winnebago avoided this vulnerability for generations, although some tribes of the Western Great Lakes chose to sign treaties to appease the United States. By the end of the nineteenth century and in the early decades of the twentieth, however, even the Fox leadership structure yielded to American paternalism as the community faced a modern age.

From the late nineteenth century to 1934, then, federal-Indian relations and white contact rapidly undermined traditional Indian leaders and their communities. Nonetheless, traditionalism represented one of the sources of community strength as Indian leadership struggled to supervise progress.

Whenever two cultures meet, some interaction and mutual exchange take place. For example, the federal policy of individualized land allotments attacked tribalism — a concept that can be interpreted to mean community life guided by traditional cultural practices. From 1887 to 1934, the allotment policy severely tested tribal communities. Their strengths prevailed, but not before considerable injustice had been done, that is, the seizure of Indian lands. Although the basic fabric of tribal societies was weakened, it held together. The continued and vibrant presence of Indian communities in the Western Great Lakes today is testimony to this survival and resiliency.

Ironically, as the allotment policies and other so-called reform measures, as well as the external forces unleashed by World War I, accelerated the rate of change in Indian communities, the mainstream American public enjoyed the "return to normalcy" of laissez-faire capitalism in the decade following World War I. The Progressive Era in American history and the "Roaring Twenties" personified national success, but the Indian population suffered.

While many Americans indulged in prosperity until the crash of 1929, Indian people in tribal communities continued to live in poverty. Only during the years preceding World War II, while Americans suffered from the economic effects of the Great Depression, did the living standards of a significant number of Americans approach that of Indian people. Generally, however, Indians probably did not even realize this fact since most remained in their communities throughout the depression years. And with their internal networks strong, tribal communities remained intact.

Thus, tribal communities changed in response to continual cultural and political pressures from the outside rather than from pressures within their traditional cultures. And although it is argued here that fundamental aspects of tribalism — kinship networks, family roles, cultural norms and leadership — survived federal policies such as assimilation, Indian communities did suffer serious hardships.


**The Meriam Report**


In 1926, Secretary of Interior Hubert Work joined with the Institute for Government Research to complete a nationwide study of Indian progress and the federal government's Indian policy. This substantial task fell to Lewis Meriam, who was selected to supervise the survey. He was assisted by technical specialists in the areas of law, economic conditions, health, education, agriculture, family life, and urban Indian communities. For seven months, the staff members visited seventy-five reservations, agencies, hospitals and schools. The task force submitted its finished project on February 21, 1928, and published it under the title "The Problem of Indian Administration."[47] The lengthy Meriam Report disclosed the horrendous conditions of Indian life in health, education and economic welfare, including those of the

Western Great Lakes states. For example, the report disclosed that Minnesota's Indian population of 14,819 in 1926 (ranked sixth behind Oklahoma, Arizona, South Dakota, New Mexico and California) suffered inferior living conditions.[48]

On the subject of family and community life and the activities of women, the Meriam Report stated, "A relatively small number of Indians make the transition from primitive to civilized life successfully; the great majority tend to shift from primitive ways to the ways of the poorest and least enterprising of the white population."[49] Most important, the report concluded that the allotment program had failed, and that such living conditions merited a new policy from the federal government.

### The Policy of Retribalization and Self-Government

With the election of the Democratic President Franklin D. Roosevelt in 1932, Commissioner of Indian Affairs John Collier introduced new ideas of reform to federal-Indian affairs. The thrust of reform came on June 18, 1934, when a Democratic Congress passed the Indian Reorganization Act (IRA). Reversing the federal policy of allotment, the measure was "[a]n Act to conserve and develop Indian lands and resources; to extend to Indians the right to form business and other organizations; to establish a credit system for Indians; to grant certain rights of home rule to Indians; to provide for vocational education for Indians . . ."[50]

As the indigenous tribes and new Indian groups struggled to adjust to reservation life during the early decades of this century, federal policy continued to significantly affect community life. In fact, the IRA had one of the most profound policy effects on Indians and their communities in twentieth-century U.S.-Indian relations. It reintroduced tribalization by reconstructing communities and tribal governments throughout the country. Still today, most tribal governments are based on provisional assistance and guidelines first set in place under this law. However, the tribal governments were reestablished according to federal guidelines, thus making them quasi-traditional and patterned after the U.S. government.

It is important to note, however, that the response of the Western Great Lakes tribes to the IRA was not uniform. For example, among Minnesota's tribal communities, the Upper Sioux do not have a constitution and are not considered a tribe for enrollment purposes because residents are enrolled at other reservations (primarily Sisseton or Flandreau in South Dakota). In 1984 the community was supervised by a board of five trustees, who are elected at large for four-year terms, under provisions for governance adopted in 1962.[51]

Of the Dakota, on the other hand, the Prairie Island and Lower Sioux Indian communities obtained similar, standard IRA constitutions (ratified in 1937). Prairie Island Reservation had its constitution and bylaws approved by the Secretary of the Interior on June 30, 1936.[52] These constitutions provided for tribal councils composed of a chairperson and four council members elected to two-year terms. The Shakopee-Mdewakanton Sioux community was affiliated with the Lower Sioux for governmental purposes until it formed a separate government on November 28, 1969, when the Secretary of the Interior approved its tribal constitution.[53] The membership of this Sioux community was based on individuals already listed on allotment rolls and their descendants. A general council continues to serve as the governing body, which consists of all qualified voters, who must be residents. Possessing authority to delegate the administration of the community to the business council, the general council selects and is governed by the chairman, vice chairman and secretary-treasurer, who serve one-year terms. Although under less traditional guidelines, Western Great Lakes communities have combined elements of traditional and American government to reclaim a semi-sovereign status as a result of the IRA.

After the implementation of the Indian Reorganization Act, tribal communities became more traditionally cohesive. Collier's efforts to restructure tribal communities brought about a federal policy that favored unifying Indian communities based on their cultural elements. It allowed the communities to restore their tribal governments, albeit according to federal guidelines. This restructuring of the communities' political bodies allowed the members to come together in a cultural coherence, yielding a kind of new traditionalism. And so, Collier's New Deal policy positively affected tribal communities until World War II.

While IRA reservation governments helped spawn a new era of communalism among Indian tribes, the entrance of the United States into World War II had adverse effects on Indian communities. Although it offered Indians many new opportunities, World War II drew many Indian individuals away from their native communities. It has been estimated that approximately 25,000 Indian men served in the armed forces, and another 40,000 to 50,000 Indian men and women served in the war industries. From 1941 to 1945, their service in the war effort unforeseeably disrupted community life.

This migration left reservation communities temporarily without family members, whose roles in the family and in the community fell vulnerable to change. When returning to the reservations after the war, those Indians who had now been exposed to mainstream values encountered a degree of indifference from those tribal members who remained. With the internal elements of family and roles undergoing transformation, the off-reservation experience undermined communities, causing a crisis of identity and fragmentation.

### The Policy of Termination and Urban Relocation

During the early 1950s, many tribal communities of the Western Great Lakes continued to experience social change. These communities and other Indian communities suffered a population drain because of the off-reservation experience. For example, in the Lac Courte Oreilles Chippewa community, men underwent a major role transformation as they sought nontraditional work in the white communities. Working as mechanics, handymen and general laborers off the reservation caused a contradiction with their traditional political, civic and religious roles.[54] Simultaneously, a new policy emerged in the 1950s known as termination. Based on House Concurrent Resolution 108, this assimilative effort proved to be a most dangerous policy for Indian people.[55] In short, termination sought once and for all to abrogate the trust relationship between Indian communities and the United States, thus forcing many Indians to move to cities.

The new federal Indian policy of relocation to urban areas, which was offered to the entire Indian population in 1952, played a major role in the migration of American Indians to U.S. cities. Today, well over one-half of the approximately 1.5 million Indians reside in cities. Although urban relocation has threatened Indian communities in the Western Great Lakes and elsewhere, the reservation communities continue to exist, which surely is indicative of their internal strength and cohesion. Moreover, Indians who had relocated to cities began to have contacts with other Indians and formed urban Indian communities, often across tribal lines. Despite the twofold policies of termination and relocation, then, which attempted to disintegrate communities and assimilate Indians, reservation communities remain, and new urban Indian communities have begun to crystallize.

### Contemporary Western Great Lakes Reservations

Of the 291 reservations in the United States presently, there are twenty-nine in the Western Great Lakes region. A brief look at selected information concerning contemporary reservations in this area indicates that these Indian communities have survived generations of contact with other peoples and cultures, albeit not without a substantial redistribution of their land base and a more recent commitment to various forms of economic development on tribal lands. As Table 1 indicates, although a number of contemporary Western Great Lakes reservations contain considerable total acreage, the amount of tribally controlled land in most instances is substantially less. For example, the largest land base is maintained by the White Earth Chippewa in Minnesota (835,200 acres), but the proportion owned by the tribe is less than 5 percent of that total (25,568 acres). The largest tribally owned land base is maintained by the Chippewa Band at Grand Portage in Minnesota (37,390 acres), while the smallest in the Western Great Lakes area is held by the Huron Potawatomi Band in Michigan (120 acres). Moreover, a number of the larger reservations have substantial portions of their total acreage individually allotted, such as those of the Minnesota and Wisconsin Chippewa. Finally, the table indicates that large portions of these reservations are non-Indian owned. The White Earth Chippewa Reservation contains over 800,000 acres which are not owned by Indians. In several instances, a large portion of this non-Indian owned land is controlled by the federal government. On the Stockbridge-Munsee Reservation in Wisconsin, for example, over 13,000 acres are owned by the federal government out of a total reservation acreage of only 15,327.

**TABLE 1**

**SELECTED CONTEMPORARY WESTERN GREAT LAKES RESERVATIONS**

| Location | Alloted | Tribally Owned | Non-Indian Owned | Total Acreage |
|---|---|---|---|---|
| **Minnesota:** | | | | |
| Chippewa Bands | | | | |
| Fond du Lac | 17,154 | 4,213 | 18,633 | 40,000 |
| Grand Portage (Cook County) | 7,283 | 37,390 | 79[a] | 44,752 |
| Leech Lake (Case Lake) | 12,693 | 14,069 | 4 | 26,766 |
| Mille Lacs (Onamia) | 68 | 3,552 | —— | 3,620 |
| Nett Lake | 11,744 | 30,035 | 63,505[b] | 105,284 |
| White Earth | 1,993 | 25,568 | 807,639[c] | 835,200 |
| Lower Sioux (Morton) | —— | 1,743 | —— | 1,743 |
| Mdewakantons of the Mississippi Dakota (Prairie Island) | —— | 534 | —— | 534 |
| Shakopee-Mdewakanton Sioux (Prior Lake) | —— | 258 | —— | 258 |

| | | | |
|---|---|---|---|
| Upper Sioux/ Sisseton Dakota (Granite Falls) | —— | 746 | —— | 746 |

**Wisconsin:**

Chippewa Bands

| | | | | |
|---|---|---|---|---|
| Bad River | 33,477 | 8,325 | 13,110[a] | 54,912 |
| Lac Courte Oreilles | 26,584 | 3,945 | 13,190[a] | 43,719 |
| Lac du Flambeau | 15,327 | 25,152 | 33,321[d] | 73,800 |
| Mole Lake | —— | 1,694 | 280 | 1,974 |
| Red Cliff | 2,145 | 5,122 | —— | 7,267 |
| St. Croix | 515 | 1,715 | —— | 2,230 |
| Oneida | 473 | 2,108 | —— | 2,581 |
| Potawatomi | 400 | 11,267 | —— | 11,667 |
| Stockbridge-Munsee | —— | 2,250 | 13,077[a] | 15,327 |
| Winnebago[e] | 4,055.9 | 333.4 | —— | 4,389.3 |

**Michigan:**

Chippewa Bands

| | | | | |
|---|---|---|---|---|
| Bay Mills | —— | 2,189 | —— | 2,189 |
| Isabella | 678 | 506 | —— | 1,184 |
| Keweenaw Bay | 8,124 | 1,610 | 4,016[a] | 13,750 |

Potawatomi Bands

| | | | | |
|---|---|---|---|---|
| Hannahville | —— | 3,408 | —— | 3,408[f] |
| Huron | —— | 120 | —— | 120 |

Source: U.S. Department of Commerce, *Federal and State Indian Reservations and Indian Trust Areas* (Washington, D.C.: U.S. Government Printing Office, 1974).

[a] Owned by the federal government.

[b] Five acres owned by the federal government.

[c] 28,555 acres owned by the federal government.

[d] Forty acres owned by the federal government.

[e] Winnebago communties are located in the Wisconsin counties of Shawano, Marathon, Clark, Wood, Adams, Juneau, Monroe, Jackson, La Crosse and Crawford.

[f] Thirty-nine acres were added in 1942.

In Minnesota, the stability of the Dakota communities has been impressive. Possessing prime agricultural land, the Lower Sioux Indian community at Morton began in the late 1880s and has continued to survive as a small community.[56] The Mdewakantons of the Mississippi Dakota have held their land since receiving it in the late 1880s from the federal government. Several of the reservation communities have strong tribal governments. For example, each of the Minnesota Chippewa band communities have local business committees of five members elected on alternate four-year terms, and the chairperson and secretary of these committees form a twelve-member tribal executive committee for the Minnesota Chippewa tribe, which was formed under the IRA. The Oneida, Stockbridge-Munsee and Winnebago communities in Wisconsin, and the Bay Mills, Isabella, Keweenaw

Bay and Hannahville communities of Michigan, all have some form of governmental body consisting of some variation of elected tribal offices and council positions, while the small Huron community has no tribal government.[57]

In recent years, bingo and other business investments have served as the basis of the economy of many Western Great Lakes tribal communities.[58] For example, the Mdewakantons[59] and the Oneidas have started "big bingo" operations, while the Menominees in northern Wisconsin have established a forest industry to drive its economy. Approximately 95 percent of the Stockbridge-Munsee tribal income in 1984 also came from forestry.[60] The Oneidas have been successful in several other business investments in recent years as well. Several tribal communities have not been as successful, however. Both the Keweenaw Bay and Hannahville reservations in Michigan have virtually no tribal economy and no tribal incomes.[61]

In summary, having maintained a land base, the tribal communities of the Western Great Lakes now have entered a critical era of economic development. Some tribes like the Oneida and Menominee, who have business investments of large proportion, are more successful than others. Meanwhile, many tribal members are migrating to and from cities. Nevertheless, in this era of dynamic change, the tribal communities have succeeded in retaining their identities.

### Policy Impact and Urban Consequences

Many of the reservation communities have been affected by the relocation of their members to urban areas. This movement has left the reservations with decreased populations as the relocatees establish themselves in the cities and in off-reservation areas. For obvious reasons, the urban Indian community possesses fewer kinship networks than the reservation community. Nevertheless, newcomers are largely dependent on relatives who act as "gatekeepers" and help kinfolk with living arrangements and employment. Because newcomers may not know anyone except their relatives, these relationships are very close in the initial stages.

Normally, the gatekeeper will introduce newcomers to their network of friends and inform them about the urban environment. Attempting to adjust socially to urban life, newcomers join this network, start one of their own, or combine members of their relatives' network of friends with new friends of their own.

The off-reservation transition offers a new socialization process for urban Indians, who, in their reservation communities, were an integral part of the communal kinship network. Making social contacts represents a new social and cultural venture for many urban Indians; it is an individual process of integrating into the urban environment while simultaneously assimilating into the mainstream to the extent desired. Initially, the newcomers rely on the gatekeeper's community of friends or establish their own friendships, but the latter frequently proves difficult. The Indian person realizes that he/she is an individual, in a strange environment consisting of many kinds of people and ethnic backgrounds. This is a shocking change from the relative homogeneity of the reservation environment. In such a transitional phase, one scholar reported that Menominee women were prone to adopting white middle-class values.[62]

The initial effort to form friendships is probably the most difficult. Having seldom if ever developed external social relationships, newcomers must nurture social skills outside of their native element. This sociocultural development does not come easy for many urban Indians. Many have to force themselves to become extroverts, at least temporarily, in order to have a few friends. Others meet persons wishing to become friends with them, and become unwillingly sociable; some Indians have less difficulty in initiating friendships because of their individual personalities. In brief, for many Indians who now live in cities, their patterns of social interaction have changed.

Relocation and urban adjustment continued throughout the Eisenhower years of the 1950s and into the next two decades. Urban Indian networking began developing the fibers of modern Indian life now present in the cities. This process of social networking consumed time, depending on the social ability of the newcomer. Operating on the traditional premise of being from a reservation background, many newcomers could relate much easier to other Indians from reservations. Attempting to find other tribal members or other Indians from the same reservation proved difficult, so that befriending another newcomer helped one to adjust to urban conditions. Ultimately, this process began to blur tribal differences among urban Indians.

### Native Identity and Urbanization

Socialization among Indians in urban areas is important in sustaining the urban community. Among the Chippewas, powwows represent a reservation and urban activity in which tribal members and relatives of other tribes can participate.[63] The powwow has helped transform the urban Indian phenomenon into an intertribal activity that promotes a general ethnic or racial identity, often termed pan-Indianism.

With many remnants of the past, the powwow has become a way for many Indians to identify themselves as Indians, and for this modern traditionalism to be introduced to non-Indians.

The Kennedy years of the early 1960s ushered in the so-called New Frontier, and simultaneously introduced a different direction in federal policy pertaining to Indian affairs. Tribal communities, which had survived the threatening termination policy, experienced relief when the newly-named Indian Commissioner, Philleo Nash, assumed office. Opposed to termination, Commissioner Nash desired to be the Indians' commissioner and worked devotedly to improve the economic situation in Indian country.[64] This effort, however, emphasized assistance to reservation communities and neglected urban Indian communities, causing future problems for the Indian majority.

During the turbulent years of civil rights activism and renewed ethnic awareness, many Indians as individuals underwent an identity crisis. In the process of transforming reservation Indians to an urban setting, the individual often remained isolated, thus creating a third type of Indianness or "Indian person" in addition to the Indian reservation community and the urban Indian community. This person frequently had to survive through the remainder of the 1960s and the next decades without a community.

President Lyndon Johnson's administration supported Nash's efforts and stressed concern for Indian rights. In a speech to Congress entitled "The Forgotten American," Johnson spoke of renewed efforts to assist American Indians: "I propose a new goal for our Indian programs: A goal that ends the old debate about 'termination' of Indian programs and stresses self-determination as a goal that erases old attitudes of paternalism and promotes partnership and self-help."[65]

Although the tribal communities had survived the termination years, they now faced a new era of civil rights. Such individual rights as were granted by law, however, threatened the sovereign freedom of tribal communities. For instance, although the 1968 Indian Civil Rights Act was hailed as a landmark law to support Indian citizenship rights, it actually limited the rights of tribal communities. For example, under Sec. 202, this measure states, "No Indian tribe in exercising powers of self-government shall — (1) make or enforce any law prohibiting the free exercise of religion, or abridging the freedom of speech, or of the press, or the right of the people peaceably to assemble and to petition for a redress of grievances."[66]

Since the "Red Power" years of the 1960s and early 1970s, American Indian communities and their members have experienced a renaissance of native identity. This interest, however, is ever changing, and has been reinforced by the people themselves. This time period overflowed with verbal protests from Indians demanding their rights and reaffirming their identity. In 1968, a fresh Indian leadership emerged with the founding of the American Indian Movement (AIM) in Minneapolis. Some Indian activism developed into militancy as with the takeovers of Alcatraz Island (1968), the Bureau of Indian Affairs building in Washington, D.C. (1972), and Wounded Knee, South Dakota (1973). Perhaps due to such protests, the American public began to see an increasingly visible Indian presence, and American Indians themselves developed an intense pride in combatting previous injustices.

Proir to the 1960s, due to such policies as termination, Indian identity was on the wane. However, there were sufficient remnants of nativism to provoke a revitalization of "Indian pride." In the 1960s and 1970s, both group racial identity and individual identity reemerged. This revitalization was both a reaction against negative mainstream stereotypes and a reinforcement of a dire psychological need to retain basic identity in the face of confusing assimilative forces.

## The Federal Policy of Self-Determination

In the mid-1970s, with the pronouncement of "Indian self-determination without termination," federal policy shifted toward the recognition of the tribal community and Indian identity. In 1974 Congress passed the Indian Self-Determination and Education Assistance Act, which President Gerald Ford signed into law on January 4, 1975.[67] Ford stated, "My Administration is committed to furthering the self-determination of Indian communities without terminating the special relationships between the Federal Government and the Indian people."[68]

This measure authorized the secretaries of Interior and Health, Education and Welfare to contract with, and make grants to, Indian tribes and organizations for the delivery of federal services. The essence of the act is that, "The Secretary of the Interior is directed, upon the request of any Indian tribe, to enter into a contract or contracts with any tribal organization of any such Indian tribe to plan, conduct, and administer programs, or portions thereof . . ."[69]

In spite of the federal policy of self-determination, federal paternalism has continued and Indian communities have experienced a dissipation of their autonomy. This reduction has occurred especially in the area of federal Indian law. For instance, if an Indian community constitutes a tribe and has a functioning government, then common legal interpretation refers to it as a "dependent Indian community."[70] This status is one to which Indian communities have adjusted, although they retain their basic elements.

Sovereignty, the essence of natural freedom, describes the Indian community in political terms. Traditionally, the communities did not think of themselves only in political terms. Sovereignty is a non-Indian term with multiple interpretations, and can be applied from both an Indian and a white perspective, especially regarding Indian-white relations. Thus, in recent years Indians have viewed sovereignty for Indians differently from sovereignty for whites, i.e., federal, state and local governments. On the other hand, whites view Indian sovereignty and the sovereignty of the various governmental levels in a mainstream way.

An example of the new Indian definition of sovereignty can be found in Minnesota from 1974 to 1984. The Dakota communities belonged to a group organization. Over the years, this group changed its name and membership until 1984 when it was disbanded. The various communities believed that their own concerns could be served better if they handled them separately.[71] Traditionally, Indian communities govern themselves using a system of autonomous self-rule. This sovereign status changed as the federal government placed more restrictive laws on Indian autonomy. Traditionally, the community functioned in its own political, social and cultural manner, and acted freely.

The decade of the 1980s has evoked a new phase for Indian America. Many tribal governments have ventured into economic development, and this entrepreneurship has had a reinforcing effect. Through economic development, tribal communities are becoming more self-governing and financially independent, although they continue to exist under a quasi-sovereign relationship with the federal and state governments. In 1982, for example, the Shakopee-Mdewakanton Sioux community ended its cigarette excise tax agreement with the state of Minnesota. With no state tax, the community could sell cigarettes much more cheaply than other vendors. However, an ordinance stipulated that only two cartons could be sold to non-Indians.[72]

In another business enterprise, the Little Six Bingo Palace at Prior Lake in Minnesota was the start of other bingo operations to follow. There, bingo was set up for seven nights a week with large jackpots. The $950,000 facility seats 1,300 people with free shuttle bus service transporting customers from the Twin Cities. In the mid-1980s, the operation employed about 130 people. By June 1983, the bingo operation at Prior Lake had earned enough profit to pay off the mortgage and to pave roads and driveways on the reservation. Profits also fund a health clinic, a day-care center and a cultural center.[73]

Tribal communities in the 1980s are based on the concept of tribalism, despite policy efforts and historical events which tend to negate Indian communities. Historian William T. Hagan has noted that during the 1960s and 1970s, tribalism derived from three basic sources: increased pride in tribal identity; federal policy changes from termination to self-determination; and financial benefits accumulating from awards for tribal members' claims and funding from federal programs.[74]

Indian people are a changing people, although in the eyes of non-Indians they are a "slowly" changing people. According to the dominant society, progress is measured by reforms and rapid change. But rapid change does not automatically translate into permanent progress. A community can change too fast via reform efforts, resulting in instability or destruction. Generally, tribal communities tend to change at their own rate as long as they are in control of their scheme of life. If outside forces interfere, then the community becomes susceptible to uncontrollable change which may become problematic.

Another pertinent but fundamental point is that Indian people are a practical people. Cultural change has occurred in many communities when goods were received and adopted from another culture in a practice of "cultural borrowing." For example, even before the white man, trade was a major intertribal activity, introducing new goods, causing changes, and constraining communities to adjust.

At another level, the twentieth century has challenged various policies in the Indian communities, and Indians have had to endure all the effects in the name of reform. As some tribal members became individualized, they succumbed to mainstream values, vices and stereotypes. The greater challenge exists within each Indian person. If the struggle for native identity is lost, then contemplation of self-destruction, by such means as alcoholism and suicide, too often results.

While a tribal community can afford to lose one or several tribal members and still retain its tribal identity, the loss of a tribal community means the loss of a people. This could result in the Ishi effect. The last of his people, the Yahi (an indigenous tribe of California), Ishi survived by finding balance within himself and peace with the white man. When he died in the early 1900s, his tribal community died with him, and history is the only record of the Yahi's existence.[75]

Contemporary conditions point to the tribal government's safeguarding of the communities, yet the tribal members cannot depend totally on the tribal government for paternalistic protection from the federal government. Since the Indian Self-Determination and Education Assistance Act of 1975,[76] tribes have openly expressed tribal nationalism. Their current area of venture is economic development, in which tribal governments utilize the full scope of their resources and interpretation of Indian sovereignty via treaties to combat any paternalistic federal policies.[77]

The community is also reinforced when its members cooperate as a group in decisionmaking. These democratic experiences always challenge the cohesiveness of the community and present dangers of communal disagreement. But, if the political infrastructure is workable, the chances of overcoming the possibility of factionalism are increased. These decisionmaking experiences have challenged Indian communities on reservations and in urban areas, yet the current existence of these communities attests to their internal political strength.

**Decisionmaking and Modern Leadership**

In their decisionmaking, Indian communities rely upon members of various types. Traditionally, wise elders assumed leadership because of their numerous experiences in dealing with similar issues and their ability to recall the history of how the community overcame a critical situation. A vital step was approval by a type of political council, whose membership was defined according to tribal law. This problem-solving process was also supported by discussion and general approval of the people. Each tribe possessed its own laws regulating the composition of the political council and the selection of its leaders.

Among the Chippewas many years ago, leadership was exercised by individuals who held a variety of positions. In the nineteenth century, the Chippewas possessed hereditary chiefs, chiefs made by agents, nonhereditary war chiefs, and a host of individuals who temporarily acted as leaders. These persons were "pipe lighters" or "speakers" who acted as spokespersons for the community, and these "Mide" leaders played an important role.[78] In contemporary times, the necessity for these leaders has diminished for the most part, and a whole new set of needs has been created based on economic and political circumstances. Nonetheless, the legacy of traditional Chippewa leadership has provided a foundation for perpetuating Chippewa identity, which is ceremonially exemplified by Chippewa "Mide" leaders and "pipe carriers." Today's Indian leaders face considerable difficulties, especially in regard to cultural continuation, funding sources for programs, and operational expenses within their communities.

From 1973 to 1981, the federal government increased its expenditures on Indian programs from $1.08 billion to $2.75 billion.[79] This sum helped a rapidly increasing American Indian population. The 1980 census reported that 1.37 million Indians lived in the United States. Approximately 25 percent lived on reservations, 11 percent lived in

Oklahoma historic areas, 23 percent lived in counties adjacent to reservations, and 60 percent in areas distant from reservations.[80] Economic development in the 1980s funded by the federal government has helped to shape reservation communities. In the mid-1980s, a Presidential Commission on Indian Reservation Economies implemented a study plan with a task force to review the status of Indian economic development.[81] President Ronald Reagan's economic policy was aimed at directing Indian communities toward economic improvement and business ventureship.

In response to the reemphasized federal-Indian concerns about economics, the Indian communities of the Western Great Lakes have responded aggressively. For example, the Red Cliff Chippewa community started the Buffalo Bay Fishing Company in 1986 after planning it for over two years.[82] The company retails and wholesales Lake Superior fish. This type of business venture emphasizes a new area of business solidarity for the community. Other examples of this experience are the Stockbridge-Munsee bingo facility in Wisconsin which opened in November 1986. Bingo operations continue to operate at the Menominee and Oneida reservations in Wisconsin, and the Oneida have constructed an industrial park and a large $12.5 million hotel across from the Green Bay airport.[83]

Given the importance of socialization to the vitality of Western Great Lakes Indian communities, powwows held throughout the year are manifestations of the importance of Indian identification. Such events include dances held at Oneida, Milwaukee, Menominee, Lac Courte Oreilles, Red Cliff, Minneapolis, St. Paul, Chicago and other sites. Cultural events and educational conferences have become a part of the recent agenda of tribal community activities as well.

The impact of external politics has caused the communities to take action as individual groups and in a pan-Indian way, especially under such organizations as the Great Lakes Intertribal Council, whose members represent the tribal governments in Wisconsin. Particularly confrontational issues, such as the off-reservation spear fishing controversy, have called for unity in the Indian communities in Wisconsin, and a similar situation has developed in Michigan. As happened hundreds of years ago, the Western Great Lakes Indian communities are being brought together by external forces which threaten them.

In the cities, Indian communities are now established and have maintained their status quo. The Indian population in the Milwaukee area in 1980 was approximately 6,500; in the Chicago area, it was approximately 11,000; and the Twin Cities area had about 16,000 Indians.[84] Within these urban populations, Indian communities have developed organizations, associations and clubs, all under the generic term "Indian." Out of the urbanization experience, an urban Indian identity has emerged which has, in many cases, superseded tribal affiliations for individuals who no longer have sufficient knowledge of their tribal heritage. Of the Indian groups in the Western Great Lakes, the Oneida are a good example of urban migration. Their families are the most important units of the community and they are larger than the average nuclear unit. Much of the Oneida population in Wisconsin lives in Green Bay; some families have moved to Milwaukee, Chicago and Detroit. In addition to the emphasis on family, the Oneidas retain strong social and emotional bonds with the reservation community, producing a "return" factor of frequent visits to the community.[85]

## The Social Justice of Indian Existence

After more than two hundred years of contact with other civilizations and the onslaught of federal policies, Indian reservation and urban communities of the Western Great Lakes continue to maintain their identities. Among the reservation communities, the eighteen Minnesota Chippewa communities are an example. They remain distinct in their individual communities, although they have contact among themselves.[86] Despite the strains of federal policies, public pressures, and other external forces, the communities have endured. All of this has been possible because the reservation communities and urban communities are steeped in the elements of nativism.

The reservation communities of the Western Great Lakes are more tribal in their composition than the urban Indian communities, which consist of intertribal community members who have networked in the metropolitan areas. The transformation of urban Indian people from tribal identity to Indian identity is a great cultural and psychological alteration, yet one which does not disturb the basic essence of nativism. In this sense, Indians of various tribal communities now identify themselves racially more than culturally. To be more precise, tribal cultures have become less emphasized, and a generic Indian culture has been the result. Interestingly, the mainstream population fosters the emergence of this generic Indian culture because it lacks knowledge about distinct Indian cultures. This ignorance is also reinforced by growing urban Indian and young reservation populations who are losing their cultural knowledge because of voluntary assimilation into the mainstream. Modern Indians in urban areas are often viewed as "cultureless" by the mainstream, who form stereotypes and imagine a single urban Indian image.[87] The unwillingness of the general urban society to accept American Indians living in cities has also caused poor race relations and discrimination towards them in the economic sector. Using the Chippewas as an example, J. Anthony Paredes points out that urban studies generally focus on the individual Indian's adaptation to urban life, and that the psychological adjustment and urban acceptance of the general Indian population are insufficiently emphasized.[88]

The Western Great Lakes Indian community, whether reservation or urban, has changed, yet it has also remained intact. Because of their ever-developing governments, tribal communities can be perceived as political bodies. They can also be viewed as social units, or even cultural units. Rather than having a single political, social or cultural dimension, however, the Indians of the region are a culmination of multiple characteristics, and they should be viewed that way. Nonetheless, the Indians of the Western Great Lakes do share areas of common cultural characteristics. For instance, a main value of the Chippewas is generosity or a willingness to share.[89] In addition, group emphasis is another imperative value in terms of bonding the community together.

In the 1980s, the communities' economies have perhaps become more important than their legal, sociological or cultural state of existence. Attempts can be made to understand them from any of the four characteristics mentioned, but their true nature is a composition of all the characteristics that explain their ethnic innateness. Exemplary of their ancestral communities centuries ago, tribes like the Potawatomi and the Chippewa operate within intrapolitical systems that are local autonomous communities.[90]

American Indians and their tribal communities present a saga of persistence, survival and sociocultural adjustment in the face of a dominant alien culture and its paternalistic policies. Throughout the history of Indian-white relations, Indian people have employed cultural tactics of learning to adjust and change, but they do so at their own will. Most Indian communities possess this important strength, and it is essential for perpetuating their identity. The evolution of traditional identity towards a more protomodern one reveals a kind of "Indian Darwinism" that corroborates Indian community survival and presence in the Western Great Lakes. It is important to recognize both the ability and desire of the tribal communities to adapt to new conditions and surroundings, and the fact that they will survive as long as they possess these in tandem. In the process, their tribal identities are perpetuated. With their identities intact, Indians can continue in their struggle to achieve social justice.

## NOTES

*The subject of this study proved too complex for any one set of data or methodology, thus a cross-disciplinary approach was employed to examine American Indian involvement in politics, culture, sociology, psychology and history. To help formulate my ideas and approach toward the paper, I enlisted the aid of several people, including anthropologists Dr. Nancy Oestreich Lurie, Milwaukee Public Museum, and Dr. Terri Strauss, NAES College, Chicago; Dr. Sharon O'Brien, Political Science, University of Notre Dame; and Dr. Bruce Fetter, History, University of Wisconsin-Milwaukee. My thanks to them for their suggestions and recommendations of literature about Indians and other ethnic communities. The research grant and the semester leave made available by the UW System Institute on Race and Ethnicity is appreciated. This support enabled me to research materials at regional libraries, to attend two conferences, and to dialogue with people in a quest to understand why Indian communities persist.

[1]Harold Hickerson, "The Southwestern Chippewa: An Ethnohistorical Study," *American Anthropologist* 64: 3, Part 2 (June 1962), Memoir 92, American Anthropological Association: 40. For insight into Chippewa life and trade relations, see Harold Hickerson, "The Genesis of a Trading Post Band: The Pembina Chippewa," *Ethnohistory* 3: 4 (Fall 1956): 289-345.

[2]Victor Barnouw, "Acculturation and Personality among the Wisconsin Chippewas," *American Anthropologist* 52: 4, Part 2 (October 1950), Memoir 72, American Anthropological Association. For general cultural information about Indians of the Western Great Lakes, see Albert E. Jenks, "The Wild Rice Gatherers of the Upper Lakes: A Study in American Primitive Economics," in Bureau of American Ethnology, *19th Annual Report, 1897-98* (Washington, D.C.: Smithsonian Institution, 1900), Part 2, pp. 1013-1137.

[3]Hickerson, "The Southwestern Chippewa," op. cit. note 1, p. 5. See also Robert W. Dunning, "Rules of Residence and Ecology among the Northern Ojibwa," *American Anthropologist* 61: 5, Part 1 (October 1959): 806-816. For general information on village unity, see Margaret Mead, *Cooperation and Competiton among Primitive Peoples* (New York: McGraw-Hill, 1937).

[4]Louise Spindler, "Menomini Women and Culture Change," *American Anthropologist* 64: 1, Part 2 (February 1962), Memoir 91, American Anthropological Association: 39.

[5]Harold Hickerson, "The Chippewa of the Upper Great Lakes: A Study in Sociopolitical Change," in Eleanor Burke Leacock and Nancy Oestreich Lurie, eds., *North American Indians in Historical Perspective* (New York: Random House, 1971), pp. 169-199 at 170.

[6]Ruth Landes, "Ojibwa Sociology," *Columbia University Contributions to Anthropology*, Vol. 29 (New York: Columbia Universiy Press, 1937). Landes did her fieldwork among the Ojibwa on the reserve at Emo, Ontario, in 1932-33, which would indicate that a length of time and mainstream contact diverted the emphasis from communalism to individualism. However, these Ojibwa lived in isolated circumstances and sustained traditionalism while hunting, trapping and trading in the white market. See also Gretel H. Pelto,

"Chippewa People and Politics in a Reservation Town," in J. Anthony Paredes, ed., *Anishinabe: 6 Studies of Modern Chippewa* (Tallahassee, FL: University Presses of Florida, 1980), pp. 242-323 at 299.

[7]Hickerson, "The Southwestern Chippewa," op. cit. note 1, p. 11, and Victor Barnouw, "Chippewa Social Atomism," *American Anthropologist* 63: 5, Part 1 (October 1961): 1006-1013.

[8]Bernard J. James, "Some Critical Observations Concerning Analyses of Chippewa 'Atomism' and Chippewa Personality," *American Anthropologist* 56: 2, Part 1 (April 1954): 283-286 at 285.

[9]Ernestine Friedl, "Persistence in Chippewa Culture and Personality," *American Anthropologist* 58: 5 (October 1956): 814-825 at 814. See also Ruth Landes, "The Ojibwa Woman," *Columbia University Contributions to Anthropology*, Vol. 31 (New York: Columbia University Press, 1939).

[10]William Caudill, "Psychological Characteristics of Acculturated Wisconsin Ojibwa Children," *American Anthropologist* 51: 3 (July-September 1949): 409-427. See also Blanche Wautrous, "A Personality Study of Ojibwa Children," unpublished Ph.D. dissertation (Northwestern University, 1949); and Inez M. Hilger, "Chippewa Child Life and Its Cultural Background," *Bureau of American Ethnology Bulletin*, Vol. 146 (Washington, D.C.: U.S. Government Printing Office, 1951).

[11]Hickerson, "The Southwestern Chippewa," op. cit. note 1, p. 55.

[12]Hickerson, "Upper Great Lakes Chippewa," op. cit. note 5, p. 183.

[13]Spindler, op. cit. note 4, p. 1. See also George D. Spindler, "Sociocultural and Psychological Processes in Menomini Acculturation," *University of California Publications in Culture and Society*, Vol. 5 (Berkeley: University of California Press, 1955).

[14]Spindler, op. cit. note 4, p. 45.

[15]Ibid., p. 99.

[16]Ibid., p. 39; and Walter J. Hoffman, "The Menomini Indians," in Bureau of American Ethnology, *14th Annual Report, 1892-93* (Washington, D.C.: U.S. Government Printing Office, 1986), Part 1, pp. 3-328. For tribal changes relating to economics, politics and socialization, see Margaret Mead, "The Changing Culture of an Indian Tribe," *Columbia University Contributions to Anthropology*, Vol. 15 (New York: Columbia University Press, 1932).

[17]Spindler, op. cit. note 4, p. 3.

[18]Hickerson, "The Southwestern Chippewa," op. cit. note 1, pp. 50-51.

[19]Jack Campisi, "Oneida," in Bruce G. Trigger, ed., *Handbook of North American Indians*, Vol. 15, "Northeast" (Washington, D.C.: Smithsonian Institution, 1978) (hereafter cited as *Handbook, Northeast*), pp. 481-490 at 485.

[20]Hickerson, "The Southwestern Chippewa," op. cit. note 1, pp. 48-49.

[21]For information on cultural artifacts of the Chippewa, see Frances Densmore, "Chippewa Customs," *Bureau of American Ethnology Bulletin*, Vol. 86

(Washington, D.C.: U.S. Government Printing Office, 1929), p. 28; and A. Irving Hallowell, "Ojibway Ontology, Behavior and World View," in Stanley Diamond, ed., *Primitive Views of the World* (New York: Columbia University Press, 1964), pp. 49-82.

[22]Sol Tax, "The Social Organization of the Fox Indians," in Fred Eggan, ed., *Social Anthropology of North American Tribes: Essays in Social Organization, Law, and Religion*, 2nd ed. (Chicago: University of Chicago Press, 1955), pp. 243-282 at 261.

[23]Truman Michelson, "Contributions to Fox Ethnology," Part 1, *Bureau of American Ethnology Bulletin*, Vol. 85 (Washington, D.C.: Government Printing Office, 1927), and Part 2, *Bureau of American Ethnology Bulletin*, Vol. 95 (Washington, D.C.: U.S. Government Printing Office, 1930).

[24]Spindler, op. cit. note 4, p. 22.

[25]Hickerson, "The Southwestern Chippewa," op. cit. note 1, p. 79.

[26]George D. Spindler and Louise S. Spindler, "Identity, Militancy, and Cultural Congruence: The Menominee and Kainai," *Annals of the American Academy of Political and Social Science* 436 (March 1978): 73-85 at 78.

[27]Hickerson, "The Southwestern Chippewa," op. cit. note 1, p. 39.

[28]Ibid., p. 49.

[29]A. Irving Hallowell, "Cross-Cousin Marriage in the Lake Winnipeg Area," *Publications of the Philadelphia Society* 1 (1937): 95-110; and Robert W. Dunning, *Social and Economic Change Among the Northern Ojibwa* (Toronto: University of Toronto Press, 1959).

[30]Fred Eggan, "Social Anthropology: Methods and Results," in Eggan, op. cit. note 22, pp. 485-551 at 532-533.

[31]Ives Goddard, "Mascouten," in *Handbook, Northeast*, op. cit. note 19, pp. 668-672 at 668.

[32]Removal Act, 4 Stat. 411-412, May 28, 1830 (21st Congress, 1st Session).

[33]See the "Oneida Treaties" in Charles J. Kappler, comp., *Indian Affairs: Laws and Treaties*, Vol. 2, "Treaties" (Washington, D.C.: U.S. Government Printing Office, 1904), pp. 5-6, 23-25, 34-39, and 502-518.

[34]Campisi, op. cit. note 19, p. 485.

[35]Marion Johnson Mochon, "Stockbridge-Munsee Cultural Adaptations: 'Assimilated Indians,' " *Proceedings of the American Philosophical Society* 112: 3 (June 1968): 182-219; and Otto J. Kowalke, "The Settlement of the Stockbridge Indians and the Survey of Land in Outagamie County, Wisconsin," *Wisconsin Magazine of History* 40: 1 (Autumn 1956): 31-34.

[36]Helen Tanner, ed., *Atlas of Great Lakes Indian History* (Norman, OK: University of Oklahoma Press, 1987), p. 166; see also the "Winnebago Treaties" in Kappler, op. cit. note 33, pp. 117-119, 130-131, 250-258, 281-283, 292-294, 300-303, 345-348, 498-500, 565-567, 690-693, 790-792, and 874-875.

[37]Campisi, op. cit. note 19, p. 484.

[38]Tanner, op. cit. note 36, pp. 166-167.

[39]Dawes Act (Indian General Allotment Act), 24 Stat. 388-391, February 8, 1887 (49th Congress, 2nd Session).

[40]William B. Miller, "Two Concepts of Authority," *American Anthropologist* 57: 2, Part 1 (April 1955): 271-289.

[41]See Francis Paul Prucha, ed., *Documents of United States Indian Policy* (Lincoln, NE: University of Nebraska Press, 1975), p. 207.

[42]Ibid., p. 215.

[43]General Citizenship Act, 43 Stat. 253, June 2, 1924 (68th Congress, 1st Session).

[44]Spindler and Spindler, op. cit. note 26, p. 78.

[45]William Jones, "Ethnology of the Fox Indians," *Bureau of American Ethnology Bulletin*, Vol. 125 (Washington, D.C.: U.S. Government Printing Office, 1939), p. 82.

[46]Miller, op. cit. note 40, p. 78.

[47]See Francis Paul Prucha, *The Great Father: The United States Government and the American Indians* (Lincoln, NE: University of Nebraska Press, 1986); and Lewis Meriam, technical director, et al., *The Problem of Indian Administration*, the Meriam Report (Baltimore, MD: Johns Hopkins Press, published for the Brookings Institution, 1928), p. 278.

[48]Meriam Report, ibid., p. 62.

[49]Ibid., p. 547.

[50]Indian Reorganization Act, 48 Stat. 984-988, June 18, 1934 (73rd Congress, 2nd Session).

[51]Judith Rosenblatt and Elizabeth Ebbott, eds., *Indians in Minnesota*, 4th ed. (Minneapolis: University of Minnesota Press, 1985), p. 56.

[52]U.S. Department of Commerce, *Federal and State Indian Reservations and Indian Trust Areas* (Washington, D.C.: U.S. Government Printing Office, 1974) (hereafter cited as *Federal and State*), p. 254.

[53]Ibid., p. 256.

[54]Bernard J. James, "Social-Psychological Dimensions of Objiwa Acculturation," *American Anthropologist* 63: 4 (August 1961): 721-746 at 729-31.

[55]House Concurrent Resolution 108, 67 Stat. B132, August 1, 1953 (83rd Congress, 1st Session).

[56]*Federal and State*, op. cit. note 52, pp. 245-246.

[57]Ibid., pp. 227-235, 559-560, 589, 591-592, and 597-598.

[58]Ibid., pp. 579-601. Additional economic data for selected Western Great Lakes communities reveal the following. Several years ago, the Bad River Reservation community had an average annual per capita income of $6,500 de-

rived from iron and copper, and some revenue generated from the forest industry. In 1984, approximately 50 percent of the Lac Courte Oreilles Reservation economy depended upon farming and 20 percent derived from forestry; an additional 30 percent came from leases. In the same year, the major business venture was a tribally-owned cranberry farm. On the Lac du Flambeau Reservation, an estimated one-third of the economy is generated from forestry and gravel sales. Also located in northern Wisconsin, Mole Lake Reservation had a per capita income of over $500 annually from forestry. On the Red Cliff Reservation, approximately 85 percent of the economy derives from forestry and the remaining 15 percent from leases. The entire St. Croix Reservation economy is derived from forestry.

[59]Ibid., pp. 243-245. Located on Prairie Island, the Prairie Island Reservation rests on low-lying land. About one-half of the community's property is in the floodplain. Prairie Island is shared with Northern States Power Company's nuclear generating plant and with the Army Corps of Engineers' U.S. Lock and Dam No. 3. The Lower Sioux Reservation in Minnesota is two miles south of Morton and six miles east of Redwood Falls. Tribal revenue is generally earned by leasing out a gravel pit and farm land. During the 1970s, the average annual per capita income was approximately $4,000 annually. About one-fourth of this income came from farmland, and the remaining revenue derived from gravel as a marketable resource. In 1984, Jackpot Junction, a bingo facility, opened approximately five miles east of Redwood Falls. The Mdewakantons of the Mississippi Dakota band reside on reservation land purchased for them in the late 1880s. The tribe has a community center and a large facility for "big bingo" that began operating in 1984. Prairie Island Indian community is considered part of the city of Red Wing, Goodhue County, having been annexed by the city.

[60]Ibid., pp. 597-598.

[61]Ibid., pp. 227-235.

[62]Spindler, op. cit. note 4, p. 60.

[63]Michael A. Rynkiwich, "Chippewa Powwows," in Paredes, op. cit. note 6, pp. 31-100. For additional social activities, see James S. Slotkin, "The Menomini Powwow: A Study in Cultural Decay," *Milwaukee Public Museum Publications in Anthropology*, No. 4 (Milwaukee: Milwaukee Public Museum, 1957).

[64]Informal lecture by Professor Sol Tax, Native American Educational Services, Inc. College (Chicago: The College, June 22, 1987).

[65]Prucha, *Documents*, op. cit. note 41, p. 248.

[66]Ibid., p. 250.

[67]Indian Self-Determination and Education Assistance Act, P.L. 93-638, 88 Stat. 2203, January 4, 1975 (93rd Congress, 2nd Session).

[68]Gerald R. Ford, *Public Papers of the Presidents, Gerald R. Ford, 1975* (Washington, D.C.: U.S. Government Printing Office, 1976), p. 10.

[69]David H. Getches, Daniel M. Rosenfelt and Charles F. Wilkinson, *Cases and Materials on Federal Indian Law* (St. Paul, MN: West Publishing Co., 1979), p. 111.

[70]James E. Lobsenz, " 'Dependent Indian Communities': A Search for a Twentieth Century Definition," *Arizona Law Review* 24 (1982): 1-27 at 20-21.

[71]Rosenblatt and Ebbott, op. cit. note 51, p. 56.

[72]Ibid., p. 93.

[73]Ibid., pp. 94-95.

[74]William T. Hagan, "Tribalism Rejuvenated: The Native American Since the Era of Termination," *Western Historical Quarterly* 12: 1 (January 1981): 5-16 at 15.

[75]Refer to Theodora Kroeber, *Ishi in Two Worlds: A Biography of the Last Wild Indian* (Berkeley, CA: University of California Press, 1961), or Theodore Kroeber, *Ishi, Last of His Tribe* (New York: Bantam Books, 1978, originally published, Berkeley, CA: Parnassus Press, 1964).

[76]Indian Self-Determination Act, op. cit. note 67.

[77]David H. Israel, "The Reemergence of Tribal Nationalism and Its Impact on Reservation Resource Development," *University of Colorado Law Review* 47: 4 (Summer 1976): 617-652 at 617.

[78]Hickerson, "The Southwestern Chippewa," op. cit. note 1, p. 47. For further information on the Midéwiwin ceremony, see Walter J. Hoffman, "The Midéwiwin or 'Grand Medicine Society' of the Chippewa," in Bureau of American Ethnology, *7th Annual Report, 1885-86* (Washington, D.C.: Smithsonian Institution, 1891), pp. 143-300.

[79]Task Force on Indian Economic Development, *Report of the Task Force on Indian Economic Development* (Washington, D.C.: U.S. Department of the Interior, 1986), p. 9.

[80]Ibid., p. 3.

[81]Ibid., p. 2.

[82]"Red Cliff Opens Buffalo Bay Fish Company," *Masinaigan* [newspaper] (October 1986), p. 2.

[83]"Oneidas Successful in Business," *The Lac Courte Oreilles Journal* [newspaper] (April 1987), p. 3.

[84]U.S. Bureau of the Census, *1980 Census of Population, Supplementary Report*, PC 80-S1-5, "Standard Metropolitan Statistical Areas and Standard Consolidated Statistical Areas: 1980" (Washington, D.C.: U.S. Government Printing Office, 1981), Table 1, pp. 6-46 at 14 and 29.

[85]John H. Dowling, "A 'Rural' Indian Community in an Urban Setting," *Human Organization* 27: 3 (Fall 1968): 236-40.

[86]Timothy Roufs, "Social Structure and Community Development in a Chippewa Village," in Paredes, op. cit. note 6, pp. 194-241 at 224. For informa-

tion about pan-Indianism in general, see Hazel W. Hertzberg, *The Search for an American Indian Identity: Modern Pan-Indian Movements* (Syracuse, NY: Syracuse University Press, 1971).

[87]J. Anthony Paredes, "Chippewa Townspeople," in Paredes, op. cit. note 6, pp. 324-396 at 324-326.

[88]J. Anthony Paredes, "Toward a Reconceptualization of American Indian Urbanization: A Chippewa Case," *Anthropological Quarterly* 44: 4 (October 1971): 256-71.

[89]Friedl, op. cit. note 9, p. 819. Also, see Vivian Rohrl, "The People of Mille Lacs: A Study of Social Organization and Value Orientation," Ph.D. dissertation (University of Minnesota, 1967).

[90]Anthony F. C. Wallace, "Political Organization and Land Tenure Among the Northeastern Indians, 1600-1830," *Southwestern Journal of Anthropology* 13: 4 (Winter 1957): 301-321 at 306.

# THE DELIVERY OF HEALTH CARE TO AMERICAN INDIANS: HISTORY, POLICIES AND PROSPECTS

Jennie Joe

*University of Arizona*

## Introduction

The nature and quality of the health of people vary considerably from one society to another. In some developed countries, the expectation of quality health care may be so much the norm that people deem it a right, not a privilege. In other societies, the health care of the population may be marked by inequities and disparities. In the United States, for example, because of perceived health care inequities and disparities between the rich and poor, equitable access to health care for the indigent has long been a public policy issue. American Indians and Alaska Natives, along with other racial minorities, make up a sizable proportion of the poor in the United States, although the former are more likely to have greater health care needs. This situation exists despite the fact that for more than one hundred years, the federal government has attempted by various means to improve the health status of American Indians. These efforts have been prompted by the actions of advocacy groups, congressional investigations, and court decisions, as well as in response to various reports and studies.

Historically, federal funding of health care services for American Indians originated as part of the trust responsibilities implied by treaty agreements between various Indian tribes and the federal government. As a result of this trust responsibility, the federal government has established and continues to maintain a number of health care facilities for American Indians and Alaska Natives, especially for those residing on federal reservations, for whom health care is provided free. This eligibility for health care enjoyed by American Indians contrasts sharply with the rest of the U.S. population, of which only a small percentage are beneficiaries of public programs and a good many lack any type of health insurance. Nevertheless, the availability of free health care has not solved the poor health status of Native Americans.

Gerzowski and Adler[1] have argued that federal responsibility for providing health services to American Indians makes them unique among minorities, but also "raises unique questions when one considers their access to health care." For example, one would assume that with free health care available, American Indians should have fewer health problems than other minority groups — but this is not the case. While health care services may be free for many Native Americans, access to timely and appropriate health care is often influenced by other factors, e.g., health care availability and proximity, sociocultural or language barriers, insurance coverage, and the particular health problem, its treatment and prognosis. The other most significant factor, however, is the willingness of government to provide adequate funds to maintain or improve health care resources. Historically, federal government funding has not been adequate and has failed repeatedly to keep up with the health care needs of the Indian population. The lack of adequate funding is also linked to the absence of a strong, comprehensive federal Indian health care policy.

In evaluating the policies governing the provision of health care to American Indians, Cecilia Gallerito, an Indian attorney, suggests a reason for some of the criticism of these policies. She notes that such policies move on a continuum, both vertically and horizontally:

> Some policies strive to raise the level of health conditions of Indians, others work against improvement. Unilateral government intervention and cultural traditions create a situation that has stirred criticism from groups of people who monitor Indian affairs.[2]

Although most reservation-based American Indians and Alaska Natives have access to free health care services under the federal Indian Health Service (IHS), these services are limited and what is available may not be appropriate for the health problems faced by many of the Indian clients. Thus the health status of the Indian population remains among the worst in the nation. The continuation of poor health status haunts policymakers, health care providers and tribal leaders. The situation is particularly disconcerting because although there have been dramatic improvements in some areas of health over the last four decades, these improvements are quickly overshadowed and/or cancelled by the emergence of other types of health problems. Despite the availability of more and better health care resources, current data indicate that the health of American Indians and Alaska Natives continues to lag behind that of the rest of the U.S. population.

This chapter will focus on selected health care policies which pose problems for the delivery of health care to Indians, identifying their historical roots and discussing some of their consequences for American Indians and Alaska Natives.

## Indians and Health Care Policies

Because many reservation-based Indians are eligible for free health care in IHS facilities, one of the frequent policy questions is whether health care for American Indians and Alaska Natives is an entitlement. Although most Indians view federal health care as an entitlement, historical and legal precedents do not necessarily support this view. There is no policy stating specifically that health care is an entitlement for American Indians.

Like many other governmental policies related to American Indians and Alaska Natives, health care policies have not been well-defined. Until the passage of the Indian Health Care Improvement Act of 1976 (amended in 1984 and reauthorized in 1988),[3] which has served to clarify some of these issues, the major policy for provision of federal health service to Indians was based on a sentence in the Snyder Act of 1921 providing for the "relief of distress and conservation of health."[4] Although Congress had allocated money annually to assist American Indians, the passage of the Snyder Act provided the necessary statutory authority for the Bureau of Indian Affairs (BIA) to care for and assist American Indians throughout the United States. With the exception of these two federal policies, most other health care policies for Indians are rooted in administrative actions or based on various court decisions.

To understand the complexities of the health situation of American Indians and Alaska Natives today, it is necessary to go beyond the typical mortality and morbidity statistics to other factors influencing the population. For example, health issues must be examined in light of the history of federal-Indian relations so that one can understand the process by which health care became available to Native Americans. The issue of health care for Indian people must also be viewed within the dynamics of various sociocultural, political and economic interactions. The argument for this approach has been cogently made by others who have attempted to explain the changing health patterns of populations in Third World countries.[5]

As conquered nations, most Indian communities continue to be dependent on the federal government for virtually all of their health and human services. This federal support, however, is periodically threatened when Congress embarks on various funding cuts to contain the federal deficit. During these times, the federal government explores or initiates various ways to decrease or terminate some of the financial support it provides to Indians. Invariably, these threats are interpreted by tribal leaders as an indication of the federal government wanting to ease out of its trust obligation to American Indians. Sometimes the federal actions include the possibility of transferring the Indian health responsibility to the states, an option strongly opposed by the tribes. Many tribal leaders fear that if such a transfer occurred, tribes would not only have no input into the decisionmaking, but also that their health programs and services would worsen or become an easy target for elimination in the future.

The federal argument for such a proposal is that the transfer will not only lessen federal expenditures, but will encourage states to assume a greater role in providing health care for its Indian citizens. However, even as the federal government pushes for greater state involvement in indigent health care, some states with sizable Indian populations resist the addition of indigent Indian clients into their sphere of responsibility, arguing that the federal government is responsible for this population. Without additional financial incentives from the federal government, most states are not anxious to expand their limited indigent health care resources to residents on federal Indian reservations.

Faced with soaring health care costs, the federal Indian Health Service (IHS) has been experimenting with a number of different health care delivery models. One of these is an IHS-initiated demonstration project utilizing a health maintenance organization model (HMO) for the Yaqui tribe in Arizona. Pressured by the passage of a congressional mandate for Indian self-determination, the IHS has also initiated a number of contracts with Indian tribes who want to manage and operate portions of their own health care programs. The Tohono O'odham Nation (formerly Papago), for example, recently received federal money to assess the feasibility of taking over the entire IHS program on their reservation with technical assistance from a private hospital in the city of Tucson. The Tohono O'odham tribal leaders view this action as a way to gain control of the federal health care dollars earmarked for their reservation.[6]

The IHS also has given considerable attention to the development of a new policy defining eligibility for free Indian health care. The government interest in eligibility criteria has been fueled not only by the increased demand for and cost of health care services, but also by population increases, such as the recent inclusion of Indian tribes heretofore unrecognized by the federal government. (As a result of a number of historical events, some tribes that were never before federally recognized are petitioning Congress for recognition and are being granted full status). These "new" tribes have placed additional demands on the limited resources of the Indian Health Service. Without a specific eligibility policy of its own, the IHS historically has followed the policy of the Bureau of Indian Affairs, which limits its service population to Indian people who: 1) have over one quarter or more Indian blood; 2) are members of federally recognized tribes; and 3) live on or near an Indian reservation.

Attempts by the IHS to establish new health care eligibility policies, however, have been opposed by many national tribal leaders who lobbied intensively against such policies. In 1987, such opposition to the IHS proposal to limit its service to federally recognized Indians with one quarter or more Indian blood quantum resulted in an IHS moratorium on this endeavor.[7] Many of the tribal leaders viewed this policy proposal as an attempt by the federal government to infringe on the right of a tribe to determine who is a member of a tribe.[8] The outcry against the IHS proposal was extremely intense: there were over sixteen thousand responses to the proposed rules in addition to the ten thousand or more pages of written testimony taken at more than 120 public hearings held on the subject.

Besides questions of eligibility for IHS health care, there are also other health care finance issues that are tangled up in various federal-state jurisdictional debates, some of which have been or are in the process of being addressed by federal court decisions. A number of these jurisdictional disputes between the IHS and the states have centered on the eligibility of indigent Indians for state-administered, publicly financed health care when that care is provided in a non-IHS facility. These cases demonstrate a related pair of key questions: Do reservation-based indigent Indians (as citizens of a particular state) have a right to participate in that state's sponsored health programs, and should the state pay for such health care costs?

## Citizenship and Eligibility

With the passage of the 1964 Civil Rights Act, the question of citizenship for Native Americans should have been put to rest, but the issue resurfaces whenever the state and federal governments disagree about which agency has the primary responsibility for paying the health care costs incurred by an indigent Indian in a non-IHS facility. The basis of the controversy is the question of which agency, state or federal, is indeed the payer of last resort. Unfortunately, until some of these legal issues are resolved, coverage for the immediate or future health care needs of those affected by the controversy is problematic. Some Indian patients, for example, find themselves and their families facing legal actions or being harassed by collection agencies while they try to find ways to pay their costly medical bills.

Many private and state health care facilities believe that Indians, as wards of the federal government, have access to unlimited federal health care resources. Some of these private facilities have grown so accustomed to billing the IHS for services provided Indian patients that they refuse to treat Indian clients without proper referral documents. On one occasion, a severely depressed mental health patient — a young Tohono O'odham man in southern Arizona — was referred on a weekend by an IHS provider to a non-IHS mental health facility. Unfortunately, when he arrived at the facility without an appropriate referral document, he was refused service. Two days later, the young man's body was found swinging from a tree a few yards away from his home. He had hung himself. The Tucson mental health facility conceded that if the young Indian patient had not indicated he came from a reservation, but was merely "walking-in" (from the streets of Tucson), he probably would have been hospitalized immediately. But because this young man was an Indian (whose care is usually paid for by the IHS), he could not be seen without prior or proper authorization.[9]

**Health Issues Then and Now**

Although the exact health status of Native Americans prior to European contact has not been documented, all references made by explorers indicate that the Indians they first encountered were healthy.[10] This situation, however, changed drastically with the arrival of the first European settlers, and since that time the health status of American Indians and Alaska Natives has continued to lag behind that of the rest of the general population. First of all, the European contact proved disastrous for the aboriginal populations because they had no immunity to the variety of communicable diseases the Europeans brought with them. Thousands of American Indians died as a result. A number of tribes were totally decimated, while others managed to survive only to face other death threats associated with warfare, land dispossession, forced relocation, and the poverty that accompanied their subsequent confinement to reservations.

In some areas, the few who survived banded with survivors of neighboring tribes in order to rebuild a tribal base. In other instances, tribes that were more isolated from the Europeans managed to keep a population stronghold, although they too suffered heavy losses from communicable diseases and warfare. The colonial domination that preceded the contact period wrought additional problems. The economic and social fabric of many tribes was destroyed or, if not destroyed, completely destabilized. In addition, after the ravages of epidemics, warfare and forced migration, a number of tribes were left homeless and therefore had no other option than to accept relocation. Once relocated onto reservations, new problems emerged, including chronic ill health, disability and poverty. These early experiences broke the spirit of many native peoples and the concomitant deterioration of their well-being left a permanent side effect that has since been imprinted on subsequent generations. The consequences of this deterioration include such pathological disorders as low self-esteem, alcoholism, poor mental health, welfare dependency and various kinds of self-destructive behaviors.

Since the federal responsibility for health care of Native Americans was transferred in the mid-1950s to the U.S. Public Health Service (PHS) from the Department of Interior, however, mortality and morbidity linked to certain infectious diseases such as pneumonia, influenza, tuberculosis and gastrointestinal diseases have decreased dramatically. Nevertheless, in addition to a variety of mental health problems, some of the major health problems present among Native Americans today include accidents, alcoholism, otitis media (middle ear infections), diabetes, nutritional deficiencies and poor dental health.[11]

Thus, despite improved health care resources and sometimes better access to modern medicine, the health status of American Indians and Alaska Natives continues to trail that of other minority groups in the United States. A special report issued in 1985 by the Secretary of the U. S. Department of Health and Human Services on minority health indicated that the average life expectancy for Native Americans is six years less than that of other minorities in the United States.[12] The report also indicated that American Indians not only have the lowest overall educational attainment, but that almost one-third of them live in poverty. The 1979 median family income for American Indians and Alaska Natives was $15,900. The report further noted that Native Americans, along with blacks, have the highest rates of injury and death from non-disease-related causes. In particular, Native Americans have the highest mortality rate from motor vehicle accidents of all minority groups.[13]

In general, there is a perception within Indian communities that insensitive governmental policies, bureaucracy and poverty are major contributors to these health problems.[14] For example, the federal government's control of most economic and political resources on Indian reservations not only perpetuates long-term welfare dependency, but also fuels the persistence of poor health for many Indian families through inadequate nutrition and exposure to a variety of health hazards. On the other hand, without government-sponsored programs, the health and welfare of most Indian tribes would indeed suffer even more than it does now.

The government-sponsored health programs, however, are far from adequate and, depending on the generosity of Congress, may improve or deteriorate over time. Within recent years, as Congress and the president initiate policies to contain health care costs for the poor, the IHS as a federal entity has not been spared from budget cuts. The annual ritual for the IHS when faced with reduced budgets has been to recommend cuts in outside clinical services to health programs operated by the tribes. Such reductions invariably have zeroed in on such popular community resources as the community health representatives (CHR), a cadre of indigenous paraprofessionals who are perhaps most vulnerable because they are hired by the tribes and work outside the typical hospital or other clinical settings. In addition to providing various health education activities and assisting with home health care of the aged, the chronically ill and the severely disabled, CHRs serve as a critical link between the communities and modern health resources. Because of their visibility in the Indian communities, the activities and contributions of CHRs are valued highly by the tribes. Thus, for the last several years, a massive annual appeal to Congress has been made by the tribes to maintain the CHR program. Such mass appeals at times have helped reinstate some of the funds previously removed from the IHS budget.

### The IHS and Health Care for Reservation Indians

As the key federal agency designated to provide health care to American Indians and Alaska Natives, the goal of the IHS is to raise the health status of Native Americans to the highest possible level.[15] Although some progress has been made towards this end, the vast majority of Native Americans, as mentioned before, either continue to experience poor health or are "at risk" for developing a variety of chronic and debilitating health problems.

Health care was not available to American Indians until a number of Indian tribes in the nineteenth century negotiated for the services of a physician or for specific medical supplies when they were asked to cede their lands to the U.S. government. Some tribes did receive some medical services as a result of their treaties with the federal government. A separate and distinct federal policy for the provision of health care for all American Indians, however, did not begin to emerge until after

1849, when Congress established the Department of Interior and it became the new administrative home for the Bureau of Indian Affairs.

Prior to 1849, the Office of Indian Affairs (as the BIA was called in those days) was administratively a part of the Department of War. While under the Department of War, the Office of Indian Affairs had no specific health programs for Indians, but would be forced periodically to provide some emergency services, especially when a nearby Indian village would pose a possible health threat to neighboring military forts or non-Indian settlements. During certain epidemics, for instance, the Army Medical Corps might be called upon to immunize Indians in these villages as a way to halt the potential spread of a communicable disease such as smallpox.[16]

During this time, the confinement of many of the tribes to federal reservations had marked epidemiological and demographic effects on their health and population.[17] First, the forced relocation of some tribes meant severe lifestyle changes, from a nomadic to a sedentary existence, as well as changes in the form of subsistence, e.g., government-issued food supplies that were often inedible. Second, the new confined land base, or reservation, was small, forcing Indian groups to live in close quarters, thereby increasing the chances of epidemics. Third, as food sources (game and vegetation) on these small reservations quickly became scarce, chronic malnutrition became increasingly prevalent.

As these forced changes ushered in new problems such as malnutrition, the young and the old became especially susceptible to other, more serious health problems and complications. Malnutrition continued to ravage many of the Indian communities, although in a number of instances the federal government shipped in food rations. However, these and other goods provided were often contaminated or nutritionally inferior to the precolonial diets of most tribes.

Poor nutrition was frequently either a secondary or a major contributing cause to such diseases as tuberculosis, trachoma, smallpox, measles, dysentery and other gastrointestinal infections, and contributed to the high mortality and morbidity rates among the elderly and the young. An important study conducted in the early 1920s (the Meriam Report)[18] reported that infant mortality for most Indian tribes was twice that of the general population, and death (of all age groups) attributed to tuberculosis was seven times higher for Indians than the general population.[19]

During these early reservation years, health care responsibilities were left to individual families and tribes except in a few instances where the government might provide some health care to "high risk" groups such as Indian students forced to attend government or mission boarding schools. Here, as a precaution against epidemics of communicable disease, a school nurse or a doctor occasionally visited the students. Despite these efforts, however, many Indian youths died while enrolled in these schools.

On the reservations, mortality rates were extremely high. Blindness due to trachoma and deaths due to infectious diseases such as tuberculosis were of special concern. For example, in one early mortality survey, Ales Hrdlicka found 641 deaths from pulmonary and other forms of tuberculosis on fifty-three Indian reservations between 1907 and 1908.[20] Other infectious diseases added to the high infant and maternal mortality rates. In 1910, the United States Census reported that only 74.4 percent of Indian newborn infants were expected to survive.[21] Few babies were born in hospitals and those delivered at home often were at risk for infections and other complications. With high mortality rates on most reservations, it is not surprising that many Indians viewed hospitals as places of death or places where one expected death, and thus refused hospitalization or even to see a physician. This negative perception of modern medicine, and especially hospitals, was greatly influenced by the fact that so many of the sick did not go to the hospitals until it was too late, and therefore they often died soon after admission.

As mortality and visible health problems of American Indians on the reservations increased, the BIA became the object of much political and public criticism. To counter the criticism, it began to employ physicians and nurses, but as mentioned earlier, the initial concerns were for young people in boarding schools with no immediate concern for Indian communities at large. Instead, different church groups and missionaries were encouraged by the federal government to build hospitals as well as to train Indian nurses. However, as the role of the churches diminished at the turn of the century, the federal government began to assume a more active role in providing health care services. The first federal hospital for Indians was built in Oklahoma at about this time.

When the federal government constructed hospitals or clinics on a reservation, planning for the facility encompassed more than just building a hospital. Because most Indian reservations were isolated from established townships or cities, it soon became evident that the construction of health facilities on Indian reservations also required construction of staff housing and other resources. Thus over the years, the necessity for comprehensive health programs on the reservation meant that the Indian Health Service has had to seek additional dollars in order to build the needed support services and facilities.

In retrospect, it can be said that the increased role of the federal government in the health care of American Indians was necessitated by its overall trust responsibility for Indian lands. Eventually this responsibility incorporated spheres of concerns such as education, welfare, health, economics, and the establishment of a variety of infrastructures to carry out programs in these areas, including political institutions such as tribal governments. At first, most of the government programs were provided to tribes on the basis of their treaty agreements with the United States. Later, these separate services became available to most federally recognized tribes as part of the overall responsibility of the Bureau of Indian Affairs. Thus, over the years the government began to formalize programs which functioned within the BIA. For example, shortly after the BIA was transferred to the Department of Interior in 1849, the bureau set up a small health program. The initial health activities of this new unit, however, were not separate from but were integrated with other programs provided by the bureau.

The development of health facilities for reservation Indian populations by the federal government was also necessitated by the fact that the states had neither jurisdiction nor program responsibilities on federal lands. Since most tribal reservations were on federal land, reservations remained outside state jurisdiction. Most federal and state policymakers viewed reservation-based populations as the responsibility of the federal government and not the states. This separation of responsibility dictated a policy trend that reinforced the notion that residents of federal reservations were not eligible for state-sponsored programs. Furthermore, as states assumed a greater role in health and welfare activities, most state officials, unless mandated to do so, saw no reason to extend their services to residents of Indian reservations. This exclusion of Indians was also partially supported by the argument that Indians, as residents of a federal land base, did not contribute to the property tax, a resource which paid for most state-supported programs and services. With no one else ready to assume the responsibility for Indians residing on federal reservation land, the federal government had to take on virtually all of the responsibilities for the health and welfare of American Indians and Alaska Natives.

Despite many decades of funding increases for BIA health programs, the health situation of American Indians in many instances continued to worsen. The concern for this problem soon became both public and political. At the urging of a number of Indian advocates during the first decade of the twentieth century, Congress in 1911 appropriated $40,000 for improving the health status of American Indians. Congress also appropriated $90,000 to the U.S. Public Health Service (PHS) and the Marine Hospital Service in 1913 to conduct a survey on the health care needs of American Indians. The results of this study and of other studies conducted by independent groups such as the American Medical Association and the Tuberculosis Association led eventually to an increased appropriation for health care services for Indians. In 1921, Congress enacted the Snyder Act to give the BIA a general authorization for many of its social programs. The act provided "moneys as Congress may from time to time appropriate, for benefit, care, and assistance of the Indians throughout the United States." As previously mentioned, it further indicated that this authorization was for the "relief of distress and conservation of health" of Indians. The act also authorized funds in the BIA budget for the "employment of physicians."[22]

Since the enactment of the Snyder Act, the BIA has relied on it as the major congressional authority to plan and operate health and other welfare programs for American Indians and Alaska Natives. Because the Snyder Act was initiated by Congress voluntarily, and because Congress has continued to provide funds for these programs, the courts have ruled on a number of occasions that these programs are not part of the federal government's trust responsibility to American Indians and Alaska Natives. In other words, the government's trust responsibilities, which include holding reservation land in trust for tribes, does not include other benefits voluntarily provided by Congress.[23]

It is clear that the Snyder Act provided the framework necessary to help improve the health of Native Americans because it authorized the subsequent growth of health care resources, albeit not always sufficiently enough to have a positive impact on all areas of mortality and morbidity.

As mentioned before, the failure of the BIA to deliver responsive health care became a source of congressional debate and continued to resurface annually until Congress decided that the health activities of the BIA should be transferred to the PHS. The PHS was viewed by many as the ideal choice to take over this charge, because it was the federal agency with expertise and responsibility regarding matters of public health. Thus in 1954, after considerable resistance from the BIA, the bureau's Indian health program was transferred to the PHS under the provision of the Transfer Act.[24] At the time of the transfer, the Indian health care business of the BIA was substantial, and the annual budget for Indian health in the bureau had grown to $21,400,000.[25]

**Progress Since 1954**

After its transfer to the Department of Health, Education and Welfare (now termed the Department of Health and Human Services), the IHS expanded its health programs for American Indians and Alaska Natives in a number of ways. Over thirty new hospitals were built. Other kinds of facilities such as health centers and health stations were also constructed in many of the remote areas of Indian reservations and in isolated Alaskan villages. Over the years, as more health facilities were constructed and staffed, there was also a growth in the demand for these services. Because of the increased exposure to hospitals, physicians and nurses, Indian people began to find modern medicine more acceptable; in fact so acceptable that almost all Indian births now occur in hospitals. In addition, hospital admissions and utilization of other services have more than doubled since 1954.[26]

Although their utilization rates are high, most IHS hospitals are small. The average number of beds is forty-five, including cribs for newborns. Only four IHS hospitals have more than one hundred beds (in Anchorage, Phoenix, Tuba City, Arizona, and Gallup, New Mexico), and three of these hospitals (Anchorage, Phoenix and Gallup) are referred to as medical centers, since they also serve as referral hospitals for more complicated cases. Because most of the other IHS hospitals are small, their range of available medical services is quite limited. Some hospitals have no obstetric services, and most do not have surgical services. For these specialty services, the IHS must either transfer patients to other IHS referral hospitals or purchase needed services for patients from nearby non-IHS medical specialists or facilities through contract care.

In recent years tribal and intertribal organizations have become increasingly involved in health care management, as well as in the delivery of health care services. The passage of two federal bills made this policy change possible. The 1975 passage of the Indian Self-Determination and Education Assistance Act[27] mandated the BIA and the IHS to contract with tribes so that they could assume the management and delivery of some programs historically handled by these two governmental agencies. By 1985, six of the 51 hospitals and 50 of the 124 health centers were administered by tribes under the act. As a result of the passage of the Indian Health Care Improvement Act in 1976, the IHS was authorized to fund health programs for Indians residing in urban areas.[28] Today there are 37 urban Indian health programs in 20 states.[29]

Previous to the passage of these new policies, the involvement of Indian people in the management of local IHS health programs was limited to a few chosen tribal representatives who were placed on the consumer health advisory boards only to react to, but not make, any policy decisions. In most instances, these advisory board members also served at the pleasure of the local IHS authorities, and thus their advisory input regarding policy or programs of the IHS was orchestrated by government officials.

### The California Situation

At the time of the transfer of the health care responsibility from the Department of Interior (under the BIA) to the Department of Health, Education and Welfare (under the PHS), the California legislature passed a resolution to discontinue federal health care programs in the state. California's action was based on hearings and the recommendations of a number of tribal leaders who felt that the federal health care resources available to them were insufficient and inferior to other health programs in the state. For example, at the time the BIA had only one Indian hospital in California (in Winterhaven, which is near Yuma, Arizona). This hospital, although located in California, was utilized primarily by Indian tribes from Arizona. The other two Indian hospitals (one on the Hoopa Reservation in northern California and the other in southern California at Saboba) were closed prior to 1950. Because these hospitals were located in very isolated areas of California, they were inaccessible to most Indians in the state.

Thus, the majority of the Indians in California had little or no experience with federal Indian health care, and the state resolution confirmed this situation. Meanwhile, political leaders in California argued that the state had adequate health resources for its Indian population. However, while the state had ample health resources, most of these resources were not available in the remote rural communities where a majority of the California Indians resided. As a result, the health situation for California Indians actually worsened following the passage of the resolution.

In 1965, the California Department of Health conducted a study which documented a number of severe health problems confronting California Indians, and recommended that federal health care for tribes in California be reinstated. In 1967, the California Department of Health obtained a federal grant to develop a health outreach program for Indians in rural areas of the state. Nine projects were initially established, followed by seven more. The California Department of Health assisted representatives from these projects to form a consortium. The group incorporated as a nonprofit organization called the

California Rural Indian Health Board (CRIHB). Soon after its incorporation, the new consortium sought private foundation funds to help set up an independent administrative infrastructure in order to take over the management of the program from the state.

These initial Indian health programs in California were basically outreach activities, with a part-time health aide who helped transport patients to doctors' offices, helped patients sign up for indigent health care services, and served as a patient advocate in the health care system. Usually there was also a part-time administrator for the project. With a staff of two or three, most projects had mainly informational functions and did not provide direct health care services. Despite this minimal provision of services, these projects were the first formal health programs in most California Indian communities.

Following the development of these projects, a number of tribal leaders lobbied the California legislature to reverse its earlier decision and to assist the tribes in getting the federal health program reinstated in California. In 1971, Congress reinstated the Indian health program in California, approving special "add-on" funds to the IHS for this purpose. The funding allocation was minimal, however, and could not support any program expansion. In many instances, the Indian communities had to search for other funds to build clinics or to obtain much needed medical and dental equipment.

Following the example of rural Indian communities, Indians in the urban areas of California also initiated a number of storefront clinics, some encouraged by the development of the urban free clinics in the 1960s. The California Department of Health helped organize these activities and provided some of the initial funding. The urban Indian clinics also organized and formed the California Urban Indian Health Council (CUIHC). This new coalition joined CRIHB in testifying before Congress for more federal health dollars for the rapidly increasing Indian population in California.

As Indian groups lobbied the state and federal governments, tribal leaders gained considerable experience and expertise in "working the Hill," i.e., the halls of Congress; their political activism also led them to push for legislation incorporating their projects into mainstream funding for the IHS. These efforts, as well as those by other tribal leaders across the country, gave impetus to the development and passage of the 1976 Indian Health Care Improvement Act.[30]

This legislation proposed to elevate the health status of Indians and Alaska Natives to a level equal to that of the rest of the nation with a specific seven-year plan. The act covered a number of health care priorities not funded or authorized to be performed by the IHS. For example, Section V authorized the IHS to support existing health programs or projects for Indians residing in urban areas. Another section of the act authorized the IHS to upgrade its clinical facilities in order to pass accreditation and licensing requirements; the upgrade would enable the IHS to compete for reimbursement from Medicare, Medicaid and private health insurance plans.

Although over the years the IHS has received additional resources for expansion, the allocation formula it utilized to support and maintain health programs came under serious criticism by California tribes who said they were disenfranchised by the formula. To seek a more equitable recourse, the Rincon band of Mission Indians in southern California sought a declaratory judgment in federal court. The Rincon band charged that the system used by the IHS to allocate its health care dollars to Indian communities violated their constitutional right to equal protection.

In handing down a decision in the case of the *Rincon Band of Mission Indians* v. *Harris*,[31] the court indicated that there was no rational basis for the methods used to determine the allocation of funds by the IHS to California Indians. The court asked that the IHS provide equity in this case. The equity judgment and the equity funds that followed aided the expansion of health programs for rural California Indians, providing more resources toward the overall improvement of their health status.

Unlike other tribes in other states, the rural and urban Indian health programs in California also have an additional resource. Through the cooperative lobbying efforts of many of the tribal and urban Indian health programs in California, the state legislature established an Indian health program for the state. The state allocates approximately 2.4 million dollars each year to help support Indian health programs in urban and rural areas. A statewide advisory board with representatives from both the urban and rural programs helps the state to develop priorities and advises it on the overall direction of the program.

### Health Care for Off-Reservation Indians

Access to health care services by Indians in off-reservation communities has been the subject of numerous reports and studies.[32] Before the advent of urban-based health care programs for American Indians, many of the earlier studies sought to document the need for health care resources for Indians residing in such cities as Los Angeles, San Francisco, Seattle and Denver. Indians in these cities felt that they should have access to some federally supported health resources because many of them were relocated by the federal government from their reservations in the 1950s and 1960s. At the behest of the federal government, many came to the cities in search of jobs and other economic opportunities not available on the reservations. Once relocated, however, many of them found themselves in urban ghettoes and in job situations with little or no benefits, especially health insurance.

Upon their arrival in the cities, most Indians were unfamiliar with the health care system and experienced rejection when they sought health care because they had neither the money nor insurance to pay for it. Many were also denied service by health facilities because of the mistaken belief that the federal government had sole responsibility for the health care of Indians, no matter where they resided. Thus many had to return to their reservations for needed health care. Indian women frequently returned to the reservation to have their babies, and other family members often endured health problems until they became life-threatening or until they were able to get back to the reservation.

As Indians in the city became more politically vocal and organized, they joined their advocates in encouraging policymakers and congressional leaders to address some of their urgent health care needs. This pressure and the successes of the first storefront health care services served as an important beginning for what later became the first formal recognition and funding of off-reservation programs under the Indian Health Care Improvement Act. This funding gave the fledgling clinics stable funds for referral services, as well as money for preventive or primary health care. Funds were not provided, however, for hospitalization.

Like the urban clinics in California, the urban Indian health programs in other states began as part of the free clinic movements of the late 1960s and organized as nonprofit entities. Their client base was generally comprised of both Indians and non-Indians. Initially storefront operations, most of the clinics depended on volunteers and donations. Although they were able to open and operate a clinic once or twice a week, most clinic administrators agreed that reliance on volunteers and donations was too unpredictable and inadequate. Consequently, a number of clinics embarked on various strategies to make their services permanent and comparable to other health care programs.

The push towards legislation to legitimize and financially stabilize these urban health programs became an important agenda item; the passage of the Indian Health Care Improvement Act helped to attain this goal. Prior to the passage of the act, a number of clinics formed consortia and sought special federal set-aside funds for their programs. As previously stated, this required annual testimony before congressional appropriation committees and constant attention to documenting unmet needs and lobbying efforts.

Nevertheless, through the act, Congress and the IHS have helped legitimate some of the urban Indian health programs by recognizing them in a policy action. Although most of these urban clinics have been funded by the IHS for a number of years, their financial situation still remains precarious. Like the annual dilemma of the reservation-based CHR program, the urban Indian health program is typically placed on the federal budget chopping block each year. As a result, annual campaigns to head off the budget cuts must be mounted by these urban programs in order to help save them.

### The Elevation of the IHS

The Indian Health Service recently became the seventh agency within the U.S. Public Health Service (PHS). According to Gene Gerber, this action indicates that the IHS has the size, scope, number of employees and comprehensiveness of mission to be ranked among the other superagencies of the PHS.[33] Such an elevation had been sought and included in the various drafts of the reauthorization of the Indian Health Care Improvement Act. When these proposed reauthorizations failed, the elevation proposal was pursued administratively.

The arguments for the elevation of the IHS to agency status included that it would provide the IHS leadership with easier access to policymakers within the Department of Health and Human Services. Furthermore, the elevation was seen as a way to involve other PHS agencies in addressing some of the major health problems of American Indians and Alaska Natives, especially in the research arena. Whether the goals associated with the elevation of the IHS will benefit Indians remains to be seen, but thus far the most visible changes have included additional offices in the administrative headquarters of the IHS and more bureaucratic paperwork, including a proposal to transfer several administrative staff and functions from Rockville, Maryland, to Albuquerque, New Mexico, thereby enlarging Headquarters West.

According to the 1980 census, the population of American Indians and Alaska Natives is approximately 1.4 million. In 1986, the IHS provided services to 930,000 American Indians and Alaska Natives. A majority of IHS clients reside on or near federal reservations, where most IHS health facilities are located. Nationwide, the IHS funds or operates approximately 27 hospitals, 26 health centers, and over 50 small health stations. While most IHS hospitals are located in or near towns or areas with sizable populations, IHS health stations are usually situated in the more remote areas of the reservations or in the bush areas of Alaska. Presently, there are approximately six hundred physicians in the IHS. This represents a ratio of 0.6 IHS physicians to 1000 Indian patients, compared to a more equitable ratio of 1.6 physicians to 1000 patients in the general population.[34] For many years, most physicians recruited to work in IHS facilities were either from the military draft, the National Health Service Corps, or were repaying scholarship debts. With the end of military conscription and especially the 1987 phaseout of the National Health Service, a critical health manpower resource which once provided the IHS and other medically underserved communities with physicians and other health professionals is no longer available. This has resulted in the closure of a number of health facilities. Essentially, the demise of the National Health Service program has made it difficult for the IHS and Indian communities to recruit physicians and other health professionals for many of the remote Indian communities and native villages.

For a number of years, many tribal entities have cooperated with the federal government to provide scholarships and other resources to Indian students interested in science and medicine. The number of these students is slowly growing as reflected in the increased membership of the Association of American Indian Physicians. Although increasing numbers of younger Indian physicians are electing to work in IHS facilities on Indian reservations, the number of available Indian physicians still remains extremely small.

**Eligibility and Health Care**

As a rule, patients eligible for IHS services are of Indian descent and belong to an Indian community served by the IHS. More specifically, the community must regard an individual as "Indian," and the individual must show either tribal membership, residence on tax-exempt land (a reservation), or demonstrate that he or she meets the BIA eligibility criteria.[35] Services that are available through the IHS include inpatient and outpatient medical care, dental care, public health nursing, and preventive care in such areas as alcoholism, diabetes and mental health. These services, however, are not available on every reservation. Each IHS facility also has in its budget a limited amount of money to pay for services not available such as deliveries and trauma care.

Although an eligible Indian patient who comes to an IHS facility is rarely refused care, the IHS can deny payment for services provided in non-IHS facilities if the clients have not been authorized or approved in advance by the IHS. In order to reserve its contract care dollars, the IHS also diligently assists the enrollment of Indians who are eligible for Medicaid and Medicare. When IHS facilities provide services to these clients, they also bill Medicaid and Medicare for reimbursement. For Medicare and Medicaid patients referred to non-IHS facilities, the IHS generally agrees to pay the patient's share of the hospitalization bill. Ultimately, the IHS views Medicare and Medicaid as the primary service providers, and itself only as the payer of last resort.

This administrative policy has evolved over time, although the federal government has never fully defined what is covered under its health care responsibility for American Indians. Unlike other federal entitlement programs that spell out what a health care package entails, the IHS has no definite policy other than to maintain that an adequate package would require a certain stable level of funding for a specific number of Indian clients. As mentioned before, there has never been an adequate funding level established or even an exploration of what would be a typical health care package for an average Indian client on a reservation.

Therefore, it is not surprising that most legal opinions rendered on IHS responsibility reaffirm that it is not an entitlement program. In underscoring this point, Daniel Press, an attorney working with Arizona tribes, noted that the annual appropriation request by the IHS is structured on a scale that has no relevance to needs and priorities:

> For entitlement programs, the government estimates what services it will be obligated to provide in the coming year to meet its obligation. . . . It then estimates how much it will cost to provide these services and appropriates sufficient money to do so. Thus the amount of money available is based on the projected need for services. IHS, on the other hand, starts with last year's appropriation which in turn was based on the prior year's [budget] or the so-called base budget. Congress then decides to give IHS a 1% or 10% or whatever increase in the various IHS categories. But neither the base budget nor the increase is based on what it will take to provide all of the services needed to all of the eligible Indians. Instead it is based strictly on historical factors and Congress' generosity, or lack thereof, in giving increases each year.[36]

Needless to say, the lack of a comprehensive health package policy and the rather haphazard method of congressional appropriation have resulted in a "band-aid" approach to health care for Indians. The Indian Health Service argues that it must do the best with what it is allocated; when resources are not sufficient, it must set priorities or deny services. The other federal agency for Indians, the BIA, has historically given priority to reservation Indians only. This policy was challenged in the 1970s in *Morton* v. *Ruiz*,[37] when the court asked how fairly the federal government (in this case, the BIA) allocated limited resources under the provision of the Snyder Act.

Ruiz, a Tohono O'odham (Papago) miner, had moved about fifteen miles away from his reservation in order to be near his place of work, but he encountered financial difficulties when he and other miners went on a strike for more wages. During the strike, Ruiz attempted to obtain some financial relief under state general assistance (GA), but his claim was denied because the state did not permit people who were on strike to enroll in the general assistance program. He then returned to his reservation and applied for GA under the Bureau of Indian Affairs. Once again, Ruiz was denied financial assistance because the bureau said its program was limited to Indians living on the reservation.

Ruiz sought relief through the courts on the grounds that he was eligible for BIA general assistance program under the provision of the Snyder Act. In the end, the U.S. Court of Appeals for the Ninth Circuit ruled in favor of Ruiz, holding not only that the BIA serves Indians "on and near" federal reservations, but also that the bureau failed to comply with the policy of the Administrative Procedure Act, which requires federal agencies to publish requirements and rules concerning programs they administer.[38] Because the BIA failed to publish its regulations, Ruiz was not aware that he was not eligible for the bureau's general assistance program.

As a result of this legal decision, the policy of the BIA as well as the IHS is to include in its service population Indians living "on or near" the federal reservation. Recent definitions of IHS service areas further identify these geographical boundaries.

### Contract Care Policy Issues

As previously mentioned, in order to maximize its limited funds, IHS policy since 1955 has stressed that it is the payer of last resort. This policy interprets the IHS sphere of responsibility to be "residual" to other non-IHS resources. If an Indian patient is eligible for Medicare or Medicaid, these resources must be utilized before the IHS will pay for the services provided. The IHS formalized this policy in 1978 by publishing its "Alternative Resources Regulations" that encouraged the use of Medicare, Medicaid, private insurance and other payment options.

One of the most critical factors in providing health care for American Indians and Alaska Natives is adequate funding. The IHS recently has begun to look to state and other resources to help shoulder some health care costs. Most states, however, disagree and view the IHS as the sole and primary health resource for reservation Indians. The federal government's position, though, is that Indians, as residents and citizens of a particular state, are entitled to all privileges and services provided to citizens of that state.

The IHS has been successful in tapping other resources. For example, prior to the enactment of the Indian Health Care Improvement Act, the Social Security Act prohibited Medicare and Medicaid reimbursement for care provided in federal facilities, including IHS facilities. This policy has now been changed to allow such third-party payments to the IHS. In order to receive additional third-party payments, many IHS hospitals and clinics began improving their facilities to meet more stringent accreditation requirements. As part of the Indian Health Care Improvement Act, funds were allocated to the IHS so that hospitals and clinics could accomplish this task.

While the cost of health care provided to Indian patients in IHS facilities is covered entirely by federal funds, the cost of care outside IHS facilities must come from other sources. As mentioned earlier, each IHS area is allocated money for contract care annually, i.e., they receive a budget that covers costs for patients who cannot be treated in IHS facilities or who require specialized medical care not offered by the IHS. Because contract care dollars are limited, the IHS has specific eligibility guidelines as well as limits on the types of contract care it is willing to buy. A person eligible for contract care must reside on the reservation within the respective IHS service area, and the patient must be an enrolled member of that tribe, or, if a minor, the patient must be a foster child or a temporary transient from another reservation. Indian students enrolled in college or schools outside their respective IHS service areas are also eligible. The specifics of the IHS alternative resource rule regarding contract care indicate that:

> Contract health services will not be authorized by the Indian Health Service when, and to the extent that, alternate resources for the provision of necessary medical services are available and accessible to the individual requesting the services or would be available and accessible upon application of the individual to the alternate resource.[39]

This alternative resource policy has been criticized by a number of Indian tribes who claim that it discriminates against indigent Indians. For example, the IHS mandates that all low-income or Indian families on welfare must enroll in Medicaid and Medicare. If they fail to do so, the IHS will declare them ineligible should they require contract care. Nonindigent Indians generally are not asked to sign up for these programs.

Within the legal arena, on the other hand, the use of the alternative resource rule by the IHS has been supported by such court decisions as *McNabb* v. *Heckler*.[40] In this particular case, a non-Indian, common law wife of an Indian gave birth to a premature infant in a non-IHS facility in Montana after being denied prenatal services and delivery at an IHS facility. According to the IHS officials, she was denied service because she could not produce a marriage certificate verifying her marriage to her Indian spouse. As a result, when the mother went into early labor, she had to enter a county hospital. The delivery resulted in the birth of a premature infant, and the child had to be placed in intensive care for several weeks. When the child was discharged from the hospital, the couple was handed a medical bill that they could not pay. They sought assistance from the IHS, but were referred back to the county. The IHS had earlier assisted the mother in applying for the county Medicaid program, but her application was subsequently denied. The county's eligibility office assumed she was eligible to receive medical care from the IHS. Caught in the middle, the couple sued both the county and the IHS. By the time the case went to court, the county changed its decision and agreed to pay for the delivery, but refused to pay for the baby's hospitalization. The county argued that, as an Indian, the child was eligible for IHS contract moneys and the court concurred, so the IHS paid the costs of the baby's hospitalization.

Although the alternative resources rule was upheld by the Ninth Circuit Court of Appeals in *McNabb* v. *Bowen*, the court criticized the IHS policy on contract care, contending that while the IHS tends to use a procedural process that is correct, it may create an unfair situation by "taking contract health benefits from the poorest Indians, who generally are most in need of health care, [and] awarding benefits to those who are less in need."[41] The court was also critical of the way the IHS abandoned the McNabb family, and declared that the IHS still had responsibility for an Indian patient even though he or she might be eligible for other sources of health financing.

The appellate court issued the following holdings:

a. The IHS alternative resource rule is valid and legal.

b. Although IHS is the primary source of health care for Indians, it is not the primary payor and can make use of other alternative sources.

c. States have obligations to provide and finance health care to its citizens, including Indians who are eligible for these services.

d. IHS can require Indians to explore alternative resources in order to receive contract care. If the third party or alternative resource refuses, however, IHS must pick up the costs and then seek reimbursement from the alternative source. The Indian person should not be burdened with the bill or the expense of recovering the cost of health care from alternative sources.[42]

Currently, the issue of who is the primary payer is also a source of legal controversy in Arizona. Arizona was the last state to participate and receive federal funds to finance health care for indigent patients. When it decided to do so in 1982, it asked to initiate some portions of the program on an experimental basis. The program, known as the Arizona Health Care Cost Containment System (AHCCCS), focuses on the provision of acute medical care and was given temporary permission to exclude certain required programs under Medicaid such as home health care, family planning and nursing home care.

As a program for the indigent, a large majority (68 percent) of individuals covered under the AHCCCS are those already on some form of public assistance. These clients consist of families on Aid for Dependent Children (AFDC) and clients on Supplemental Security Income (SSI). For this population, the AHCCCS receives full reimbursement from the federal government for health care. The remaining 32 percent of AHCCCS clients, however, must have their medical expenses covered totally by the state. This group includes persons or families defined as medically needy and/or medically indigent, families that are poor but are not enrolled in AFDC or SSI, and pregnant women and young children from families with a higher income, though still an insufficient one to cover health care.

The legal tug-of-war centers on the threat that the AHCCCS feels will come from the state's reservation Indian population, who fall within the other 32 percent described above. The state fears that many Indian clients will be "dumped" on them, and consequently break the AHCCCS "bank." This has resulted in the state of Arizona filing a legal complaint in 1986 seeking declaratory relief and requesting a determination of whether the state or the federal government is responsible for the provision of health care to American Indians residing on Arizona reservations.

While this legal standoff continues, the question of who is the payer of last resort is being debated among congressional as well as tribal people. In a response to the director of the Arizona AHCCCS program, Arizona Congressman Morris K. Udall stated his disagreement with the AHCCCS director's interpretation of the decision in *McNabb* v. *Bowen* : "The Court has found that IHS has a positive duty to assist Indians in accessing alternative health resources, and where it fails to, it has to pay for the service." [43]

Although the *McNabb* v. *Bowen* decision did uphold the right of the IHS to ask Indian patients to apply for and utilize alternative resources to pay for their health care, it did not resolve adequately the issue of what happens when both the federal and state agencies claim to be the payer of last resort. In any case, it did call attention to the need for a policy that addresses how the federal government should interact with the states in providing health care to indigent clients who reside on Indian reservations.

Despite the focus on health care costs, there is a dearth of information on health care expenditures for American Indians. The Office of Technology Assessment reported that in fiscal year 1984, "IHS was reimbursed $12.7 million from Medicare and $14.1 million from Medicaid for services provided to eligible Indians in IHS facilities."[44] The report also noted that collection from state Medicaid programs has been more difficult for the IHS because it does not always have the resources to stay abreast of different and changing Medicaid requirements or the staff necessary to enroll eligible Indians into Medicare and Medicaid programs.

Recent legal decisions have favored IHS health care payment policies, but the reality of the situation is that a number of indigent Indian families and individuals are still faced with medical bills and collection agencies. They are pawns in the game of "Who pays?" For example, one Navajo family received a letter from the IHS indicating that the IHS had been billed $2000 for medical services incurred by their child while hospitalized in a non-IHS facility. The letter stated that the IHS would not pay the bill and advised the family to apply to the AHCCCS for payment. The family was also instructed to provide the IHS with a copy of their AHCCCS application outcome. The letter stressed (with the sentence underlined) that the family must complete the AHCCCS application process and supply the necessary documentation within thirty days from the date of receiving the letter. The letter also emphasized that if the family failed to comply with the instructions, the IHS would not authorize any future payment for other medical care received by the family outside IHS facilities.[45]

Another case of denial of payment involved an Indian family who within a few days of moving to South Dakota was involved in an automobile accident. From the scene of the accident, they were taken by a private ambulance to the nearest hospital (a non-IHS facility) for treatment. The IHS area facility refused to pay the bill because the family was not from that area, and the county also refused to pay for the same reason, i.e., the family did not meet the length of residency rule in South Dakota for Medicaid eligibility. After months of debate and letter writing, Medicaid and the IHS agreed to pay for some of the medical bills, but only after the family sought legal help.

An interesting example of the game of "Who pays?" or "Who is responsible?" is also illustrated by the *White* v. *Califano* case in South

Dakota.[46] In 1976, an IHS psychiatric social worker on the Pine Ridge Reservation determined that the condition of a mental health client had worsened and required immediate psychiatric treatment. The client had previously been hospitalized at the state hospital, but in order to get the patient back into the state facility, the social worker had to petition authorities to obtain approval for involuntary commitment. The local county's Board of Mental Illness and the state attorney general were contacted, but both refused to issue support for the petition, stating that the county and state did not have authority on federal reservations. The social worker then approached the tribal court, and the tribal court judge placed the patient in the individual's custody and approved the order to commit the patient. The state mental health hospital officials, however, said they could not accept the tribal judge's recommendation without endorsement of the petition by the state attorney general. When contacted, the state attorney general reiterated his earlier decision, saying that the state could not accept or act upon petitions filed for involuntary commitment of Indian persons who reside on federal reservations. Citing this as a state responsibility, the federal government also refused to provide services.

After this frustrating series of denials, the client's guardian filed suit in the federal district court against both the federal and state governments. The federal government claimed to refuse service because the state was violating the "civil rights" of the Indian. Although *White* v. *Califano* did not resolve the responsibility issue, it did uphold the state's claim that it lacked jurisdiction on federal land and that the IHS had, within its mandate, a duty to provide mental health services. These and other legal decisions indicate the complexities of the health care policies confronting Indian tribal members today, especially those who are indigent and have to tangle with eligibility rules and conflicting policies of state and federal health care financing. As the life expectancy for American Indians increases, new health care costs are also emerging — coverage for long-term care, transplants, chronic disability, and the high cost of caring for terminal patients with conditions such as cancer and AIDS. At present, the IHS does not receive contingency funds for catastrophic illnesses such as these. Thus it appears that the question of health care financing will continue to be a primary concern for many tribes in the future.

**Summary Comments**

Ever since the 1831 Supreme Court decision in *Cherokee Nation* v. *Georgia,* that declared Indian tribes to be "domestic dependent nations" whose relationship to the United States government "resembles that of a ward to his guardian,"[47] federal policies affecting American Indians have vacillated between retaining and terminating that guardianship status. Invariably, these policy fluctuations not only have complicated the relationship between Indians and the federal government, but also have affected the policies and relationship between Indians and state governments.

It is within this context and the history of the federal-Indian relationship that policies concerning the health care of American Indians also unfold. In addition to a variety of congressional actions, state and federal court decisions are also central factors in determining whether American Indians are eligible for health care services, where they receive them, and who pays.

Although Congress has routinely allocated funds for Indian health care, the courts have consistently viewed this annual budgetary action as a voluntary one for Congress and therefore not a part of its trust responsibility. Health care for American Indians is thus not an entitlement; instead, like other federal dollars that come into Indian communities for schools or for welfare, the dollars for health care are provided because most American Indians and Alaska Natives do not have the financial resources to afford it.

The transfer of the health responsibility for Indians to the PHS has to some extent helped to improve the health status of American Indians and Alaska Natives. For example, since the PHS assumed the administrative responsibility in 1954, infant death rates have declined from 62.7 to 14.6 per 1,000 live births.[48] Deaths from infectious disease such as tuberculosis, gastrointestinal diseases, pneumonia and influenza have also decreased by more than 70 percent.[49]

However, as the statistics for morbidity and mortality due to physical health problems have lowered, the statistics for rates of mental health problems and other conditions not readily amenable to antibiotics or surgical interventions have risen sharply. Not only are there limited resources for many of the aforementioned health problems, but the health care delivery system also is increasingly finding itself unprepared to treat or cure the "new" types of health problems facing American Indians and Alaska Natives. In many of the remote areas of "Indian country," the frustrations of poverty and hopelessness often prove to be unbearable, especially for young people, as was recently highlighted by a young journalist in Alaska:

> Something is stalking the village people. Across the state, the Eskimos, Indians and Aleuts of Bush Alaska are dying in astonishing numbers. By suicide, accident and other untimely, violent

means, death is stealing the heart of a generation and painting the survivors with despair.[50]

In January 1988, the *Anchorage Daily News* ran a special ten-part series about the despair and problems of Alaska natives living in the remote, or bush, areas. The series began with an examination of a suicide epidemic in one remote village of 550 that began in 1985 when a 22-year-old young man shot himself in the heart.[51] This tragic episode was the beginning of a sixteen-month suicide epidemic that eventually took the lives of seven more young adults between the ages of 19 and 29. Six of the eight suicides were accomplished with shotguns; two of the victims hung themselves. All but one were male. The national suicide rates for young men between the ages of 20 and 24 is 25.6 per 100,000, but the rate of suicide among Alaska Natives is 257 per 100,000, ten times the rate in the general population. [52] The death of a Native American, however, is rarely a media event despite the high mortality rates.

This sense of helplessness and the self-destructive behavior are deemed "unnatural" by many village leaders, who attribute some of these behaviors to the negative influences of Western culture and the problems of acculturation. These things happen, according to some of these elders, because Western culture has destroyed much of the traditional culture, and when young Alaska Natives attempt to enter the mainstream culture, they find little acceptance. The sense of not "belonging" creates such unbearable pain for some that the only option might be alcoholism or suicide.[53] IHS leadership has recently referred to this change in the health pattern of American Indians and Alaska Natives as a direction which will "require changes in personal and community behavior rather than intensified medical services." [54]

While the federal entities wrestle with the problem of adequate funding and quality medical care, it is evident that many of the health problems confronting Indian communities today require more innovative and holistic approaches — ones that go beyond mere diagnosis and treatment to dealing with prevention and addressing such issues as low self-esteem and poverty. Such approaches will also require a more active role from the tribes if these problems are to be resolved.

## NOTES

[1]M. Gerzowski and G. Adler, "Health Status of Native Americans," paper presented at the American Public Health Association Annual Meeting (Montreal: APHA, 1982).

[2]Cecilia Gallerito, "Indian Health, Federally or Tribally Determined? Health Recommendations of the American Indian Policy Review Commission," *New Directions in Federal Indian Policy: A Review of the American Indian Policy Review Commission* (Los Angeles: American Indian Studies Center, University of California, 1979), pp. 29-44 at 29.

[3]Indian Health Care Improvement Act, P.L. 94-437, 90 Stat. 1400, September 30, 1976 (94th Congress, 2nd Session); and Indian Health Care Amendments, P.L. 100-713, 102 Stat. 4784, November 23, 1988 (100th Congress, 2nd Session).

[4]Snyder Act, 42 Stat. 208, November 2, 1921.

[5]See Merrill Singer, "Developing a Critical Perspective in Medical Anthropology," *Medical Anthropology Quarterly* 17: 5 (November 1986): 128-129; and Hans Baer, Merrill Singer and John H. Johnsen, "Toward a Critical Medical Anthropology," *Social Science and Medicine* 23: 2 (Winter 1986): 95-98.

[6]Tom Shields, "Health-Care Takeover: Tohono O'odham Want Control," *Tucson Citizen* (January 20, 1988).

[7]Indian Health Service Final Rule, 42 CFR Part 36, *Federal Register* 52: 179 (September 16, 1987), pp. 35044-35050.

[8]Ibid., p. 35044.

[9]"Young O'odham Man Commits Suicide," *Tucson Citizen* (February 8, 1988).

[10]See Sherburne F. Cook, "Demographic Consequences of European Contact with Primitive Peoples," *Annals of the American Academy of Political and Social Science* 237 (January 1945): 107-111; and Henry F. Dobyns, *Their Number Became Thinned: Native American Population Dynamics in Eastern North America* (Knoxville, TN: University of Tennessee Press, 1983).

[11]Indian Health Service, *Indian Health Service: A Comprehensive Health Care Program for American Indians and Alaska Natives* (Washington, D.C.: The Service, 1986). See also the section on the Indian Health Service in a congressional report, *Final Report and Legislative Recommendations: A New Federalism for American Indians* (Washington, D.C.: U.S. Government Printing Office, 1989).

[12]U.S. Department of Health and Human Services, *Report of the Secretary's Task Force on Black and Minority Health*, Vol. 1, *Executive Summary* (Washington, D.C.: U.S. Department of Health and Human Services, 1985), pp. 58-59.

[13]Ibid., p. 58.

[14]The late Jake Whitecrow, as the executive director of the National Indian Health Board, made these comments in a speech delivered at the National Native American Developmental Disabilities Conference (Mesa, AZ: April 13, 1988).

[15]Indian Health Service, op. cit. note 11, p. iv.

[16]Bertram S. Kraus and Bonnie M. Jones, *Indian Health in Arizona* (Tucson, AZ: Bureau of Ethnic Research, University of Arizona, 1954), p. 4.

[17]See Diane T. Putney, "Fighting the Scourge: American Indian Morbidity and Federal Policy, 1897-1928" (Ph.D. Dissertation, Marquette University, 1980); and Gregory R. Campbell, "Don't You See Our People Are Starving and Dying?: The Epidemiological Consequences of Removal to Indian Territory," paper presented at the 42nd Annual Plains Conference (Lincoln, NE: 1984).

[18]Lewis Meriam, technical director, et al., *The Problem of Indian Administration*, the Meriam Report (Baltimore, MD: Johns Hopkins Press, published for the Brookings Institution, 1928).

[19]Ibid., pp. 198-199, 201.

[20]Ales Hrdlicka, *Tuberculosis among Certain Indian Tribes of the United States* (Washington, D.C.: U.S. Government Printing Office, 1909).

[21]U.S. Bureau of the Census, *Indian Population in the United States and Alaska, 1910* (Washington, D.C.: U.S. Government Printing Office, 1915).

[22]Snyder Act, op. cit. note 4.

[23]U.S. Congress, Office of Technology Assessment, *Indian Health Care*, OTA-H-290 (Washington, D.C.: U.S. Government Printing Office, 1986), p. 9.

[24]The Transfer Act, P.L. 83-568, 68 Stat. 674, August 5, 1954 (83rd Congress, 2nd Session), authorized the transfer of the Indian Health Service from the Bureau of Indian Affairs to the Public Health Service.

[25]Kraus and Jones, op. cit. note 16, p. 23.

[26]Indian Health Service, op. cit. note 11, p. 14.

[27]Indian Self-Determination and Education Assistance Act, P.L. 93-638, 88 Stat. 2203, January 4, 1975 (93rd Congress, 2nd Session).

[28]Indian Health Care Improvement Act, op. cit. note 3, p. 1400.

[29]Office of Technology Assessment, op. cit. note 23, p. 12.

[30]Indian Health Care Improvement Act, op. cit. note 3.

[31]*Rincon Band of Mission Indians* v. *Harris*, 618 F.2d 569 (9th Cir. 1980).

[32]See, for instance, Willy De Geyndt, "Health Behavior and Health Needs of Urban Indians in Minneapolis," *Health Services Reports* 88: 4 (April 1973): 360-366; Jack O. Waddell and O. Michael Watson, eds., *American Indians in Urban Society* (Boston: Little, Brown, 1971); Eloise Richards Barter and James T. Barter, "Urban Indians and Mental Health Problems," *Psychiatric Annals* 4: 11 (November 1974): 37-43; Michael Fuchs, "Health Care Patterns

of Urbanized Native Americans" (Ph.D. Dissertation, University of Michigan, 1974); Alan L. Sorkin, *The Urban American Indian* (Lexington, MA: Lexington Books, 1978); and Jennie R. Joe, Dorothy Miller and Trudie Narum, *Traditional Indian Alliance: Delivery of Health Care Services to American Indians in Tucson* (Tucson, AZ: NARTC, University of Arizona, 1988).

[33]Gene Gerber, "Elevation of IHS to Agency Status," unpublished manuscript (1988).

[34]Everett Rhoades, et al., "The Indian Burden of Illness and Future Health Interventions," *Public Health Reports* 102: 4 (July-August 1987): 361-368.

[35]42 CFR 36.12. (See note 7.)

[36]Daniel Press, "Legal Issues in the AHCCCS Controversy," unpublished manuscript prepared for the Tohono O'odham Conference on AHCCCS (January 1988), p. 46.

[37]*Morton* v. *Ruiz*, 415 U.S. 199 (1974).

[38]Administrative Procedure Act, 60 Stat. 237, June 11, 1946 (79th Congress, 2nd Session).

[39]42 CFR 36.23(f). (See note 7.)

[40]*McNabb* v. *Heckler*, 628 F. Supp. 544 (D. Mont. 1986).

[41]*McNabb* v. *Bowen*, 829 F. 2nd 787 (9th Cir. 1987).

[42]Ibid.

[43]Letter from Rep. Morris Udall (D. Ariz.) to the state director of the Arizona Health Care Cost Containment System (AHCCCS), January 15, 1988.

[44]Office of Technology Assessment, op. cit. note 23, p. 18.

[45]See the *McNabb* v. *Bowen* decision, 829 F. 2nd at 791.

[46]*White* v. *Califano* 437 F.Supp. 543 (D.S.D. 1977), *affirmed*, 581 F.2d 697 (8th Cir. 1978).

[47]*Cherokee Nation* v. *Georgia* , 30 U.S. (5 Pet.) 1 (1831).

[48]Indian Health Service, op. cit. note 11, p. 16.

[49]Ibid.

[50]"A People in Peril," special reprint from the *Anchorage Daily News* (Anchorage, AK: Anchorage Daily News, 1988), p. A2.

[51]The suicide note found with the body indicated that the young man was deeply troubled. He wrote: "The future is shit. I've been clashed into a rapidly changing culture. Tried my best to keep up...." Ibid.

[52]Alaska Division of Public Health, "The Recording and Epidemiology of Suicide in Alaska, 1983-84," reprinted in "A People in Peril," op. cit. note 50, p. A3.

[53]"A People in Peril," op. cit. note 50, p. B8.

[54]Rhoades, et al., op. cit. note 34, p. 368.

# THE EDUCATION OF AMERICAN INDIANS: POLICY, PRACTICE AND FUTURE DIRECTION

## John W. Tippeconnic III

*Arizona State University*

The concept of "education" is a powerful tool in our society. Formal education housed in schools provides the dominant society with the means to exert control over the socialization process of young, developing individuals. In the United States, we proclaim pride in living in a democracy based on the principles of equality, freedom and social justice for all. Yet, we know that these democratic concepts are more relevant for some than for others, especially the poor and powerless. Education, especially public education, has been viewed as the instrument in our society to promote American ideals. [1]

Education and schools are very visible in our society. It seems that whenever there are political, economic, social or health problems, education becomes part of the solution. An example is the recent reform movement in education. Since 1983, federal officials, governors, business leaders, politicians and others have joined with educators to raise critical questions about the results of education and to suggest ways to bring about "quality" and "excellence" in teaching and learning. As Ernest Boyer points out, "This is a school reform movement, in short, driven by political and economic interest, not by educational and human ones."[2]

The discussion thus far points out two factors which help define the context in which this chapter will discuss the education of American Indians. [3] First, the formal education of American Indians takes place in schools—institutions that are not part of the Indian culture. Furthermore, formal education uses teaching and learning methods different from traditional means used by Indians. This will not change. Even tribal or Indian-controlled educational efforts are housed in schools.

Second, numerous outside factors influence formal education, helping to shape what goes on in schools. Political, economic and social conditions provide a mixture of forces, multidimensional in nature, that make education a complex and confusing process in our country. As we will see below, this is especially so for American Indians because of the special relationship they have with the federal government, which means that the federal government plays the dominant role in their education.

There is a third factor that is important in understanding the education of American Indians. American Indians represent less than 1 percent of the total United States population. There are more blacks, more Hispanics, and more Asians in this country. Numbers are critical in a democratic system where votes and political pressure often dictate attention and the allocation of resources. Not only are American Indians few in number, but there is great diversity with approximately three hundred different tribes, each with its own cultural identity. At times this diversity prevents unity among American Indians.

The purpose of the chapter is to discuss the education of American Indians from a broad perspective in order to present and discuss information that will give a greater understanding to the complex nature of Indian education. First, some observations based on an analysis of the history of Indian education will be presented. Then, the current status of American Indian education will be discussed. Next, a sampling of population, economic and social data will be presented and discussed in light of selected key issues in the education of American Indians. Finally, the future of Indian education will be presented in an attempt to show the importance of educational equity in the achievement of social justice.

## An Analysis of the History of Indian Education

The history of the formal education of American Indians in the United States has been described as "a national tragedy—a national challenge."[4] The intent here is not to provide a detailed history of the education of American Indians,[5] but rather a number of key observations based on an analysis of the history. This will provide the context in which the rest of the chapter will be developed.

A first observation is that formal education was recognized and used early in the history of this country as the means to change the American Indian. Once the idea of extinction was ruled out, the federal government turned to a policy of "civilizing" and Christianizing the American Indian. The teaching of reading and writing, combined with religious instruction, became the practice in education. Schools, including boarding schools, emerged as the institution that would implement this policy. To this day, formal education is viewed as an important ingredient in resolving the economic, social, health and political problems confronting American Indians.

It must also be noted that assimilation, either forced, through persuasion, or self-directed, has been the dominant and consistent foundation on which educational policy and practice have been realized for American Indians. Regardless of the federal policy toward American Indians, be it treatymaking, removal, reform, termination or self-determination, assimilation has been central to educational practice. The boarding schools of the nineteenth century practiced forced assimilation by taking Indian students from their families and tribal environments and transporting them great distances to institutions that de-emphasized "Indianness," utilizing training programs based on learning individualism, sedentary farming, and reading and writing in English.

The reforms in the federal-Indian relationship of the 1930s, spurred by the Meriam Report in 1928,[6] also changed American Indian education. Foremost was a change in educational practice. Day schools instead of boarding schools were emphasized. Bilingual-bicultural approaches were employed. Nevertheless, assimilation continued to be part of the policy, except it was viewed in a more humanistic perspective. Today, the federal policy toward American Indians is one of self-determination. Assimilation continues to be present in our educational approaches, only now American Indian people are somewhat in control of the educational process.

It is clear that the education of American Indians does not take place in isolation, but is dependent on the larger political, social and economic conditions of the United States. For example, the acquisition of land by non-Indians was the primary force behind the federal policies of treatymaking, removal and termination. Education was viewed as a way to facilitate the acceptance of relinquishing land, accepting individual ownership, and assimilating into the mainstream society.

As mentioned earlier, American Indian education has strong ties to the federal government. This connection is based on the special relationship established during the treaty period from 1778 to 1871. Approximately four hundred treaties were entered into between the U.S. government and Indian nations. One hundred twenty of these treaties had provisions that specifically mentioned education.[7] Since the end of treatingmaking in 1871, numerous congressional acts, Supreme Court decisions and executive orders have solidified this special relationship and provided the legal basis for federal responsibility and involvement in the education of Indian people.

This special relationship means that the federal government has played a dominant role in the education of Indian people, especially those individuals who are federally recognized as tribal members and those who reside on or near reservations. What it also means is that, in general, Indian people look toward the federal government to provide educational services, often to the extent of becoming overly dependent. However, this special relationship has also resulted in a high level of political savvy and sophistication about the federal government. Indian people have become quite knowledgeable and effective in lobbying federal agencies, including Congress.

As we will see later, the number of American Indian students who attend public schools continues to increase yearly; today over 80 percent of Indian students attend public schools. Actually, the policy of having Indian students attend public schools goes back to the 1890s, when the federal government passed legislation subsidizing public schools to educate Indian students. The legislation provided the

> authority [for] the policy of integrating Indians into the white culture, thus establishing the goal of assimilation and the public schools as the vehicle for attaining that goal. It established the precedent of providing subsidies to public schools in order to get them to assume responsibility for Indian education. The Federal subsidy was necessary, both because there was a reluctance on the part of Indians to enter the schools and because the school district was reluctant to assume the extra costs (in many cases the Indian students lived on nontaxable trust land) and problems anticipated with Indian students. The subsidy was, in effect, an inducement which the State or school district was almost always willing to take in exchange for providing a chair and a desk in a classroom for an Indian.[8]

The Johnson-O'Malley Act of 1934[9] further subsidized public education by authorizing the Bureau of Indian Affairs (BIA) to contract with states to provide funds to educate American Indians. In 1950, Congress passed P.L. 81-815 and P.L. 81-874, known as federal impact laws. Although the laws were intended to provide funds to public schools to educate students who lived in areas that felt the impact of federal programs, primarily military bases, American Indian students were included when amendments to the laws were enacted. These laws were viewed as a means of providing payments in lieu of taxes for students living on federal land, including reservations. A fourth piece of legislation that provides federal funds to public schools to educate American Indians is the Indian Education Act of 1972, Title IV of P.L. 92-318, as amended. Title IV, as it is known, provides funds on an entitlement basis to public schools to develop and operate supplemental programs to meet the special educational and culturally related academic needs of Indian students. Title IV was amended in 1988 by P.L. 100-297, which changed the law in a number of ways by, among other things, allowing BIA schools to receive Title IV funding, and creating gifted and talented centers to serve American Indians.

Federal subsidies clearly have been successful as an incentive for public schools to educate Indian students, so successful that the federal government is questioning its role of providing elementary and secondary schools through the BIA. Whether the BIA will continue to operate a national school system is subject to debate. The BIA proposed, in a 1988 initiative, to "localize the administration of BIA elementary and secondary schools by contracting management to tribes under P.L. 93-638 or to states if the tribes opt not to contract."[10] This of course met strong opposition, especially from Indian tribes. The result has been an effective lobbying effort in a supportive Congress which included in P.L. 100-297 a mandate prohibiting the BIA from terminating, contracting or transferring any BIA school without approval from the appropriate tribal governing body.

There have been a limited number of national studies on the status of Indian education in this country. The Meriam Report is recognized as the first major assessment of the economic, social and educational conditions of the American Indian.[11] The Brophy Report[12] followed in 1966, the Kennedy Report[13] in 1969, the Havighurst Report[14] in 1971, and the report of the American Indian Policy Review Commission[15] in 1976. Although each study would have to be treated separately to ascertain its full focus and treatment of Indian education, it can be said, in general terms, that the condition of Indian education in this country is poor. The Kennedy Report termed both BIA and public school education a "national tragedy."[16] Numerous recommendations emerged from these reports that addressed virtually every aspect of education, e.g., teachers and teaching practices, curriculum, funding, Indian control, bilingual-bicultural education, boarding schools and parental involvement.

There have also been numerous studies of individual programs; most have been evaluative in nature and conducted at the request of Congress. The Title IV programs are an example. Virtually every program authorized in the Indian Education Act has been evaluated. The problem with these efforts is that they often are politically motivated and address how services are delivered and how funds are allocated, rather than focusing on teaching and learning questions. As such, research in Indian education has been very limited, although there appears to be more interest in these questions recently.

Lack of parental involvement also has been a concern throughout the history of Indian education. The national studies mentioned above acknowledged this problem and recommended that more parents be involved in the education of their children. Title IV mandated parental involvement through a parent committee that would actively participate in the operation of the program. Even with this mandate and other similar efforts, parental involvement continues to be a concern today.

Fortunately, the leadership in Indian education has changed in recent years. Prior to the 1960s and 1970s, the leadership was primarily non-Indian, and decisions were made with little or no involvement from Indian people. The policy of self-determination and the opportunities associated with the Great Society programs in the 1960s resulted in Indian people assuming positions of leadership in Indian education programs at national, state and local levels. However, the bureaucratic structures, especially at the national level, have continued to impede efforts to provide effective leadership to improve the status of Indian education. For example, during the Reagan administration the two top-level jobs in Indian education at the federal level, one in the BIA and the other in the Department of Education, were held by individuals functioning in acting capacities. It was not until 1987 that Indian individuals were selected on a permanent basis to fill these positions.

A final observation based on the history of Indian education is that awareness, interest and concern about the education of Indian people, from a national perspective, seems to be diminishing as the world shrinks during the information age. The education of American Indians appears to be forgotten and insignificant in the larger scheme of things. The recent national reform movement in education is a good example. Since 1983, when *A Nation at Risk*[17] was released, virtually every major professional organization concerned about education has released its own version of what constitutes "excellence and quality" in education. And while governors, federal bureaucrats, business leaders, religious groups and others have joined educators to suggest ways to improve the educational system in our country, a recent review of fourteen reform documents found only one reference to the education of American Indians, the *American Indian/Alaska Native Concerns Study Committee*. Moreover, this reference was only part of a larger report, . . . *And Justice for All*,[18] published by the National Education Association. The failure to consider the educational concerns of American Indians in the findings and recommendations of these reports is even more surprising given the numbers of at-risk American Indian youth. When specific minority groups are mentioned, the focus is primarily on Hispanics or blacks, or even Asians, with American Indians too often grouped under the "other" category.[19]

**The Education of American Indians Today**

There are over 360,000 American Indians attending elementary and secondary schools today.[20] As Table 1 shows, 82 percent of the total attended public schools in 1987. The number of Indian students in public schools continues to increase, while the number of students in BIA schools has decreased by 8,680 students since 1978.[21]

TABLE 1

STUDENT ENROLLMENT BY TYPE OF SCHOOL, 1978 AND 1987

| Type of School | 1978 | Percent | 1987 | Percent |
|---|---|---|---|---|
| Public Schools | 215,000 | 78 | 298,107 | 82 |
| Bureau of Indian Affairs | 47,000 | 17 | 28,810 | 8 |
| Contract or Tribal Schools | 2,500 | 1 | 11,180 | 3 |
| Mission/Private | 9,000 | 3 | 25,448 | 7 |

Sources: Robert J. Havighurst, "Indian Education: Accomplishments of the Last Decade," *Phi Delta Kappan* 62: 5 (January 1981): 329; and Bureau of Indian Affairs, *United States Department of the Interior Budget Justification, FY 1988* (Washington, D.C.: Bureau of Indian Affairs, 1988).

In 1987, the BIA operated 57 boarding schools, 57 day schools, and 14 dormitories where students attended public schools. In addition, the BIA provided funds to support 58 tribal or contract schools. The U.S. Department of Education reported that in 1980 there were 305,730 American Indians attending school; this represented 0.8 percent of the total public elementary and secondary school enrollment for the country. Blacks had the largest minority enrollment with 16.1 percent; Hispanics followed with 8 percent and Asians with 1.9 percent of the minority enrollment.[22]

There were approximately 90,000 American Indians attending colleges and universities in 1986, compared to 76,000 in 1976. Included in the 90,000 are 5,000 Indian students at the graduate level and 1,000 attending professional schools. The majority of American Indians, 56.2 percent, attend public or private two-year institutions.[23] There are 20 tribally controlled community colleges that enroll approximately 4,000 students.[24]

Even though a majority of American Indian students attend local public schools, the federal government continues to play a dominant role in their education. The BIA, housed in the Department of the Interior, and the Department of Education are the two executive branch agencies responsible for the education of American Indians. The BIA has provided educational services since 1870. Currently the BIA operates a national school system, a Johnson-O'Malley program that provides supplemental support for eligible Indian students attending public schools, and a higher education program that includes support for adult education, three postsecondary schools, tribally controlled community colleges, and a higher education grant program for individual students.

The Department of Education administers a number of programs that benefit American Indians, the most important of which are the programs mandated by the Indian Education Act of 1972. Title IV, as it is commonly known, provides support to public schools, BIA schools, Indian-controlled schools, tribes, Indian organizations, Indian institutions, institutions of higher education, and fellowships to individuals. Impact aid, bilingual education programs, Chapter 1 programs, and vocational and adult education are among other Department of Education programs that benefit American Indian people.

The condition of Indian education today can be demonstrated with selected data:

- 16.2 percent of American Indians, 25 years old and over, living on reservations have completed less than five years of school. The percentage is even higher, 37.4, for the Navajo.[25]

- Fifty-six percent of American Indians, 25 years old and over, are high school graduates. The percentage for the total U.S. population is 66 percent. The percentage decreases to 43.2 percent when considering only reservation Indians.[26]

- Eight percent of American Indians had four or more years of college, compared to 16 percent of the total population.[27]

- The dropout rate for 1980 high school sophomores was 29.2 percent for American Indian and Alaskan natives, compared to 13.6 for the general public. The dropout rate for Hispanics was 18, for blacks it was 17, for whites it was 12.2, and for Asian Americans it was 3.1.[28]

- Among American Indians, the college dropout rate ranged from 45 percent to 62 percent.[29]

A recent survey of a national sample of Indian educators attempted to gain some understanding about their thinking concerning the current status of Indian education. The survey was similar to the Gallup Poll on the public's attitudes toward the public schools that is conducted each year.[30] Respondents were asked the following question: "Would you say that the education of American Indians, from a national point of view, has improved, gotten worse, or stayed the same during the past five years?"

Thirty-five percent indicated that the education of American Indians had improved over the past five years, 33.3 percent said it had gotten worse, 28.1 percent said it had remained the same, and 3.5 percent did not know. The same question was asked from a state point of view. Again, 35.1 percent indicated the education of American Indians had improved at their state level, 22.8 percent said it had gotten worse, 36.8 percent said it had stayed the same, and 5.3 percent did not know.[31]

It was also asked, "How has Indian education fared under the Reagan administration?" Seventy percent said that Indian education had fared "poorly" under the Reagan administration, 14 percent indicated "fair," 12.3 percent said "no change," and 3.5 percent said "good." The results are not surprising given that the education of American Indians is tied to the federal government. The respondents were more critical of the Reagan administration than of what was going on in general nationally, or in their states.[32]

### Population Data

Population figures for American Indians differ according to who is doing the counting and the definition of "Indian." For example, two common sources of population data are the BIA and the Bureau of the Census, but both reflect different counts based on dissimilar ways of defining American Indians. The BIA estimated it provided services to 755,201 American Indians in 1983. The BIA's definition of Indian includes those from one of the 291 federally recognized tribes or 197 Alaskan village communities.[33] Urban Indians are generally not included in the BIA count.[34]

On the other hand, the Bureau of the Census uses self-identification to identify American Indians. The 1980 census reported 1,366,676 American Indians in the United States.[35] An additional 56,367 Eskimos and Aleuts, located primarily in Alaska, were also included in the 1980 census. Although the total figure of 1,423,043 represented less than 1 percent of the total U.S. population of 226,545,805, it is still a 72 percent increase over the 1970 census figure. The rapid growth in ten years is due in part to a high birthrate, but is also attributable to the Census Bureau's improved methods of counting American Indians. Even with this increase, many tribes feel their population figures are higher; there are some estimates of two million American Indians in this country. Also, because American Indians are a relatively young population, with a median age of 22.9 compared to the total U.S. median age of 30.0,[36] an even larger potential for growth exists.

TABLE 2

AMERICAN INDIAN POPULATION BY YEAR

| Census Year | Population | Percent Increase From Previous Decade | States With Largest Population—Ranked |
|---|---|---|---|
| 1980 | 1,366,679 | 72.4 | Cal., Okla., Ariz., N.M., N.Car. |
| 1970 | 792,730 | 51.4 | Okla., Ariz., Cal., N.M., N.Car. |
| 1960 | 523,591 | 46.5 | Ariz., Okla., N.M., Cal., N.Car. |

Sources: U.S. Bureau of the Census, *Census of the Population: 1980*, Supplementary Report PC80-S1-13, "American Indian Areas and Alaskan Native Villages: 1980" (Washington, D.C.: U.S. Government Printing Office, 1984), Table A, p. 2, and Table 1, p. 14; U.S. Bureau of the Census, *Census of Population: 1970*, Subject Reports, Final Report PC(2)-1F, "American Indians" (Washington, D.C.: U.S. Government Printing Office, 1973), Table II, p. xi; and U.S. Bureau of the Census, *Census of Population: 1960*, Subject Reports, Final Report PC(2)-1C, "Nonwhite Population by Race" (Washington, D.C.: U.S. Government Printing Office, 1963), Table 10, pp. 12-15.

As Table 2 also reports, California had more American Indians than any other state in 1980. Five states, California (198,275), Oklahoma (169,292), Arizona (152,498), New Mexico (107,338) and North Carolina (64,536) accounted for 50.6 percent of the total Indian population.[37]

The 1980 census identified 278 federal and state reservations, with eleven states containing five or more reservations. One-fourth of all American Indians (339,836) lived on reservations, with Arizona having the largest reservation population (113,763), followed by New Mexico (61,876). It is interesting to note that non-Indians make up about 51 percent of the total reservation population in the United States. The Navajo have the largest reservation; they also have the largest population (104,978).[38]

Five metropolitan areas were identified as having an Indian population of 20,000 or more. They are the Los Angeles-Long Beach, California area with 48,158; Tulsa, Oklahoma with 38,498; Oklahoma City, Oklahoma with 24,752; Phoenix, Arizona with 22,900; and Albuquerque, New Mexico with 20,788.[39]

The 1980 census also identified American Indians in the historic areas of Oklahoma, excluding urban areas. These include areas which were reservations during the period from 1900 to 1907. A total of 121,108 Indians lived in this area, including those on the Osage Reservation.[40]

*Economic Data*

The 1980 census reported the unemployment rate for American Indians was twice that of the total U.S. population; 13.0 and 6.5 percent respectively. (The 1970 rates were 11.1 percent for American Indians and 4.4 for the general population.) The median family income for American Indian families in 1980 was $13,678; for Eskimo families, $13,829; and for Aleut families, $20,313. On the Navajo reservation the median family income in 1979 was $8,397. These figures compare to the national median family income of $19,917. The poverty rate for American Indians was 27.5 percent compared to 12.4 percent for the total U.S. population. The poverty rate for individuals on the Rosebud and Navajo reservations was 51.4 and 52.4 percent respectively.[41]

As noted above, the economic situation on reservations is much worse. A recent investigation by the *Arizona Republic* newspaper found that

> Indian reservations still lead the nation in indicators of despair. For example, it's not uncommon for a reservation's unemployment rate to exceed 80 percent. On many reservations, the only Indians with jobs are those who work for the tribe or the federal government.

> The Indian unemployment rate, the highest for any minority in America, is decried by U.S. Senators familiar with Indian issues. Sen. Daniel Inouye, D-Hawaii, chairman of the Senate Select Committee on Indian Affairs, calls unemployment on reservations a "national disgrace." Sen. John McCain, R-Ariz., compares economic conditions on Indian reservations to those in Third World countries: "The employment that there is—and this is why the statistics lie so much—is provided by the federal government or by the tribal governments themselves. There is no economic enterprise to provide meaningful jobs which make people move up on the economic ladder."[42]

As part of their investigative study, the *Arizona Republic* asked a national sample of 450 American Indians a series of questions. As the results in Table 3 indicate, unemployment was considered the second greatest problem facing Indians today. Moreover, additional questions revealed that 39 percent of the sample felt that, socially and economically, Indians are in about the same condition as they were ten years ago. Nearly 30 percent felt Indians were worse off than they were ten years ago.[43]

TABLE 3
WHAT IS THE GREATEST PROBLEM FACING INDIANS TODAY? (N = 450)

| Problem | Total Percent |
| --- | --- |
| Alcohol/Drug Abuse | 43.3 |
| Unemployment | 36.0 |
| Education | 16.4 |
| Cultural Loss | 14.9 |
| Termination/Sovereignty Threats | 10.9 |
| Health Care | 10.4 |
| Housing | 6.0 |
| Teen Pregnancy | 1.8 |
| Suicide | 1.8 |
| Other Problems | 3.6 |
| All of the Above | 12.2 |

Source: "Fraud in Indian Country: A Billion-Dollar Betrayal," *The Arizona Republic*
(October 11, 1987).

*Social Data*

The 1980 census presented some interesting social data.[44] For example,
55.8 percent of the housing units on reservations with an American Indian, Eskimo or Aleut householder or spouse had no telephone. An
amazing 87.3 percent of the housing units on the Papago Reservation
in Arizona had no phone, as well as 83.4 percent of the homes on the
San Carlos Apache Reservation in Arizona. Other data concerning
housing units on reservations included:

- 15.9 percent of the housing units were without electric lighting.
  The percentage was 47.1 on the Hopi reservation.

- 16.6 percent did not have a refrigerator. The percentage was 46.9
  on the Navajo reservation.

- 20.8 percent had an outhouse or privy. The percentage was 55.5
  on the Hopi and 53.5 on the Papago reservations.

- 38.8 percent had more than 1.01 persons per room. The percentage was 65 for the Navajo and 58.8 for the Hopi reservations.

As Table 3 indicates, one could go on to discuss alcohol and drug
abuse, health care, housing, teen pregnancy, suicide, or any other social, economic or political indicator. Chances are the data would
present a picture similar to the one shown above. American Indians are
at the bottom, with those living on reservations at the very bottom.
But rather than discussing these areas, our attention here is on education. Education is seen as a critical area and often identified as the

means to change the kind of bleak economic and social conditions cited here.

The education of American Indians is complex and difficult to understand given the diversity in tribes, the state and tribal approaches to education, and the different federal programs that benefit Indian students. It is hard to specifically identify critical issues, since there are so many concerns in Indian education, tending to vary in importance from state to state, tribe to tribe, community to community, and/or school to school. There are issues associated with teaching and learning, characteristics of successful students, testing, control and governance, funding, research, higher education and leadership. The discussion here will be limited to the issues of responsibility for Indian education, teaching Indian students, education on and off reservations, and higher education.

### Responsibility for Indian Education

Who has responsibility for the education of American Indians? Is it the federal government or the states? Or, is there a shared responsibility? In 1976 the American Indian Policy Review Commission (AIPRC) reported that state departments of education were asked two questions: What is the state's role in the education of Indian children? And, what is the federal government's role in the education of Indian children? The responses to these questions were:

> The overwhelming majority of those states responding to the question concerning the state's role in the education of Indian children indicated that the state's role was no different for Indian children than for all other children. In a typical reply, the respondent from Colorado said, "The state has the same responsibility for Indian children as any other child."

> In regard to the question concerning the Federal Government's role in the education of Indian children, nearly all respondents indicated that they viewed the Federal Government only as a funding agency.[45]

The Education Commission of the States, in discussing the involvement and relationships between federal, state and tribal governments, reported that conflict does exist:

> For instance, state laws and regulations often clash with federal directives and sometimes prevent either entity from effectively serving Indian children. Conflict and confusion, moreover, sometimes arise from how the various entities—the federal government, the state and the tribe—define who is an Indian. Determin-

ing who qualifies as an Indian raises questions of program duplication, program eligibility, fiscal entitlement and program accountability. Local school districts sometimes find it very difficult to determine what funding they are entitled to. Many of them also do not apply for funding that could aid Indian children, simply because they do not believe that the paper work and consultation with Indian parent committees are worth the amount of added funding they would receive.[46]

In spite of the conflict and the strong tie to the federal government, there is increasing evidence that the states are assuming more responsibility, at least in practice, in the education of Indian students:

- The number of BIA students and schools have decreased significantly over the past ten years.

- Over 80 percent of the Indian students in schools are enrolled in public schools.

- The BIA continues to promote public education and recently proposed that their schools be turned over to tribes or to the states.

- In 1978 Congress mandated that the BIA develop and implement educational standards for their schools. The states in which BIA schools are located directly or indirectly influence the standards since teachers and academic programs have to be certified at the state level.

- State departments of education have become very active in the education of Indian students. Arizona, Oregon, New Mexico, Wyoming, Washington, Oklahoma, Michigan, Montana, California, North Dakota, South Dakota, Utah, North Carolina, Wisconsin and Minnesota all have very active units at the state level.

- During its tenure, the Reagan administration placed emphasis on states' rights, including an increased role at the state level and a decreased role at the federal level.

- Finally, the national reform movement in education has brought attention to education with specific actions which have taken place in state legislatures around the country. Focus has been on the states and their plans to address quality and excellence in education.

A related concern is the future of BIA education. This could be discussed as a separate issue, but because state public school systems stand to gain Indian students, it is presented here as part of the federal-state responsibility debate.

As has already been noted, the BIA proposed, as a 1988 initiative, transferring all BIA schools to local public school districts if tribes did not take over their operation. The BIA's proposal stems from the substandard education received in its schools and the feeling that Indian students would be better served in public schools.

There was a tremendous amount of opposition from tribes, Indian educators and others to the BIA's proposal. Several reasons were given against the transfer. First, the transfer of BIA education to public schools or even to tribes would violate the federal government's trust responsibility for Indian education. Second, the BIA did not consult with the tribes about the proposed transfer of schools. Third, the proposed transfer would place the tribes in a difficult position of assuming control of BIA schools before they were ready and with no assurance that tribes already had or would receive adequate resources to operate the schools. Finally, the BIA offered no evidence that Indian students would actually do better in public or tribal schools. Furthermore, there was no assurance that parents or tribal leaders would have any say in how their students were educated in public schools.[47]

The concern about the transfer resulted in a provision in P.L. 100-297 noted earlier, prohibiting the BIA from transferring the operation of any BIA-funded school or substantially curtailing any program at such a school without permission of the appropriate tribal governing body. Thus, Congress has stopped the transfer of BIA schools to public schools for the moment.

However, in April 1988 the BIA released its *Report on BIA Education: Excellence in Indian Education Through the Effective School Process.*[48] The document was a result of a request by Congress in the 1987 appropriations process for a comprehensive education plan (CEP) from the BIA. The report was billed as a new effort to prepare a CEP, but was not called a CEP "because it does not attempt to plan comprehensively or answer all the future questions that may be important to the future of Indian students attending BIA schools."[49] Rather, the report provided information and presented options for review in order to facilitate the resolution of these broader issues.

There are three main sections to the report. The first section addressed the current condition of BIA education. In the second section, the BIA proposed to improve their schools by implementing the characteristics of "effective" schools. The "effective school" movement is based on research, some conducted with American Indians, identifying the key characteristics that work in schools, e.g., high expectations of students, a clear sense of mission and purpose, strong leadership at the level of the school principal, emphasis on learning the basic skills, holding students academically accountable, providing a safe and orderly learning environment, and involving parents and the local community in the educational process. The third area of the report presented five possible alternatives for the future of BIA education. They were:

- Replacing BIA-administered education with tribal systems of education.
- Transferring BIA schools to public school districts.
- Individually-contracted BIA schools.
- Individual education vouchers.
- A revitalized BIA education system.

A recent survey of Indian educators asked the question, "Should the Bureau of Indian Affairs turn over its education function to the tribes and states?" Fifty percent of the sample said "yes" and 50 percent said "no." [50] Given these mixed opinions, a reasonable approach, supported by many tribes, might be that the BIA remain in the education business by revitalizing its system and moving toward a gradual process of providing adequate resources for tribes to assume control of BIA schools. The key factor is a legal concern as to the federal trust responsibility for Indian education. The BIA is viewed as the federal agency that has the trust responsibility for Indian education. Unless there are guaranteed assurances that the trust responsibility for education will transfer to other agencies, especially public schools, there is no chance that tribes will support the elimination of BIA education.

Thus, responsibility for Indian education remains a difficult and confusing issue. It remains a shared responsibility, with over 80 percent of all Indian students attending public elementary and secondary schools, and with the federal government providing supplemental funds to public education while simultaneously operating a national BIA school system. It appears this shared responsibility will continue indefinitely because Indian tribes and other constituencies will likely resist any efforts by the federal government to relinquish its legal responsibility for the education of Indian people.

### Teaching Indian Students: A Conflict in Values and Approaches

A criticism throughout the history of Indian education has been that the education Indian students receive is not relevant or does not meet their needs. Teachers, methods of teaching, curriculum and materials, school types, student achievement and parental involvement have all been subject to criticism within this context.

As noted earlier, a central issue is how education is defined, operationalized and used in our society. Formal education in schools, with a set curriculum and a teacher in charge, was foreign to the way American Indians learned prior to European contact. However, the educational system and its formal approach were recognized early in the history of this country as the means to change the American Indian—to assimilate the Indian into the white man's way of living.

The issues of relevancy and need are generally focused in areas of culture, including language, and academics, usually basic skills development. These two areas are closely related, but have not always been used together to promote learning. Prior to the 1930s and during the 1940s and 1950s, the culture of American Indians was viewed as an impediment to assimilation via education. The practice in schools was neither to recognize nor use the culture and language of American Indians in the learning process. In fact, both their culture and language were openly degraded and considered inferior, causing Indian students to feel ashamed of their heritage.

From the 1930s until the start of World War II, and again from the 1960s to the present, the culture and language of American Indians have received some recognition and respect in the schools. However, since the degree of recognition and respect varies according to time, place and, often, individual leadership, the acknowledged importance of American Indian culture and language in the learning process has not been consistent.

Today there are opposite forces working, each gaining momentum, that will help determine what happens in the future. First, the recent educational reform movement in the United States has focused on academic achievement, higher standards, testing, and common standardized approaches to solving educational problems. Reform has not emphasized individual and group differences. This is especially true for the American Indian, who for various reasons has not been recogized by a vast majority of the reform reports. Yet, American Indians are affected by what is happening. Indian educators were recently asked, "What impact has this national reform movement had on the education of American Indians?" They responded as follows: 14.3 percent said there was "no impact"; 30.4 percent said "little impact"; 33.9 percent indicated "some impact"; 14.3 percent said "significant impact"; and 7.1 percent did not know.[51]

The high response level for "no impact" and "little impact" may reflect the fact that the education of American Indians has received little attention in the reform reports, as well as the feeling that the education of Indian students takes place in isolation from education in general in this country. Regardless, the educational reform movement is making its presence felt in Indian education. An example is the change in focus of Title IV, Indian Education Act programs. Like education in general, Title IV has shifted its focus from cultural areas to academics, usually the basic skills, with emphasis on student achievement and program accountability.

On the other hand, Vera John,[52] Susan Philips,[53] Arthur More[54] and Karen Swisher and Donna Deyhle[55] have all shown that the culture of American Indians affects how they learn in our schools. According to these studies, many American Indian students prefer learning styles that are different from the way most educators usually teach students in our society.

What does all of this mean? Surprisingly, it is not commonly accepted that culture and language make a difference in how students learn. In fact, there appears to be a belief among some educators that students are students and should be treated the same regardless of cultural background. Only in areas where there are large numbers of American Indian students, or where individual educators of Indian students promote different learning and teaching styles, is it likely that the pedagogical approach will be culturally sensitive. Otherwise, American Indian students continue to experience difficulties with the educational process.

### Reservation vs. Off-Reservation Education

Is there a difference between the type of education American Indian students receive on reservations compared to that received off reservations?[56] If so, what is the difference? In general terms, key differences between reservation and off-reservation schools are:

- Reservation schools tend to have a higher percentage of Indian students in the student body of each school. They are thus very visible. In many of the off-reservation schools, especially those in urban areas, this is not the case. Indian students are often a numerical minority, lost in the crowd, and recognized only by supplemental programs like Title IV, Chapter I, or bilingual education.

- Reservation schools tend to serve a more homogeneous group of Indian students, usually from one tribe, that are more likely to speak their tribal language and practice their tribal culture. Off-reservation schools, on the other hand, are more likely to serve students from many tribes, a large number of whom will have limited knowledge and involvement in their tribal language and culture.

- The above has important implications for teaching and learning. Contract or tribal schools, as alternatives to BIA, public and mission education, are more likely to emphasize tribal language and culture in the educational process. This is also true for a number of public and BIA schools that are on reservations.

- Reservations will likely have four systems of education—BIA schools, contract or tribal schools, public schools and mission schools—operating near one another. Off-reservation areas will also have a mixture of public and private schools, but not including BIA schools and contract or tribal schools.

- Reservation schools will generally have a closer tie to the tribe and federal government. Tribal activities in education are more likely to influence reservation schools. The presence of the federal government is felt more in the total operation of the school, especially in BIA and contract or tribal schools, than in public schools, although public schools on reservations also feel the federal government's presence, especially in funding.

- Reservation schools also tend to have a stronger relationship with the parents and community being served. In all reservation schools, it is more likely to find American Indians serving on school boards and other institutional means for parental involvement, e.g., PTAs, parent committees, etc., than in off-reservation schools.

The above differences have an impact on the kind of education that is delivered and the perceptions or attitudes about the quality of education on and off the reservation. There appears to be a prevailing attitude that the quality of education on the reservation is not as good as education off the reservation. There are a number of factors that contribute to this thinking:

- The economic, social and health conditions on reservations are in a depressed state. In such situations education is, first, lower in priority for both tribal governments and individuals and, second, required to cope with economic, social and health situations that affect student learning.

- For a variety of reasons, it is difficult for the schools on reservations to recruit and retain effective teachers, administrators and other school professionals; to construct and maintain school facilities; and to obtain the necessary funds to support high-cost items associated with reservation education.

- Since Indians are so visible in schools on reservations, their educational problems may be magnified. It may not be that off-reservation schools, especially urban schools, are doing a better job; it might just be that Indians are almost invisible because of their low numbers. Or it may be that many Indian students who attend off-reservation schools are so much more assimilated or further from their culture that they are doing better in American schools.

A 1985 evaluation of Indian-controlled schools found that on the average, eighth-grade students in Indian-controlled schools were not scoring as well on achievement tests in reading and math as were students in public and BIA schools.[57] Also, twelfth-grade students in Indian-controlled schools scored better in reading, math and science than twelfth graders in BIA schools, but not as well as twelfth graders in public schools. According to the author of the evaluation, the findings were not surprising to representatives of Indian-controlled schools, who faulted the test design for comparing achievement test scores. They would have preferred a longitudinal study comparing current and past student performances.[58]

From the perspective of integrating tribal language and culture into the curriculum and treating them as strengths in the learning process, certain reservation schools are probably doing a better job of educating Indian students. Bicultural-bilingual education is practiced more in contract or tribal schools than in BIA, public or mission schools.

It is clear that the education of Indian students differs according to whether it occurs on or off reservation. However, the situations are very complex and gross generalizations should be avoided. In any event, both reservation and off-reservation schools have many concerns which make educational goals difficult to achieve.

### American Indians and Higher Education

Are American Indians attending schools of higher education and obtaining degrees? In what fields? Are colleges and universities preparing more American Indian teachers, school administrators and counselors?

A study by the Center for Education Statistics reported two trends that should result in more American Indians enrolling in colleges and universities. First, the number of Indians between the ages of eighteen and twenty-four, considered college age, more than doubled from 1970 to 1980. And second, the percentage of American Indians who graduated from high school increased from 51 percent in 1970 to 60 percent in 1980.[59]

The number of American Indians in undergraduate education increased to 88,000 in 1982, compared to 76,000 in 1976. However, the number decreased by 5.7 percent to 83,000 in 1984.[60] A recent study by the U.S. Department of Education reported that there were 84,000 American Indians in undergraduate school in 1986.[61] Most of these students, 86.6 percent in 1984, were enrolled in public colleges and universities; the remainder (13.4 percent) attended private schools. Among those in two-year institutions, more Indians were enrolled in public institutions—52.7 percent in 1986.[62] Thirty percent of the American Indians who entered two-year colleges in 1983 later transferred to four-year institutions. In 1984, American Indians represented 0.7 percent of the total undergraduate enrollment, but only 0.3 percent of the total graduate enrollment, meaning a cumulative loss of American Indians as they advanced through the educational pipeline.[63]

In 1976, more American Indians (23.1 percent) received bachelor's degrees in education than in any other field. By 1984 the emphasis had shifted, with science and technology (26.6 percent of the degrees) and business (24.9 percent) leading all other fields; only 14.2 percent of the degress were in education.[64]

There is some cause for optimism when considering the above data. However, in reality, the dropout rate among American Indians in colleges and universities is extremely high. A major issue for many institutions is the retention of those Indian students who have been admitted.

Of particular concern is the number of American Indians preparing to be educators. The number of American Indians receiving education degrees decreased from 765 in 1976 to 527 in 1984.[65] In addition, American Indians represent 0.9 percent of all the students in public schools, but only 0.6 percent of the teachers.[66] This gap can only widen if the number of Indian students continues to increase while the number of Indian teachers decreases.

Why are there not more American Indians entering teaching? When American Indians first started attending colleges and universities, it was common practice to major in education. After all, schools were very visible and represented opportunities for employment in home communities. During the 1960s and 1970s Indian education was criticized often, with teachers receiving part of the blame for the failure of Indian education. A way to improve Indian education was to train and employ more Indian teachers. Opportunities increased for American Indians to major in education. As the 1970s gave way to the 1980s, however, American Indians, like many other young people, looked toward other fields that provided more opportunity, more money, and a greater degree of respect and professionalism—namely, the fields of engineering and business.

There currently appears to be a renewed interest in education as a major. However, teacher education programs at colleges and universities and state certification requirements have changed over the past five years as a result of the national reform movement in education. Admission standards to teacher education programs have changed, becoming more rigid and dependent on the successful completion of mandatory competency exams like the Pre-Professional Skills Test (PPST) or the National Teachers Examination (NTE). An immediate result is that fewer minorities, including American Indians, have been admitted into teaching. A high failure rate among American Indians also discourages potential education majors before they have a chance to start. Many states also require the passing of mandatory competency exams before certification can be granted. American Indians, like blacks and Hispanics, pass at a much lower rate than whites, resulting in even fewer teachers.

This situation has received a lot of attention lately, with a number of research studies in progress analyzing why minorities are faring poorly on these standardized competency tests.[67] Also, colleges and universities are evaluating their set of admission criteria and their relevance to minority students.

## Future Direction

If history is an indicator, the quality of education that American Indians experience will continue to be fragmented, divisive and piecemeal in nature because of the complex differences in Indian education. At all levels, advocates of self-determination will focus on politics and the mechanics of control rather than on the teaching and learning process in the classroom. The BIA will continue to operate schools, facing criticism about the way they educate students, but receiving support when the concept of federal trust responsibility for education is threatened or challenged, as with proposals for the elimination of BIA education. Tribal schools will continue to provide an alternative approach that will focus on bilingual-bicultural education, but will be plagued by limited resources. Public education involvement and activity will increase as the enrollment of Indian students increases.

However, there are some trends that suggest or provide an opportunity for change. First, the national reform movement in education has recently focused attention on "at risk" or "disadvantaged" students. Since many American Indian students fall into these categories, one can be hopeful that greater emphasis will be placed on relevant and quality education for Indian students. A second trend is the promotion of early childhood education. Head Start programs work, and the federal government is being encouraged to increase their funding levels. The point is that the young, the very young, are the key to American

Indians achieving educational equity and social justice. Efforts to provide a meaningful and quality education, including a bicultural and/or bilingual approach, will return dividends in the long run.

The third area is the increasing recognition that education cannot function in isolation from society at large. Economic, social and political issues directly affect education and must be included in attempts to address problems. Schools must enter into partnerships with other institutions, agencies and various interest groups, in both the public and private sectors, to be effective in educating students. This is especially true for Indian education where there is a tendency, because of tribal and school differences or because of the special relationship with the federal government, to view education in isolation from various other public, private and tribal agencies.

As has been noted, states have been increasing their activity in Indian education during the past decade and will continue to do so in the future. In fact, the potential for greater state involvement is very real as the federal government, including the BIA, continues the policy of promoting public school education for Indian students. It is conceivable that the BIA, in its efforts to reduce its educational responsibility, will turn over schools to the tribes before many tribes are ready or have adequate resources to guarantee success. Without tribal readiness or sufficient resources, there is a danger that failure will occur in the process of tribes assuming control. In the long run, this may translate into state control of Indian education. The probability of this happening can be avoided if tribes deal with the federal government and increase their involvement with the states.

Another area that is likely to influence the future education of American Indians is research. Although there is not an abundance of research being conducted right now, educators and policymakers have a greater interest in both conducting and using research. There will continue to be evaluations, need assessments, feasibility studies and task force reports to justify budgets, program growth and legislative efforts. Together with research in teaching and learning, the quality of the classroom experience for Indian students should be enhanced.

There is reason to be cautiously optimistic about the future of Indian education in the United States, but it will take a broader approach. This approach should include a partnership among tribes, states, the federal government and other interest groups that will provide leadership and minimize politics while maximizing quality education for Indian students.

## NOTES

[1]A discussion about the role of education in our society is found in Daniel Selakovich, *Schooling in America* (New York: Longman, 1984). Of particular interest is the discussion about Marxism, class conflict theory and the structural functional approaches to educational research.

[2]Ernest Boyer, "How Not to Fix Schools," *Harper's* (February 1987): 39-51.

[3]The term "American Indian" includes American Indians, Eskimos, Aleuts, and other Alaska Natives.

[4]U.S. Senate, *Indian Education: A National Tragedy — A National Challenge*, Committee on Labor and Public Welfare, Special Subcommittee on Indian Education (Washington, D.C.: U.S. Government Printing Office, 1969).

[5]Detailed descriptive histories of Indian education can be found in the American Indian Policy Review Commission, *Report on Indian Education* (Washington, D.C.: U.S. Government Printing Office, 1976); U.S. Senate, op. cit. note 4; and Margaret Connell Szasz, *Education and the American Indian: The Road to Self-Determination Since 1928* (Albuquerque, NM: University of New Mexico Press, 1974).

[6]Lewis Meriam, technical director, et al., *The Problem of Indian Administration*, the Meriam Report (Baltimore, MD: Johns Hopkins Press, published for the Brookings Institution 1928), pp. 140-148.

[7]American Indian Policy Review Commission, op. cit. note 5, p. 30.

[8]U.S. Senate, op. cit. note 4, pp. 31-32.

[9]Johnson-O'Malley Act of 1934, 48 Stat. 596, April 16, 1934 (73rd Congress, 2nd Session).

[10]Bureau of Indian Affairs, *Indian News, Week-in-Review* (Washington, D.C.: Bureau of Indian Affairs, March 23, 1987).

[11]Meriam Report, op. cit. note 6.

[12]William A. Brophy and Sophie D. Aberle, *The Indian: America's Unfinished Business* (Norman, OK: University of Oklahoma Press, 1966).

[13]U.S. Senate, op. cit. note 4.

[14]Robert J. Havighurst, *The Education of Indian Children and Youth. Summary Report and Recommendation: National Study of American Indian Education. Series IV, No. 6* (Chicago, IL: University of Chicago, 1970).

[15]American Indian Policy Review Commission, op. cit. note 5.

[16]U.S. Senate, op. cit. note 4.

[17]U.S. National Commission on Excellence in Education, *A Nation at Risk: The Imperative for Educational Reform: A Report to the Nation and the Secretary of Education* (Washington, D.C.: The Commission, 1983).

[18]National Education Association, American Indian/Alaska Native Concerns Study Committee, . . . *And Justice For All: Report of the American Indian/Alaska Native Concerns Study Committee* (Washington, D.C.: National Education Association, 1987).

[19]John W. Tippeconnic III, *Education Reform Reports and the American Indian,* unpublished paper (1988).

[20]Robert J. Havighurst, "Indian Education: Accomplishments of the Last Decade," *Phi Delta Kappan* 62: 5 (January 1981): 329-331. The number of American Indians actually in school depends on what definition of Indian is used and who is doing the counting. There are some estimates of over 500,000 students in school. As indicated earlier, gathering accurate and consistent data continues to be a problem in assessments of American Indian education. The Bureau of Indian Affairs, the Department of Education, and the U.S. Census Bureau are sources of often conflicting data.

[21]Havighurst, ibid.

[22]Center for Education Statistics, *The Condition of Education* (Washington, D.C.: U.S. Government Printing Office, 1986).

[23]U.S. Department of Education, *Trends in Minority Enrollment in Higher Education* (Washington, D.C.: U.S. Department of Education, 1988), cited in "Minorities' Share of College Enrollments Edges Up, as Number of Asian and Hispanic Students Soars," *Chronicle of Higher Education* (March 9, 1988), pp. A33-A36.

[24]Bureau of Indian Affairs, *United States Department of the Interior Budget Justification, FY 1986* (Washington D.C.: Bureau of Indian Affairs, 1985).

[25]U.S. Bureau of the Census, *1980 Census of Population,* Subject Reports, Vol. 2, PC80-2-1D, Part 2, "American Indians, Eskimos, and Aleuts on Identified Reservations and in the Historic Areas of Oklahoma (Excluding Urbanized Areas)," (hereafter cited as *Census 1986*) (Washington, D.C.: U.S. Government Printing Office, 1986), Table 7, pp. 50, 54.

[26]Ibid., p. 50; and U.S. Bureau of the Census, *Statisical Abstract of the United States 1991,* (hereafter cited as *Statistical Abstract 1991*) (Washington, D.C.: U.S. Government Printing Office, 1990), Table 43, p. 38, and Table 44, p. 39.

[27]*Statistical Abstract 1991,* ibid.

[28]Center for Education Statistics, op. cit. note 22.

[29]Center for Education Statistics, *The American Indian in Higher Education, 1975-76 to 1984-85* (Washington, D.C.: U.S. Government Printing Office, 1987).

[30]Alec M. Gallup and David L. Clark, "The 19th Annual Gallup Poll of the Public's Attitudes Toward the Public Schools," *Phi Delta Kappan* 69: 1 (September 1987): 17-30.

[31]John W. Tippeconnic III, *Survey: Education of American Indians,* unpublished data (1988). Also, see John W. Tippeconnic III, "A Survey: Attitudes Toward the Education of American Indians," *Journal of American Indian Ed-*

*ucation* 28: 1 (October 1988): 34-36, for some of the major findings of the survey.

[32]Ibid.

[33]The Bureau of Indian Affairs, Bureau of the Census, and Department of Education have different definitions of "American Indian." The BIA's definition is that an individual must be a member of a tribe, band or group of Indians recognized by the federal government, and for some purposes, be of one-fourth or more Indian blood. The Census Bureau uses a self-identification method in counting American Indians. The Department of Education implements Title IV, the Indian Education Act of 1972. Title IV's definition is an individual who is a descendant, either in the first or second degree, of a member of an American Indian tribe. The definition of "American Indian" is a very political issue today, in part because resources, through eligibility requirements, are allocated according to the number of American Indians. However, it is recognized that tribes have the right to define conditions for their own tribal membership.

[34]Bureau of Indian Affairs, *American Indians: U.S. Indian Policy, Tribes and Reservation, BIA: Past and Present, Economic Development* (Washington, D.C.: U.S. Government Printing Office, 1984).

[35]U.S. Bureau of the Census, *1980 Census of Population*, Supplementary Report PC80-S1-13, "American Indian Areas and Alaska Native Villages: 1980," (hereafter cited as *Census 1984*) (Washington, D.C.: U.S. Government Printing, 1984), Table A, p. 2, and Table 1, p. 14; and U.S. Bureau of the Census, *Census of Population: 1970*, Subject Reports, Final Report PC(2)-1F, "American Indians" (Washington, D.C.: U.S. Government Printing Office, 1973), Table II, p. xi.

[36]Ibid.; *Statistical Abstract 1991*, op. cit. note 26, Table 22, p. 18.

[37]*Census 1984*, op. cit. note 35, p. 3.

[38]Ibid., Table L, p. 11.

[39]U.S. Bureau of the Census, *1980 Census of Population*, Supplementary Report PC80-S1-5, "Standard Metropolitan Statistical Areas and Standard Consolidated Statistical Areas: 1980," Table 1, pp. 6-46.

[40]*Census 1984*, op. cit. note 35, Table G, p. 4.

[41]*Census 1986*, op. cit. note 25, Table 10, pp. 81-82; *Statistical Abstract 1991*, op. cit. note 26, Table 44, p. 39; and U.S. Bureau of the Census, *1980 Census of Population*, Vol. 1, Characteristics of the Population, PC80-1-C1, Ch. C, "General Social and Economic Characteristics," Part 1, U.S. Summary (Washington, D.C.: U.S. Government Printing Office, 1983), Table 73, pp. 1-11, Table 162, pp. 1-159, Table 164, pp. 1-161, and Table 165, pp. 1-162.

[42]"Fraud in Indian Country: A Billion-Dollar Betrayal," *The Arizona Republic* (October 11, 1987), p. 26.

[43]Ibid., p. 34.

[44]U.S. Bureau of the Census, op. cit. note 25. All the data presented in this section are from this source.

[45]American Indian Policy Review Commission, op. cit. note 5, p. 137.

[46]Education Commission of the States, *Indian Education: Involvement of Federal, State and Tribal Governments, Report No. 135* (Denver, CO: Education Commission of the States, 1980), p. 54.

[47]Association on American Indian Affairs, Inc., *Indian Affairs* 113 (Spring 1987), a special issue of a newsletter on Indian education.

[48]Bureau of Indian Affairs, *Report on BIA Education: Excellence in Indian Education Through the Effective School Process* (Washington, D.C.: Bureau of Indian Affairs, March, 1988). The report is a final review draft that was used to obtain input from Indian educators prior to the final report.

[49]Ibid.

[50]Tippeconnic, *Survey*, op. cit. note 31.

[51]Ibid.

[52]Vera John, "Styles of Learning — Styles of Teaching: Reflections on the Education of Navajo Children," in Courtney Cazden, Dell Hymes and Vera John, eds., *Functions of Language in the Classroom* (New York: Teachers College Press, 1972), pp. 331-343.

[53]Susan Philips, *The Invisible Culture: Communication in Classrooms and on the Warm Springs Indian Reservation* (New York: Longman, 1983).

[54]Arthur J. More, "Native Indian Learning Styles: A Review for Researchers and Teachers," *Journal of American Indian Education* 27: 1 (October 1987): 17-29.

[55]Karen Swisher and Donna Deyhle, "Styles of Learning and Learning of Styles: Education Conflicts for American Indian/Alaskan Native Youth," *Journal of Multilingual and Multicultural Development* 8: 4 (1987): 345-360.

[56]The discussion here is limited to federal reservations. It is recognized that some of the statements in this section may also apply to nonreservation areas that have high concentrations of American Indians, e.g., Oklahoma and Alaska.

[57]Abt Associates, Inc., *An Evaluation of Indian Controlled Schools* (Cambridge, MA: Abt Associates, Inc., 1985). This evaluation was prepared for the U.S. Department of Education. The document was considered a draft final report.
Indian-controlled schools include tribal or contract schools, usually located on reservations, which receive funding through contracts with the Bureau of Indian Affairs; they may also receive grants from the Department of Education. Indian-controlled schools also include schools that are not tribally operated, and may be located in urban areas, but are under the control of an Indian school board.

[58]Ibid.

[59]Center for Education Statistics, op. cit. note 29, p. 10.

[60]Shirley Vining Brown, *Minorities in the Graduate Education Pipeline,* a research report of the Minority Graduate Education (MGE) Project, jointly sponsored by the Graduate Record Examinations Board and the Educational Testing Service, Educational Testing Service, 1987.

[61]"Minorities' Share of College Enrollments," op. cit. note 23.

[62]Ibid., p. A35.

[63]Brown, op. cit. note 60, pp. 4-6.

[64]Ibid., p. 6.

[65]Ibid.

[66]American Association of Colleges for Teacher Education, *Minority Teacher Recruitment and Retention: A Call for Action* (Washington, D.C.: American Association of Colleges for Teacher Education, September 1987), p. 3.

[67]See the "Special Section on Testing," *Phi Delta Kappan* 70: 9 (May 1989): 683-722. Seven articles are included in this section.

# ECONOMIC DEVELOPMENT AND EMPLOYMENT OPPORTUNITIES FOR AMERICAN INDIANS

## Gary D. Sandefur

*University of Wisconsin-Madison*

Policymakers and students of American Indians have a particular interest in the issue of economic development in Indian country. The importance of this issue to the Reagan administration was demonstrated in the early 1980s by the creation of the Presidential Commission on Reservation Economies. The commission's report generated considerable controversy by proposing that Indian governments relinquish some of their rights in order to attract private business to the reservation.[1]

Although economic development per se has received a good deal of attention, it can be argued that it is a secondary issue compared to the more urgent need to provide better work opportunities for American Indians. Observers from both sides of the political spectrum agree that many American Indians, especially those on isolated reservations, are unable to secure adequate employment. According to the 1980 census, 13.2 percent of the national Indian population aged sixteen and older and 27.8 percent of the reservation Indian population aged sixteen and older were unemployed. In contrast, approximately 12 percent of blacks, 8.9 percent of Hispanics, and 5.8 percent of whites were then unemployed.[2]

The federal government and American Indian tribes have explored a number of alternatives for improving employment opportunities. One solution involves providing financial assistance and special social services to Indians who are willing to move from reservations and isolated rural areas to urban areas, where better jobs are supposedly available. This voluntary relocation program was implemented in the early 1950s and continues now, though at a much lower level of funding than in the past. A second solution involves cooperative efforts between the federal government and tribes to develop tribally-owned business enterprises, ranging from bingo parlors and convention centers to lumber and pencil companies. Third, recent presidential administrations, especially the Reagan administration, have encouraged tribes to forego establishing their own businesses and concentrate their efforts on attracting private enterprises to reservations. This is an extension of the old Bureau of Indian Affairs (BIA) policy of leasing Indian-owned resources to individuals or non-Indian businesses. Fourth, affirmative action programs, and the Indian preference program in the BIA and tribal organizations, have attempted to open existing jobs to Indians both on and off reservations. Finally, health, education and training programs have attempted to improve the human capital of the Indian labor force in order to allow them to better compete for those jobs which are available.

The consensus among Indian and non-Indian policymakers seems to be that these programs, singly and in combination, have not worked. This conclusion is based, however, on the simple but compelling observation that Indian unemployment remains quite high, rather than on an analysis of the evidence regarding the effects of each of these programs. The purpose of this chapter is to carry out such an analysis. It will first examine evidence on the employment and earnings of American Indians. Second, it will outline the unique governmental context within which efforts to improve economic opportunities for American Indians must take place. Finally, it will identify possible solutions and assess their potential effectiveness in encouraging more economic development and employment opportunities for American Indians.


## American Indian Income, Earnings, and Employment


It is clear that a strong relationship exists between economic development, employment opportunities, and individual and family economic well-being. Groups of people who experience employment problems are also likely to have low incomes and high poverty rates. At the time of this writing, the most recent evidence that we have on the national Indian population (from the 1980 census) indicates that American Indians are considerably poorer than whites. An examination of the poverty rates for all households in 1980 shows that whites had the lowest poverty rate (11 percent), and that the Indian rate (22 percent) was somewhat lower than that for blacks (29 percent). Among particular types of households, the poverty rate of blacks and American Indians was much closer: whereas 5 percent of white married couples with children were in poverty, the corresponding figures were 15 percent for blacks and 16 percent for Indians.[3]

Low family incomes and high poverty rates in the American Indian population are in large part due to low earnings. Analyses of data prepared by the Census Bureau show that although the earnings of American Indians increased between the years 1959 and 1979, the dollar figures remained considerably lower than those of whites.[4] The tremendous growth in earnings of most Americans during the 1960s resulted from economic growth, job creation, and low inflation during that decade. The 1970s, on the other hand, were characterized by slow or no growth and high inflation. Although Indian male weekly earnings grew from 63 percent to 84 percent of white male earnings between 1959 and 1979, Indian female earnings changed little and were only 50 percent of white male weekly earnings in 1979. The lower earnings of Indians obviously translate into lower family incomes and higher poverty rates. This problem is compounded by the fact that, among all U.S. racial and ethnic groups, American Indian men and women were those least likely to be employed the full year throughout the 1959-to-1979 period. Although the gap between Indians and whites narrowed, in 1979 only 59 percent of Indian men as compared to 79 percent of white men worked the full year; 35 percent of Indian women as compared to 42 percent of white women did so.

*Employment on Reservations*

**EMPLOYMENT AMONG RESERVATION AND NONRESERVATION
INDIANS, 1980**

|  | All Indians | Res. Indians | Blacks | Whites |
|---|---|---|---|---|
| Percentage in Labor Force (Age 16+) | 58.6 | 65.3 | 59.4 | 62.2 |
| Percentage Unemployed (Age 16+) | 13.2 | 27.8 | 11.8 | 5.8 |
| ***Type of Work among Employed Individuals*** | | | | |
| Private | 66.3 | 34.5 | 70.3 | 76.0 |
| Self-Employed | 4.8 | 6.5 | 2.4 | 7.5 |
| Unpaid Family | .4 | .4 | .1 | .6 |
| Total Nongovernment | 71.5 | 41.4 | 72.8 | 84.1 |
| Tribal Government[a] | — | 28.1 | — | — |
| Federal Government | 10.8 | 19.3 | 7.4 | 3.4 |
| Other Government | 17.7 | 11.1 | 19.7 | 12.6 |
| Total Government | 28.5 | 58.5 | 27.1 | 16.0 |
| TOTAL | 100.0 | 99.9 | 99.9 | 100.1 |

Sources: U.S. Bureau of the Census, *General Social and Economic Characteristics of the Population, 1980* (Washington, D.C.: U.S. Government Printing Office, 1983); U.S. Bureau of the Census, *American Indians, Eskimos and Aleuts on Identified Reservations and in the Historic Areas of Oklahoma (Excluding Urbanized Areas),* PC80-2-ID (Washington, D.C.: U.S. Government Printing Office, 1986).

[a] Only the special report on American Indians on reservations included a category for tribal government. For the other groups in the table, tribal government employees are included in the "Other Government" category.

The general employment statistics for American Indians disguise the truly depressing conditions on reservations. The lack of opportunities for gainful work in these areas is illustrated in the preceding table. In 1980, 65.3 percent of reservation Indians reported that they were in the labor force, i.e., employed or seeking work. A greater percentage of reservation Indians were in the labor force than any other group identified in the table, yet the unemployment rate was much higher for them than for any other group. In general, Indians had a higher unemployment rate in 1980 than blacks or whites.

The dearth of private sector employment on reservations is demonstrated by the distribution of types of work shown in the table. On reservations, 28.1 percent of employed persons work for tribal governments, and 58.5 percent of the employed work for some governmental unit. Only 34.5 percent of Indians on reservations work for a private employer. This compares with 66.3 percent of the national Indian population, and 70.3 and 76 percent for blacks and whites respectively. These figures indicate that government employment is relatively more important for Indians and blacks than for whites.

*Causes of Economic Disadvantages*

The reasons for high poverty rates, low incomes, low earnings and the poor employment prospects of American Indians have been debated for years. Research on the causes of these problems nevertheless has succeeded in identifying a number of factors that are clearly related to these disadvantages. These factors can be divided into those concerning the attributes of individual Indians (i.e., human capital), and those concerning the types of labor markets in which many Indians must seek employment.

Education and health are two of the most important individual attributes that are related to Indian employment, earnings and income. A considerable amount of research in the social sciences has confirmed a strong relationship between education and employment and between education and earnings. Much of the difference in the earnings of American Indian men and white men can be accounted for by the lower levels of education of the former as compared to the latter.[5] Fortunately, the average educational level of American Indians has been rising for some time; by 1979 the mean level of education achieved by American Indians and the proportion of American Indians who graduated from high school were very close to that of white Americans.[6] On the other hand, the gap between Indians and whites in terms of the proportion who graduate from college has not narrowed significantly.

In part the persisting differences in earnings and employment are due to this gap in the college completion rates of whites and Indians.

As previously stated, health status is another factor contributing to the relatively low earnings and high unemployment of American Indians. A 1983 study of factors related to American Indian income and education levels found that American Indian men were more likely than either white men or black men to have health conditions that limited their ability to work.[7] It is thus encouraging to note that recent data indicate that the health of American Indians has been improving dramatically in the past few decades.[8] Alcohol-related diseases, diabetes and other illnesses are still more prevalent among Indians than other groups, but the general trend is one of improvement.

These deficiencies in human capital are compounded by problems in the labor markets in which American Indians have to seek employment. The statistics in the earlier table indicate that many American Indians live on reservations or in isolated rural areas, where there are few opportunities for good jobs. These conditions have led many policymakers to believe that a possible solution to the employment problems of Indians was for them to move to metropolitan areas with better opportunities. The evidence on the effects of such mobility is, however, mixed. A recent study found that the wage rates for Indians in metropolitan areas were higher than those for Indians in nonmetropolitan areas, but in other ways the benefits of mobility were limited. These findings suggest that migration alone is insufficient to improve the lives of American Indians.[9]

In sum, the contemporary American Indian population is characterized by low incomes and high poverty rates relative to whites. This comparatively low level of economic well-being can be traced to persistent low earnings and high unemployment, despite the fact that the Indian population has in general made considerable progress since 1960. These continuing problems are in part due to the low levels of education and the poor health of American Indians. The problems appear to be particularly serious on reservations, and increasingly so in central cities where large American Indian populations have concentrated.[10]

### Government Policies

A number of programs and policies have been enacted to redress the problems discussed above. Because policy implementation has occurred within a very complicated governmental framework, it is impossible to understand the effects of efforts to improve economic and employment opportunities for American Indians without first examining this context.

## The Federal Government

The role of the federal government in Indian affairs was first set forth in the U.S. Constitution and has been modified and delineated through a series of Supreme Court decisions and legislation since that time.[11] Because of this history, the federal government has a relationship with American Indians that is distinct from its relationship with any other minority group in the United States. While this relationship cannot easily be summarized, it can be characterized as having two major facets: government-to-government dealings (for example, the federal government can and does cooperate with tribal governments in the same way that it does with state governments); and the provision through legislation, represented by the Snyder Act of 1921,[12] of special services such as health care and education which are not offered to any other group.

Over time this role has resulted in the development of a complex set of bureaucracies that administer federal Indian policy. Although not all of the programs are directed at improving employment prospects, many of them have either direct or indirect effects on employment.

### Bureau of Indian Affairs

The Bureau of Indian Affairs (BIA) has existed since the early 1800s, first within the War Department and then within the Department of the Interior. From time to time consideration has been given to moving the BIA to the Department of Health and Human Services (DHHS). The bureau traditionally has focused its efforts on the reservation and Oklahoma Indian populations. In 1981, it estimated its service population as 734,895, about half the size of the entire Indian population counted in the 1980 census.[13] Part of the BIA's budget is spent on educational programs, both to operate schools for children in reservation areas and to aid non-Indian schools with Indian students, the latter through the Johnson-O'Malley program.[14] Another part of its budget is allocated for Indian services, including those to tribal governments, social services, law enforcement and housing. A third category covers economic development and employment programs. The BIA also has natural resource development programs, trust responsibilities (the responsibility to act in the best interests of Indians in managing Indian-owned land and other resources), facilities management, and general administration expenses.

### Indian Health Service

Established as a part of the Public Health Service in 1954, the major responsibility of the Indian Health Service (IHS) has been to provide health care to Indians on reservations and in Oklahoma. Its estimated service population in 1980 was 850,000.[15] It administers comprehensive health care to American Indians, half of its funding being devoted to the operation of hospitals and health clinics throughout the country, and another large share supporting contract health care. The latter provides specialized services that are not available through IHS clinics or hospitals. These programs reflect a significant part of the expenditures by the federal government on comprehensive health care for Indians. It should be recognized, though, that each hospital and clinic do not offer a complete range of expensive and/or rarely used services.

Two other categories of IHS expenditures, the equity health care fund and health care for urban Indians, reflect efforts to meet the needs of a changing Indian population. The equity fund is being used to move gradually toward a system in which expenditures in various areas match the need in those areas. This marks a departure from previous IHS policy, which funded health programs on the basis of past funding rather than current need. IHS-administered health care for urban Indians is also a fairly recent innovation, and provides services to the growing Indian population in large cities.

### Department of Agriculture

The Farmers Home Administration (FHA) and the Food and Nutrition Service (FNS), both within the Department of Agriculture, are not agencies for Indians only, as are the BIA and IHS, but they do provide direct funding to tribes to administer programs specifically for American Indians. FHA expenditures are often used to develop and/or improve the water and waste disposal systems in Indian communities, and over half of the FNS expenditures for Indian programs support food stamp programs that are administered through tribes. The FNS also sponsors programs for child nutrition, commodity distribution, and the Special Supplemental Food Program for Women, Infants, and Children (WIC) through tribes.

Office of Elementary and Secondary Education

This office administers the Title IV Indian education programs,[16] which provide various forms of financial assistance to school systems with Indian students. Title IV monies are used to support a variety of services, ranging from cultural programs to counseling. The office also administers compensatory education programs for American Indians.

Federal Employment Programs

Although a high proportion of federal expenditures for Indians goes toward health, health-related (i.e., nutritional, sanitation and water supply), and educational programs, a small amount is directed specifically at creating employment opportunities. In fiscal year 1983, the Department of Labor spent $87 million on Comprehensive Employment and Training Act (CETA) programs through Indian tribes, and in fiscal year 1984 it spent $76 million on Job Training Partnership Act programs through the tribes. In 1984, the BIA also spent approximately $60 million, 6 percent of its budget, on economic development and employment programs.[17]

*State Governments*

The U.S. Constitution designated the federal government as the party responsible for dealing with Indian affairs, prohibiting the state governments from taking a strong role. Subsequent Supreme Court decisions also have delimited the actions of states in Indian affairs. The Johnson-O'Malley Act of 1934,[18] however, gave state governments responsibility for providing educational and other services to Indians. Also, tribes over time have intentionally and unintentionally allowed state and county governments to assume responsibilities that could have been reserved to tribal governments. This has led to a complicated situation in which states are uncertain of their authority to legislate and regulate Indians living on reservations.

The confusing situation of state relationships with Indians is illustrated by the controversy concerning Chippewa fishing rights in Wisconsin. Treaties between the Chippewa and the federal government preserved fishing rights for Chippewa people in waters outside the reservations on which the Chippewa agreed to live. The state regulates the fishing of non-Chippewa people in these waters, so it is perplexing to many state legislators and non-Indian citizens of Wisconsin that the state cannot regulate the fishing of the Chippewa in the same way.

*Tribal Governments*

The federal government has at various times tried to eliminate tribal governments. Allotment policy in the late 1800s and early 1900s was designed to do so, as well as to divide tribally-owned lands into plots owned by individual Indians, thus ostensibly aiding in their assimilation. More recently, the termination policy of the 1950s was intended to end the special government-to-government relationship between the federal government and tribal governments. At other times, the federal government has sought to strengthen and "modernize" tribal governments. For example, the 1934 Indian Reorganization Act enabled tribal governments to reorganize, but in ways that were consistent with the model of government deemed appropriate by the majority society rather than the traditional models of government used by different Indian groups.[19] The current policy of self-determination was initiated in the mid-1970s and is supported by the Bush administration. Under it, tribes have gradually assumed more control over programs delivered to their citizens.

Although the Reagan administration also endorsed self-determination, the Presidential Commission on Reservation Economies viewed some features of tribal government as major barriers to the economic development of Indian reservations. A controversial suggestion made by the commission was that tribes should relinquish those rights that pose risks for companies which might desire to locate on Indian reservations — i.e., the commission argued that the rights of sovereign immunity guaranteed to tribes by the Constitution and Supreme Court decisions made private companies reluctant to do business on reservations, since the companies had limited legal recourse for dealing with problems that might arise.

**A Typology of Indian Employment Policy**

The complex history of federal, state and tribal relations and the elaborate structure of the bureaucracies and legislation that deal with American Indians have led to a number of strategies to address their employment problems. Although these policies can be categorized in several different ways, it is useful to think of them in terms of three major types: (1) those that emphasize Indians as members of distinct tribal governments, somewhat akin to state governments; (2) those that emphasize Indians as members of a minority group in the same way that blacks are members of a minority group; and (3) those that emphasize

Indians as part of a larger group of disadvantaged individuals in need of better education and training.

The policies that emphasize tribal governments can be further subdivided into two types: those that are designed to develop tribally-owned businesses and those that are designed to help tribes attract private businesses to reservations. Although a number of tribes own businesses, federal policy in the early 1980s discouraged tribes from doing so. The Presidential Commission on Reservation Economies argued instead that tribes should act as governments, providing incentives for private companies to locate on reservations. The development of tribal businesses has nonetheless had a tremendous impact. As one author noted, the traditional council in many tribes has been replaced by the business committee as the most important decisionmaking unit.[20]

Affirmative action is the major employment policy that treats Indians as a minority group, covering them just as blacks, Hispanics and other groups are covered. Among the policies that have treated Indians as disadvantaged individuals are the Employment Assistance Program (begun in 1952), which was designed to help Indians leave reservations and other isolated rural areas for urban areas with better employment chances, the Comprehensive Employment and Training Act of 1973, which provided training and public service employment for Indians along with other disadvantaged minority and majority individuals, and its successor, the Job Training Partnership Act of 1982, which took effect in fiscal year 1984.

**Evidence on Policy Effectiveness**

As mentioned at the beginning of this chapter, most observers seem to feel that the policies discussed above singly and in combination have failed to improve significantly the employment of American Indians. This view is not based on a careful review of the existing evidence, however, and it is to such a review that this chapter now turns.

The traditional model for tribal government-based strategies was for Indian tribes to lease land or other natural resources to private individuals or companies. C. Matthew Snipp has assessed the benefits to tribes from these leases.[21] His analysis suggests that Indians have, in general, been harmed from the leasing of agricultural lands and water to non-Indians for two major reasons. First, some of the best land controlled by Indians has been leased, which prevents Indian farmers and ranchers from utilizing it. Second, the leases were traditionally negotiated by the federal government acting on behalf of the Indians, resulting in leases that were favorable to non-Indians at the expense of the original Indian owners.

Snipp points out that Indians have benefited more from leases of timber than of land or water, but only a few tribes have sufficient timber resources that are attractive enough to provide lease income. A growing source of such income comes from the minerals, including oil and gas, that have been discovered on Indian lands. Indian tribes rarely, however, have the necessary expertise to negotiate favorable leases. Snipp states: "Managing energy resource development and effectively negotiating lease agreements require highly specialized technical skills about geological formations and market behavior. Most tribes, and BIA officials, lack this expertise."[22] Recognition of this problem among Indians has led to their pooling of expertise and knowledge as, for example, in the formation of the Council of Energy Resource Tribes (CERT) in 1975. CERT has assisted a number of tribes in the negotiation of natural resource leases.

The dissatisfaction of many Indians with lease arrangements has led several tribes to attempt to develop their own natural resources. Some tribes, such as the Menominee, have built their own lumber mills. Others have attempted to exert more control over water in order to irrigate additional land for agricultural purposes.[23] Other tribes have attempted to engage in other tribally-sponsored enterprises. The Chickasaws in Oklahoma, for example, own a cabinetmaking company, a service station with a convenience store, and a motel.

The Presidential Commission on Reservation Economies suggested that tribes forego establishing their own enterprises and attempt to attract private businesses to the reservation. As Joanne Nagel and her colleagues point out, however, there are a number of problems that inhibit the ability both to develop tribally-owned enterprises and to attract private businesses.[24] The geographical isolation of Indian reservations makes them unlikely choices for many businesses, and the small size of many tribes means that there are few tribal consumers for any products produced by a business. Air or train travel to many reservations is not feasible.

In sum, the evidence suggests that strategies relying on tribal governments have achieved only limited success in improving the employment opportunities of Indians. Further, current knowledge does not clearly identify other strategies for overcoming barriers to economic growth on reservations. This is not something that is peculiar to the Indian situation. Both the Kerner Commission's report of 1968 and, more recently, the work of William Julius Wilson in analyzing employment problems in urban areas, have emphasized economic growth as a major way of overcoming urban unemployment.[25] As Edward Gramlich has written, however: "The frustrations involved in economists' search to find ways of stimulating employment are immense and long-standing. . . . Vigorous booms cannot be created."[26] This is true of both the national economy, to which Gramlich was referring, and local economies, such as those in central cities and on Indian reservations.

There has been very little research on the impact of affirmative action on the employment of American Indians; most of what we can say about this is based on research concerning blacks. Basically, the results indicate that affirmative action has improved the employment opportunities of blacks, but has had little long-term impact on their earnings.[27] The few studies that have examined American Indians indicate that affirmative action has improved their employment opportunities.[28] More specifically, companies that are federal contractors and those that are monitored by the Equal Employment Opportunity Commission have increased the representation of minority group members in their ranks.

There has also been very little attention devoted to the impact of individual-oriented employment strategies on American Indians. The wider body of research on this topic shows that public sector employment through CETA and additional training programs did improve the employment record of the most disadvantaged workers.[29] Since many Indians are very disadvantaged, it is plausible to argue that these programs may have worked to their benefit as well. For example, Alan Sorkin looked at employment and training programs directed specifically at American Indians.[30] Focusing on adult vocational training, on-the-job training, and direct relocation, he concluded that these programs were relatively efficient compared to similar programs that were open to all individuals.

### Summary and Conclusions

The evidence in the first section of this chapter indicates that American Indians continue to experience problems in securing adequate employment. These employment problems result in low earnings, which correspondingly result in low family incomes and high poverty rates. Lack of economic development on Indian reservations is a major source of employment problems, but efforts to develop reservation economies have met with limited success. Further, although there is some evidence that direct relocation programs lead to long-term benefits for some individuals, leaving the reservation is not a clear solution to the problem.

The evidence reviewed above and elsewhere also indicates, however, that American Indians have made considerable progress over the past several decades.[31] The incomes, earnings and employment of Indians have improved relative to those of whites. Expenditures on programs discussed above have led to improvements in health, housing and general living conditions on reservations. So, although many problems remain, it is important to remember that a great deal of progress has been made.

All of this leads to some modest suggestions. First, the federal government should maintain its current policy of self-determination and continue to provide financial support to tribes for the administration of important health, housing, educational and employment programs. The lack of economic development means that tribes will continue to need financial assistance well into the future. Second, we should renew our commitment to affirmative action, which has improved the employment opportunities of American Indians. Third, resources should be recommitted to public sector job creation on the reservations, where a wide variety of tasks, such as road repair and housing renovation, could be accomplished by this means. The evidence indicates that job creation programs have had long-range impacts on participants. Fourth, we should recommit resources to the Employment Assistance Program so that individuals who wish to leave isolated, underdeveloped areas can do so. On the other hand, individuals who do not wish to leave should not be urged to migrate. There frankly are no easy solutions to the problem of encouraging economic development on reservations. Nevertheless, we cannot afford to wait for economic development alone to solve employment problems. Perhaps the most worthwhile actions for now are those which simply provide jobs for American Indians.

## NOTES

[1]See Presidential Commission on Reservation Economies, *Report and Recommendations to the President of the United States* (Washington, D.C.: U.S. Government Printing Office, 1984).

[2]U.S. Bureau of the Census, *Census of the Population, 1980: General Social and Economic Characteristics of the Population* (Washington, D.C.: U.S. Government Printing Office, 1983); U.S. Bureau of the Census, *American Indians, Eskimos, and Aleuts on Identified Reservations and in the Historic Areas of Oklahoma (Excluding Urbanized Areas)* (Washington, D.C.: U.S. Government Printing Office, 1986).

[3]Gary D. Sandefur and Arthur Sakamoto, "American Indian Household Structure and Income," *Demography* 25: 1 (February 1988): 71-80.

[4]Gary D. Sandefur and Anup Pahari, "Racial and Ethnic Inequality in Earnings and Employment," *Social Service Review* 63: 2 (June 1989): 199-221.

[5]See, for example, Gary D. Sandefur and Wilbur J. Scott, "Minority Group Status and Wages of White, Black, and Indian Males," *Social Science Research* 12: 1 (March 1983): 44-68.

[6]Sandefur and Pahari, op. cit. note 4.

[7]Sandefur and Scott, op. cit. note 5.

[8]Gary D. Sandefur, "The Duality in Federal Policy toward Minority Groups," in Gary D. Sandefur and Marta Tienda, eds., *Divided Opportunities: Minorities, Poverty, and Social Policy* (New York: Plenum Press, 1988), pp. 207-229; U.S. Congress, Office of Technology Assessment, *Indian Health Care* (Washington, D.C.: U.S. Government Printing Office, 1986).

[9]C. Matthew Snipp and Gary D. Sandefur, "Earnings of American Indians and Alaskan Natives: The Effects of Residence and Migration," *Social Forces* 66: 4 (June 1988): 994-1008.

[10]A recent report prepared by the Applied Population Laboratory of the University of Wisconsin-Madison indicated, for example, that American Indians residing in central cities in Wisconsin were doing as poorly as those living on reservations.

[11]There are a number of analyses of the development of federal Indian policy. See, for example, Francis P. Prucha, *The Great Father: The United States Government and the American Indians*, Vols. 1-2 (Lincoln, NE: University of Nebraska Press, 1984).

[12]Snyder Act, 42 Stat. 208, November 2, 1921 (67th Congress, 1st Session).

[13]Theodore W. Taylor, *The Bureau of Indian Affairs* (Boulder, CO: Westview Press, 1984), Table 1, p. 163.

[14]Johnson-O'Malley Act of 1934, 48 Stat. 596, April 16, 1934 (73rd Congress, 2nd Session).

[15]U.S. Congress, Office of Technology Assessment, op. cit. note 8, p. 6.

[16]Indian Education Act, P.L. 92-318, 86 Stat. 334, June 23, 1972 (92nd Congress, 2nd Session).

[17]Presidential Commission on Reservation Economies, op. cit. note 1, pp. 92, 94.

[18]Johnson-O'Malley Act, op. cit. note 14.

[19]Indian Reorganization Act, 48 Stat. 984, June 18, 1934 (73rd Congress, 2nd Session).

[20]William Carmack, "Indian Governments," paper presented at the Conference on the Kerner Commission Report: Twenty Years Later (Racine, WI: Wingspread Conference Center of the Johnson Foundation, March 1988).

[21]C. Matthew Snipp, "Public Policy and American Indian Economic Development," in C. Matthew Snipp, ed., *Public Policy Impacts on American In-*

*dian Economic Development* (Albuquerque, NM: Institute for Native American Development, University of New Mexico, 1988), pp. 1-22.

[22]Ibid., p. 8.

[23]See F. Lee Brown and Helen M. Ingram, *Water and Poverty in the Southwest* (Tucson, AZ: University of Arizona Press, 1987).

[24]Joanne Nagel, Carol Ward and Timothy Knapp, "The Politics of American Indian Economic Development," in Snipp, op. cit. note 21, pp. 39-76.

[25]National Advisory Commission on Civil Disorders (Kerner Commission), *Report, the New York Times Edition* (New York: E. P. Dutton, 1968); William Julius Wilson, *The Truly Disadvantaged: The Inner City, the Underclass, and Public Policy* (Chicago: University of Chicago Press, 1987).

[26]Edward M. Gramlich, "The Main Themes," in Sheldon H. Danziger and Daniel H. Weinberg, eds., *Fighting Poverty: What Works and What Doesn't* (Cambridge, MA: Harvard University Press, 1986), pp. 341-347.

[27]See, for example, James Smith and Finis Welch, *Forty Years of Progress* (Santa Monica, CA: The Rand Corporation, 1986).

[28]See, for example, Jonathan Leonard, "The Impact of Affirmative Action on Employment," *Journal of Labor Economics* 2: 4 (October 1984): 439-463.

[29]See Laurie Bassi and Orley Ashenfelter, "The Effect of Direct Job Creation and Training Programs on Low-Skilled Workers," in Danziger and Weinberg, op. cit. note 26, pp. 133-151, for a careful review of the research on employment and training programs.

[30]Alan L. Sorkin, *American Indians and Federal Aid* (Washington, D.C.: Brookings Institution, 1972).

[31]See Sandefur, "The Duality in Federal Policy Toward Minority Groups," in Sandefur and Tienda, op. cit. note 8, especially pp. 218-224, for a more detailed review of health and educational programs.

# AMERICAN INDIAN CRIMINALITY: WHAT DO WE REALLY KNOW?

Donald E. Green

*University of Wisconsin-Milwaukee*

## Introduction

The study of the American Indian experience has produced a sizable scholarly interest in a wide range of academic areas including history, anthropology, literature and sociology. Within each of these traditional disciplines, strong research traditions have developed on such topics as state building and population revitalization, treaty rights and federal Indian policy, and socioeconomic analyses of the quality of Indian life. Unfortunately, one aspect of the Native American experience has continually been neglected — the study of American Indian criminality. This chapter represents one effort to stimulate renewed interest in this topic by conducting a critical review of the available literature. More specifically, the chapter will review the literature to date which has attempted to measure crime patterns and criminal justice outcomes for Native Americans.[1] This literature includes empirical studies of the frequency of American Indian involvement in illegal behavior, their detection or arrest rates for engaging in that illegal behavior, the sentencing patterns of those convicted of such behavior, as well as their post-adjudication experiences. The review's approach is from a sociological perspective, which has traditionally considered the substantive field of criminology to be of central concern to the discipline.[2] Finally, the chapter will conclude with a discussion of the implications of what we know about American Indian criminality for the issues of social justice and public policy.

### Statement of the Problem

A review of the literature on the issues of race, involvement in criminal behavior, and criminal justice outcomes reveals that for the most part, Native Americans, in comparison to other American ethnic groups, have been virtually ignored by criminologists and sociologists interested in the etiology of, and social reaction to, crime. For example, Leonard Savitz reports that over five hundred articles have been published on black crime rates and/or their criminal justice outcomes.[3] The literature on American Indian criminality is considerably less impressive relative to the volume and levels of sophistication now being reached in the more traditional black/white comparative research on involvement in criminal behavior and criminal justice outcomes. In fact, an extensive literature search has produced only twenty scholarly works which have focused on some aspect of Native American crime patterns and/or criminal justice outcomes.[4] These works are reviewed here within categories derived on the basis of the type of indicators of criminal involvement and/or criminal justice outcomes employed by each study. Before beginning the review, however, it is crucial to note how the present effort differs significantly from two other reviews of the literature on American Indian criminality which have been published in the 1980s, those of Sidney Harring and Phillip May.[5]

To their credit, both Harring and May have contributed to this area of criminological research in several ways. Harring argues that American Indian crime patterns primarily have been studied by anthropologists, and calls for a major effort to generate data on the Native American experience and their involvement in criminal behavior from both tribal and nontribal sources in order to fill the research void in this area of criminology. In addition, he strongly challenges mainstream criminologists to consider some of the anomalies posed by the limited data available to date on American Indian crime patterns in relation to the current theoretical positions on the etiology of crime in general. On the other hand, May provides one possible framework to examine the literature on contemporary American Indian crime — a descriptive versus inferential dichotomy — and highlights the contributions of selected empirical studies to our understanding of this important social problem. These efforts notwithstanding, Harring too hastily dismisses the contribution of anthropology to the study of American Indian criminality, and fails to discuss a number of these works, while May uncritically accepts the findings of previous studies, particularly those of the anthropologists, and fails to acknowledge that some of these efforts are simply better able to contribute to our understanding of the problem at hand than others.

The present attempt to review the literature on American Indian criminality is an improvement on these earlier efforts for a number of reasons. For example, this review includes several studies which have been published since Harring and May presented their work. In addition, this effort provides a more critical review of the literature by comparing these studies to the research standards which are the "state of the art" in the field of criminology today. In doing so, considerable emphasis is placed on the methodological problems associated with attempts to obtain an accurate picture of American Indian criminality and the criminal justice outcomes for this unique American ethnic group. Finally, this effort attempts to incorporate the significant findings from these diverse studies to better guide future research efforts devoted to the understanding of American Indian criminality.

### Measuring Criminality Among American Indians

As Harring has recently noted, there are a number of problematic methodological issues facing those who attempt to obtain reliable indicators of American Indian criminality.[6] The most formidable of these is the fact that official records of Native American crime are reported in a bifurcated fashion. The more readily available measures are those that come from the Federal Bureau of Investigation (FBI) in the form of Uniform Crime Reports (UCR).[7] In fact, the UCR are the most widely available and frequently cited comprehensive source of data on crime in the United States. The UCR data report the number of actual crimes known to police, as well as the number of arrests made for these offenses. In most instances, the arrest reports include information on the individuals' age, race, sex, and location of the arrest. These reports are systematically compiled by local police agencies across the United States on a voluntary basis, and forwarded to the FBI in Washington, D.C., which publishes the data annually. It is estimated that approximately 98 percent of all police agencies in the country routinely submit these crime reports to the FBI. These data then provide one measure of the number of Native Americans (as well as other racial groups) who have been arrested for criminal offenses throughout the United States.

In spite of these impressive records, the limitations of the UCR have been widely discussed.[8] For example, police simply cannot know about all crimes which occur in society because many offenses are not reported by victims and/or witnesses. In addition, police departments across the country do not use uniform procedures for recording these crimes. Individual police discretion to report and/or arrest for any particular crime can also significantly affect the number of crimes known to police agencies. Administrative and bureaucratic changes in the size, location or method of reporting crimes can also influence these official reports of crime. Moreover, when criminal activity involves more than one offense, only the most serious crime is reported to the FBI, and the reports may include the same individuals more than once for any particular offense.

Although these are problems that apply across the board for all racial groups, American Indians face additional reporting problems. As Harring has pointed out, UCR data are only 80 percent complete for rural areas of the country, which is where approximately one-half of all Native Americans reside.[9] In addition, some individuals who are culturally Indian may not be recorded as such because of the failure of the reporting officer to perceive them as so, or because the officer fails to distinguish beyond a simple black/white dichotomy. On the other side of this issue, an officer may incorrectly identify individuals as Indian when in fact they are not. Perhaps more important, however, is the fact that reservation arrest data — the second source of information on American Indian criminality — are not included in the UCR figures. The Bureau of Indian Affairs' (BIA) records on crimes reported on reservations across the country suggest that this omission results in an automatic exclusion of almost 50 percent of all Native American crime from the UCR figures.[10] Finally, federal crimes, which are more common on reservations due to the jurisdictional differences that exist in these areas, are also excluded from the UCR data. These problems suggest that caution is warranted when considering official UCR data on American Indian criminality.

As just mentioned, a second measure of Native American crime is the official records collected by the BIA for only those crimes committed on reservations in the United States. These crimes are reported by tribal police agencies, recorded by reservations across seven regional districts, and aggregated nationally.[11] However, these data too are problematic in that, as in the case of the UCR data, some crimes may go unreported and therefore not be included in the BIA figures. In addition, reports of crime which are considered unfounded by police are not included in the BIA data. Still another methodological problem for this data source is that the seriousness of the offenses in these reports is limited because of jurisdictional issues.[12] Many offenses committed on reservations fall outside of the control of tribal police agencies and courts. Furthermore, some Indian reservations, as a result of Public Law 280, have concurrent jurisdiction with the various states contiguous to the reservation boundaries.[13] Perhaps the most formidable problem for research in this area of criminology is that these reports are not widely available, as is the case with the UCR data, and that the data are not directly proportional to that recorded by the FBI. Consequently, we cannot simply add the two sources together to obtain a total crime figure for Native Americans in general. Nor can we say one source is quantitatively better than another because the total population of American Indians in the United States is almost equally divided, with approximately one half living on reservations and the other half residing in urban areas.

A third measure of criminality is that of self-reported behavior. Typically, self-reports of frequency of involvement in illegal behavior are conducted with adolescent and/or college populations due to their convenient availability in classroom settings. However, some adult surveys of self-reported behavior based on randomly selected respondents from general populations have been conducted.[14] The data are collected through interviews or anonymous questionnaires which focus on crimes likely to be committed by the target group being studied. A major advantage of this method of measurement is that it allows researchers to examine frequency of involvement in crimes not necessarily reported and/or detected by police agencies. In fact, one significant contribution of self-report studies to the criminological literature on measurement of crime has been the realization that a large portion of all crime is not reported.[15]

Several disadvantages to this method have been discussed in the literature. For example, critiques of this measure of criminality have noted that some individuals have the tendency to underreport their involvement in illegal behavior out of fear of being caught and/or the social undesirability of admitting involvement in various criminal activities. On the other hand, it has been suggested that individuals might overreport their involvement, while still others may have simply forgotten over time. In addition, the self-reporting method has been criticized because the majority of past studies have focused on relatively minor offenses such as littering or lying to someone, and have also demonstrated a lack of concern with minority populations. However, a widely cited study by John Clark and Larry Tifft has minimized some of these concerns.[16] Clark and Tifft compared respondents' self-reports of involvement in illegal behavior with lie detector results and found virtually no intentional misinformation in the self-reported behavior by the subjects in the study.

Qualitative studies of criminal behavior provide still another method to measure involvement in illegal behavior. These studies include participant observation, life histories, and case studies of groups of individuals who engage in particular forms of deviant behavior. The qualitative method stresses the need to conduct in-depth studies of relatively small numbers of individuals who are involved in crime in order to obtain a greater understanding of the deviants themselves. Studies may involve various degrees of participation in the activities of these individuals or groups and/or a reliance on alternative measures such as diaries, letters or biographies of individuals who are actively involved in various criminal behaviors.

For the most part, these studies have provided criminological literature with rich accounts of the lives and activities of deviant individuals or groups. However, the methods have been criticized because of the risk of the researcher losing objectivity and overidentifying with the subjects. In addition, these methods are typically very time-consuming and require the researcher to make sense of an extensive volume of qualitative data.

## Measurement of American Indian Criminality

In the following sections, studies of American Indian criminality will be reviewed according to the method by which involvement in criminal behavior has been measured.

### Official Records

Norman Hayner provided the then-fledgling field of sociology with one of its first examinations of American Indian crime patterns.[17] Based on the frequently cited Meriam Report,[18] Hayner analyzed criminal behavior among Native Americans of the Plains and Pacific Northwest regions. More specifically, he focused his study on the Colville-Spokane and Yakima reservations in eastern Washington, and the Klamath from the Warm Springs Reservation in north-central Oregon. His primary thesis was that the criminal behavior patterns of these tribal groups were associated with the variables of intensity and character of contacts with white civilization, and the source and adequacy of sustenance.

Although drunkenness and sex offenses were the most frequently committed offenses, Hayner argued that federal liquor laws discriminated against Native Americans in such a way as to motivate deviant drinking patterns, facilitating the typical drunk and disorderly cases noted by federal, state, local and Indian courts. Moreover, reaction to alcohol among Native Americans, according to Hayner, varied both within and between tribes and familial units. As such, an explanation for these alcohol-related crimes must be grounded in situational factors, rather than in racial ones.

Hayner continued by linking these situational factors to regional differences illustrated by the three reservations. For example, he noted that while contacts with whites had been more disastrous for Indians of the Northwest than for those of the Southwest, the greatest differences in the extent and character of American Indian crime existed between specific reservations in the same region. Using data included in the Meriam Report on crime rates for Indians in the Dakotas, Montana, Washington and Oregon, he argued that the unusually high rates for the Klamath reservation in southern Oregon, in comparison to those for the Colville-Spokane and Yakima jurisdictions in eastern Washington, illustrated the importance of isolation. In 1942, the Colville reservation contained 1,385,086 acres and 4,126 Indians, making it the largest jurisdiction in the Pacific Northwest. However, at that time, it had never been crossed by either a railroad or an interstate highway.

The isolation of the Colvilles, according to Hayner, had been coupled with modest economic resources. For example, the average annual family income on the Colville reservation in 1938 was estimated to be $431.60, derived mostly from livestock. The crime rate for the Colville reservation in 1930 was a modest 0.9 per 1,000 population. In contrast to the Colville jurisdiction, Hayner noted that the Yakimas had experienced a longer and more intense period of contact with whites. The reservation was crossed by a main line of the Northern Pacific railroad, and by U.S. 97, the principal north-south highway east of the Cascades. The city of Yakima was only a few miles away, and much of the reservation's one hundred thousand acres was owned or leased by whites and Japanese immigrants. In fact, of the reservation's total population of sixteen thousand, fewer than three thousand were American Indians. Hayner reported that the crime rate for the Yakima reservation was 4.7 per 1,000 population in 1930. Moreover, Hayner argued that the crime rate on this reservation seemed to vary with economic prosperity. The highest number of offenses appeared during periods when money was paid for grazing and farm leases.

Finally, Hayner argued that the greatest degrees of assimilation were evident among the Klamaths. Hayner noted that many Klamaths dressed like whites, drove newer cars, and lived in homes similar to those of middle-class whites. The Klamaths also had a large amount of valuable timber in their fifty-mile square reservation, and had frequent contacts with seasonal workers attracted to the local logging camps and sawmills. During that period, only one-fourth of the five thousand people on the Klamath reservation were Indians. In terms of sustenance, the Klamath Indians typically received three to four hundred dollars per month as royalties from the timber cutting, and Hayner suggested that the leisure time created by the non-work-related payments provided more opportunities for criminal behavior. In fact, according to the Meriam Report, the overall crime rate for the Klamath reservation in 1930 was 13.1 per 1,000 population, the highest of the three groups examined. Moreover, Hayner noted that the Klamath had murder and assault rates which were three times that of the next highest rates, those of the Blackfeet and Crows of Montana.

Although Hayner suggested that these particularly high rates of violent crime could partially be attributed to "quarrels and blood feuds" dating back to earlier times, he added that distinctive customs such as these "tend to become less important factors for explanations of criminal behavior as acculturation progresses."[19] Hayner argued that the criminal behavior among American Indians was primarily linked to tribal disorganization. More specifically, he stated that "the extent to which an aboriginal culture has disorganized seems to be in large part determined by the degree of isolation, on the one hand, and the source and adequacy of sustenance, on the other."[20]

Hans Von Hentig examined crime patterns among American Indians by employing UCR arrest rates, prison admission rates, court records and the Meriam Report.[21] Based on arrest records between 1935 and 1944, Von Hentig pointed out that Indian arrests had increased during the period. Comparisons with whites revealed that between the years 1936 and 1940, Indian arrests among males per 100,000 population were 2,510.3, while the white rate for a similar period was 835.5. Moreover, prison admission rates per 100,000 indicated that between 1937 and 1941, the rate of imprisonment for Indian males was 487.7 compared to 94.2 for white males. Similar discrepancies were revealed among the two races for female offenders.

Von Hentig also presented court records which indicated that drunkenness was the most frequent offense charged, and jail time and fines were the most frequent sentences imposed. However, a breakdown of type of sentence imposed by type of court (Indian and regular) revealed that regular courts were much more likely to impose a fine, while Indian courts typically preferred jail time and probation. Relying heavily on the Meriam Report, Von Hentig suggested that explanations for Indian criminality differ from that of other racial groups. For example, he argued that the moral commitment of Indians to the U.S. code of law was weak, and that social disapproval from significant others in the Indian community for engaging in various forms of illegal behavior was infrequent.[22]

While Von Hentig was aware of some of the major problems with studying Indian criminality such as the mixed-blood factor, multiple jurisdictions, and a bifurcated court system in several states, his analysis suffers from several methodological shortcomings. For example, he presented a table entitled "Arrests of Indians" for the years 1935 to 1944 which lacked explanations concerning what crimes were included and/or excluded. Moreover, many of the conclusions he drew were based on speculation from information provided by the Meriam Report, rather than through measures of association and statistical inference.

Omer Stewart was the first researcher to compare UCR arrest rates for Indians, whites and blacks.[23] According to his 1960 data, Indian arrest rates for all offenses were nearly seven times that of the national average. Compared to the other racial groups considered, Stewart reported that the Indian arrest rate for all offenses was nearly three times that of blacks and eight times that of whites. The actual 1960 arrest rates per 100,000 population for each group were as follows: Indians — 15,123; blacks — 5,908; and whites — 1,655. These figures compare to a total arrest rate for all three groups in 1960 of 2,157 per 100,000.

According to Stewart, drunkenness accounted for over 70 percent of all Indian arrests reported in 1960. Moreover, Indian arrests for alcohol-related crimes were twelve times greater than the national average and five times greater than that for blacks. In a breakdown of urban and rural arrests, Stewart indicated that Indian arrest rates nationally were higher in urban areas than they were in rural areas, although in both instances the Indian rates remained significantly greater than those for non-Indians.

Stewart also provided comparative data on arrests and convictions for selected crimes for South Dakota, BIA data on reservations of the Southwest, and the city of Denver. The data suggested that Indian rates of arrest and incarceration in South Dakota were higher than national averages for Indians. In addition, BIA data on southwestern reservations indicated important differences within groups. For example, rates of conviction for adults on the San Carlos Apache Reservation were approximately four and five times greater than the total number of adult criminal cases for the Navajo and Jicarilla Apache reservations respectively. Stewart argued that the only similarities among these groups were that the majority of the cases were alcohol-related, and that based on selected categories and jurisdictions for which the gender of the offender was indicated, males were disproportionately represented in all crime categories except family-related offenses. Based on these data, Stewart argued that if the reasons for excessive drinking among Indians were determined, the factors explaining their high crime rates would also be known.

It is important to note that Stewart presented arrest rates computed on total population figures rather than on age-specific populations. Criminological literature on the incidence of crime in general suggests that involvement in criminal behavior is directly related to age, and that employing total population bases for computing arrest rates can produce misleading data. Moreover, Stewart failed to report offense-specific rates of criminality, which is problematic for analyses of American Indian criminality because of the tendency of Indian crime to be concentrated in particular offense categories.

On the other hand, Charles Reasons provided a more extensive longitudinal examination of UCR arrest data by racial categories than Stewart by including data at three-year intervals between 1950 and 1968, as well as by presenting a breakdown of that arrest data by offense categories (including alcohol- and non-alcohol-related offenses).[24] In addition, Reasons's data were based on age-specific arrests (fourteen years and older).

Although some differences emerged when comparing alcohol-related crime rates, findings from Reasons's analysis generally support Stewart's 1964 work. For example, Reasons's data indicated that Indian arrest rates were approximately ten times that of whites and three times that of blacks. However, according to Reasons's data, Indian arrests for alcohol-related crimes were eight times that of blacks and over twenty times that of whites. It is important to note that direct comparisons of Reasons's data with that of Stewart's work are problematic because Reasons based his analysis on selected years between 1950 and 1968, while Stewart only considered data from 1960. Moreover, Stewart's figures are based on the total American Indian population, while Reasons's analysis is based only on Indians fourteen years and older.

When examining American Indian arrest rates over time, Reasons reported that Indian arrest rates for alcohol-related offenses went from 1,953 per 100,000 population fourteen and older in 1950, to 27,407 in 1968. In fact, for all offenses, Indian arrests increased from 3,492 in 1950 to 36,584 in 1960, while arrests for whites had increased from 572 in 1950 to 3,271 in 1960, and for blacks from 1,957 in 1950 to 12,256 in 1960. A somewhat different picture emerged, however, when focusing on arrest rates which were not alcohol-related. Indian arrests topped that of all others in only two of the seven years considered, while black rates were highest in the remaining five years. Nevertheless, Indian arrests more closely approximated those of blacks in all years considered, with nonwhite rates in general being over four times that of whites.

Reasons also provided offense-specific breakdowns by race for the first time. According to the data, Indians had the highest arrest rate for auto theft of all racial groups, and in no instance were Indian arrest rates for specific crimes lower than that of whites. In general, Indian arrest rates for the index crimes he considered remained higher than that for whites, but somewhat lower than those of blacks.

Reasons has made an important contribution to the literature on American Indian criminality by employing age- and offense-specific rates of arrest. However, like most of his counterparts in this area of study, he attempted to use various theoretical perspectives to account for these rates of offending without utilizing measures of these concepts. For example, he discussed the importance of economic factors, anomie, and cultural conflict as explanations of American Indian criminality, but failed to measure these concepts and include them in statistical analyses to confirm his hypotheses. Moreover, he neglected to acknowledge the contribution of earlier works which strongly pointed to the need to control for intragroup differences in rates of offending.

Laurence French and Jim Hornbuckle attempted to examine violent criminal behavior among one group of Native Americans — the Eastern Cherokees — by employing a combined "cultural frustration/subcultural control" perspective which linked traditional culture with the current social situation.[25] The authors presented the picture of a typical Native American as being "marginal" or split between two cultures, Indian and white. They argued that their aboriginal cultural heritage has given Native Americans an "established frame of reference regarding latent subcultural controls" which, combined with the imposed legal control of the federal government (i.e., federal paternalism), created the conditions for outbursts of violent behavior.[26]

In presenting the argument for their thesis, the authors provided a historical account of the Eastern Cherokees, pointing out that traditional mechanisms of releasing aggression had deteriorated while the formal controls to which Native Americans had been subjected were strengthened. These conditions, according to French and Hornbuckle, coupled with a high rate of stress and alcoholism in the reservation environment, resulted in a subculture of violence much like that identified in the widely cited work of Marvin Wolfgang and Franco Ferracuti.[27]

Three sets of data were used to demonstrate this pattern of violence among the Eastern Cherokees: official records on the number of violent personal crimes such as criminal homicide, forcible rape, aggravated assault and armed robbery; information on the relationship between the victim and offender; and twelve descriptive accounts of actual violent episodes derived from court records. In the comparisons of violent offenses, the data indicated that with the exception of forcible rape and armed robbery, the percentage of violent crime was higher among the Eastern Cherokees than it was for all other regions of the country and/ or the national average.

In addition, data on the victim/offender relationships were presented which indicated that for the most part, Cherokee violence was an intraracial phenomena. Moreover, the data also suggested that in most instances, the offender and victim were either acquaintances or relatives. Finally, the twelve cases examined revealed that much of the violence was victim-precipitated and that alcohol was involved in the majority of these acts of violence. In summary, the authors concluded that "violence among the Qualla Cherokees is due mainly to intensive in-group tensions generated by the restrictive reservation environment" with marginal enculturation, limited social mobility, complex subcultural interaction and alcohol being contributing factors.[28]

While French and Hornbuckle presented a persuasive argument in their study, it too has methodological problems which limit its generality. For example, the research was a single case study of one tribal group in the eastern part of the United States. Moreover, the sample size was extremely small, and a number of legal and extralegal variables common to dispositional studies in criminology were not included in the analysis.[29]

Archie and Bette Randall provided limited information on arrests for the city of Spokane, the state of Washington, and the United States in general.[30] For the most part, the authors were concerned with indicators of differential treatment of Indians in the criminal justice system. For example, they reported that Indians made up 1.5 percent of the total arrests in the United States during 1974, but accounted for only .37 percent of the total U.S. population. For the same year, they reported that 11.36 percent of all Indians were arrested, while only 3 percent of all whites and 6.92 percent of all blacks were subjects of arrest. Identical categories for Spokane pointed out even larger differences in arrest rates among racial groups. For example, in 1974, American Indians made up 18.55 percent of all arrests in Spokane, and 8.05 percent in 1975. Based on this information, they concluded that ". . . Native Americans have the highest per capita arrest rates in the country."[31]

Although the authors indicated that they had observed differential treatment of American Indians by Spokane social control agents, their efforts to support these findings were somewhat simplistic. They also failed to control for legal and extralegal variables which traditional criminological studies of arrests have routinely included in their analyses.[32] Moreover, the study failed to control for tribal group differences, and was limited in terms of being able to generalize beyond the community examined.

### Official Indicators of American Indian Criminal Justice Outcomes

While most reviews of research on involvement in illegal behavior, for space reasons alone, would not include studies on post-detection and conviction outcomes, the brevity of literature on American Indian criminality allows us to also consider those studies which focus on these criminal justice outcomes for Native Americans. In fact, these studies are perhaps the more methodologically sophisticated of all research on American Indian criminality.

## Sentencing Patterns

Edwin Hall and Albert Simkus examined the sentencing patterns of Indians and whites in a western state by utilizing two overlapping populations of offenders.[33] The first included all offenders (white and Indian) sentenced to probationary types of sentences for having committed felonies under state jurisdiction between July 1966 and March 31, 1972; the second was based on a cohort sample of virtually all convicted felony offenders between July 1966 and July 1967. Unlike the majority of studies previously reviewed, this one controlled for a number of legal and extralegal variables which past research had found to be important factors in explanations of this measure of criminal justice outcomes. The legal variables included were type of offense, number of prior felonies, length of sentence, whether the offender had prior juvenile offenses, and whether the offender had previous institutionalizations as a juvenile. Education level, employment status, occupation, marital status, age and sex were the extralegal variables included in the study.

Descriptive statistics on the two populations revealed that Native Americans had lower education levels, less occupational prestige, and were less likely to be employed prior to the offense than whites. Somewhat surprisingly, the data also indicated that more Native American offenders were female. In addition, Native American offenders were more likely to have been convicted of forgery, burglary, second-degree assault and auto theft, adjudicated delinquent, committed to a juvenile institution, and had a record of prior felony convictions. Hall and Simkus also looked at the relationship between these legal and extralegal variables and the type of sentence imposed, using both a bivariate and multivariate analysis.[34] The findings indicated that even when controlling for the effects of both sets of variables, Native Americans were more likely than whites to have received sentences which included some incarceration and less likely to have received deferred sentences.[35]

## Parole Decisions

Several studies have examined the treatment afforded American Indians in the decision to release on parole. Bert Swift and Gary Bickel conducted a 1974 study of the parole treatment of Native Americans in the federal prison system.[36] Controlling for the offense committed, American Indians served 15 percent more time in prison prior to being released on parole than did all others considered. Moreover, the study also found that American Indians received longer sentences than did whites. Although these findings suggested that the differential parole treatment afforded Native Americans in the federal prison system may in fact be linked to prior courtroom decisionmaking, it is important to point out that Swift and Bickel did not control for other legal variables which have traditionally been significant predictors of the prison release decision, such as prior criminal record and major disciplinary rule violations while incarcerated.[37]

In a more recent study, Tim Bynum incorporated the legal variables of prior record and major infractions while in prison with selected social characteristics of the offenders in an examination of the parole release decisionmaking process in an upper plains state with a relatively large population of Native Americans.[38] In order to allow for sufficient time for parole consideration and/or release upon completing the imposed sentence, data were gathered in 1976 on a cohort sample of 255 offenders admitted to the state prison system during 1970. After excluding those who either had committed crimes for which parole was denied by statute, had sentences which were too long to be considered for the analysis, and/or those for whom the crimes committed were so unique or infrequently charged that their inclusion would have distorted the results, 137 offenders remained for further analysis. Of this group of offenders, who were primarily convicted of property crimes, fifty-four (39 percent) were American Indian, two were black, and the remainder were white.

Bynum overcame some of the limitations from the previous research by considering the parole decision as a continuous variable. He measured this criminal justice outcome not only by the length of sentence imposed, but also in terms of how much of the imposed sentence was served prior to release on parole. Findings indicated that for all cases, American Indians served an average of 86 percent of their sentence while all others served 75 percent, a difference statistically significant at the .01 level. An offense-specific analysis revealed similar statistically significant disparities for American Indians convicted of burglary (84 percent versus 64 percent). Conversely, for all crimes, the mean length of sentence given American Indians (18.6 months) was significantly less ($p < .001$) than that received by non-Indians (26.5 months), as was the mean length for burglary (16.2 compared to 24.8 months; $p < .01$). A multivariate regression analysis also indicated that when controlling for both legal and extralegal variables, American

Indians received a significantly lower sentence but served a greater proportion of it (age and number of major infractions were also significant variables).

Although the findings suggested a major anomaly in the data, Bynum provided two plausible interpretations.[39] The first posited that, theoretically, a parole board functions as a moderator of sentence disparities, and there was one finding which suggested this balancing effect. When Bynum considered an indicator of total months served (the proportion of sentence served times the sentence imposed), he did find that American Indians served an average of 13.6 months while non-Indians served an average of 15.3 months. The difference, though, was not statistically significant. An alternative explanation suggested by Bynum was that American Indians were in fact being treated more harshly than non-Indians, even within similar offense categories. In other words, Indians received incarceration for offenses for which non-Indians received nonincarcerative sentences. Moreover, all else being equal, American Indians served proportionately more time in prison as well.

Unfortunately, the few studies on American Indian criminality which utilized various official measures of involvement in illegal behavior have faced a number of criticisms based on comparisons with more sophisticated methodological approaches now employed by criminologists to explain variation in criminal behavior.[40] For example, most of these studies provided only descriptive information on arrest rates by race and offense categories, and most attempts to explain these differences based on variables such as economic inequality, anomie, cultural conflict and drinking behavior were speculative at best.[41] Analyses such as these which fail to control at the same time for variables of particular theoretical significance, such as drinking behavior and degree of cultural conflict, really tell us little about what factors best explain American Indian involvement in criminal behavior. However, it is important to note that two of the more methodologically rigorous studies which employed official records found evidence that regardless of a number of legal and extralegal intervening variables, American Indians did receive more severe criminal justice outcomes compared to other racial groups.[42]

## Official Records from Tribal Agencies

Jerrold Levy and his colleagues provided an analysis of patterns of criminal homicide among the Navajo between 1956 and 1965 based on data obtained from Wind Rock/Navajo police records.[43] For the most part, the research was an attempt to replicate an extensive study by Wolfgang and Ferracuti of criminal homicide in Philadelphia between 1948 and 1952.[44] Descriptive statistics revealed that the typical Navajo offender was male, between the ages of twenty-five and thirty-nine, married, and often had children. In addition, the typical Navajo victim was the wife or lover of the offender, and the common motives were marital strife, domestic quarrels and sexual jealousy. While these figures tend to parallel Wolfgang's earlier study, Levy and his colleagues reported one finding which was a significant departure from previous research. A very high proportion of Navajo homicide offenders committed suicide immediately after the homicidal event. The research suggested that both acts were performed for similar reasons, even though there was little support for the notion of a "Navajo subculture of violence." Nevertheless, according to the researchers, both behaviors were part of a larger phenomenon that warranted further investigation. Levy and his colleagues also suggested that although drinking frequency was related to arrest rates in general, use of alcohol did not account for differences between homicide offenders and the average Navajo.

These researchers should be given credit for attempting to replicate one of the most widely cited empirical studies in the field of criminology.[45] However, the research suffers from problems similar to those studies reviewed previously. For example, the sample consisted of only forty-three Navajo offenders over a ten-year period. Moreover, the authors noted that their data were inconsistent with that reported by both the Navajo police and the Navajo Yearbook,[46] two sources of annual crime statistics from the Navajo reservation. In addition, the study's sole focus on the Navajo tribe resulted in an inability to make comparisons between different tribal groups. As previously suggested, the little information we do have on American Indian criminality indicates tribal differences in involvement in illegal behavior, and these differences should be accounted for by comparative studies. Finally, unlike other studies which attempted to assess the degree to which a "subculture of violence" was in existence within a particular group in society, these researchers provided no direct measure of variables which operationalize important concepts from the subcultural violence thesis.[47]

Mhyra Minnis examined the relationship between the social structure of the Shashone-Bancock tribe and their rates of criminal involvement by analyzing data from a large-scale study of the Fort Hall Indian Reservation funded by the BIA in 1960.[48] For the most part, the data on the social structure of the community were based on 130 completed eighteen-page interview schedules, comprising a stratified sample representing one-third of the population, families and houses on the reservation. Measures of criminal involvement among the Shashone-Bancock tribe were based on records from the Tribal Law and Order Office. Selected indicators of the general social structure of the community included living conditions (types of houses, room occupancy rates, living conveniences such as number of rooms, indoor plumbing and bathrooms, utilities such as electricity and telephones, televisions, newspapers, magazines and automobiles), land utilization, population and family structure, educational status, percent on welfare, economic status, and rates of crime and delinquency. Overall, this descriptive information indicated that the Shashone-Bancock Indians on the Fort Hall Reservation had poor housing conditions and low standards of living.[49]

The population structure on the reservation was heavily concentrated in the lower age groups in comparison to the general United States population. With few tribal members in the middle or productive age groups, the nineteen-and-below age group made up 48.58 percent of the population (compared to 38.32 percent of the general United States population). Moreover, with few women in the labor force, Minnis noted that the major economic support of tribes came from approximately 25 percent of the population. She also stressed that the lack of economic opportunities was reflected in the fact that many males did not establish families until after reaching thirty-five years of age.[50]

Minnis also provided the following information on reservation crime rates. According to the Tribal Law and Order Office, of the 130 households sampled by the questionnaire, seventy-five (58 percent of all households) had some record of law violation. Over the years 1934 to 1960, the data indicated that a total of 527 offenses were committed (including recidivism) by members of 130 sample households. Using 1959 figures, Minnis reported that the reservation arrest rate was 161 per 1,000 population, compared to 46.4 for all cities in the United States (based on UCR data). In addition, a review of all arrests between 1955 and 1960 indicated a rise in crime from 13.3 percent of the reservation population to 34.3 percent in 1959. Minnis noted that many of the offenses were misdemeanors rather than felonies, with most of those falling in the categories of vagrancy, drunkenness and disorderly conduct.[51]

Minnis also analyzed the relationship between the factors of education, economic status, welfare and crime rates within categories of degree of crowding. Her findings indicated that those living in the most crowded conditions had the highest crime rates and percent on welfare as well as the lowest number of years of education, although their economic status was somewhat higher than others.[52] Based on these findings, Minnis suggested that there was a "lost generation" of young people who had few economic opportunities, high dropout rates and little job training.[53] These factors, coupled with prejudicial communities nearby and differential treatment in relation to drunkenness and disorderly conduct, pointed to a condition of "cultural clash."[54] Moreover, she argued that the Shashone-Bancock tribe was insulated in their own world, imitating their white neighbors in minor behavior patterns and communicating with the outside world only through radio and television. In conclusion, Minnis stressed that the close on-reservation surveillance by tribal police, coupled with their high visibility off the reservation, made minor offenses committed by American Indians more obvious and their punishment inevitable.[55]

Minnis's study made a sizable contribution to the literature on American Indian criminality by attempting to link social structural variables to the incidence of crime on the Fort Hall Reservation. Nevertheless, her work was also plagued by several of the problems common among studies on American Indian criminality, such as small sample sizes and relatively simplistic bivariate analyses of important relationships. In addition, her figures on criminal involvement were not broken down by sex or age, nor was there any indication that the census population figures on which her arrest rates were computed were age-specific counts. It is also unfortunate that while comparisons were made with other tribal groups on the social structural variables considered in the study, Minnis failed to make similar comparisons with crime rates.

Morris Forslund and Ralph Meyers presented a descriptive and cohort analysis of juvenile offenders by employing data on 1047 juvenile cases adjudicated by the Court of Indian Offenses on the Wind River Reservation during the years 1967 to 1971.[56] Their data indicated that males were more likely to have been delinquent than females (two out of three), and that the majority of the offenders were in the 16-to-17-year-old age group. It is interesting to note, however, that an overwhelming majority of the cases were referred to court by a juvenile officer on the reservation. Studies of non-Indian juvenile delinquency indicate that court referrals are typically given by school agents and/or parents.[57]

According to the data gathered by Forslund and Meyers, the largest percentage of offenses were alcohol-related — minor in possession, public intoxication, or driving while under the influence of alcohol. They also noted that there were some important differences between males and females in terms of offenses charged. For example, males were more likely to be charged with malicious mischief, theft, disturbing the peace, and inhaling noxious substances, while females were more likely to be charged with running away from home, maintaining public nuisance, and those offenses categorized as "other offenses." Nevertheless, a measure of association between the rank ordering of offense types by gender revealed a high degree of similarity of involvement in respective delinquent behaviors.[58]

Information on the adjudication process was also reported. A large majority of the offenders were found guilty (87.2 percent), and slightly more than one-third were sentenced to detention, while slightly less than one-third were placed on probation. More males were sentenced to detention than females, while more females were placed on probation. In addition, comparisons were made in terms of rates of delinquency charges by sex and age. Males had a higher rate of court appearances than females, with the older age group of 14-to-17-year-olds having the highest rate of court appearances. Finally, a comparison was made between court appearances on the reservation with that of all juvenile courts in the United States. Although an overwhelming majority of appearances by Wind River youth were for relatively minor offenses, Forslund and Meyers's data indicated that the reservation rate at the time of their study was approximately five times the national average.[59]

The cohort analysis utilized data derived from juvenile officer records. These findings revealed that nearly one-half of all males and over one-third of all females under the court's jurisdiction had at least one official contact with the juvenile officer during 1971, with the majority of the charges against these juveniles being alcohol-related. Moreover, the actual percentage of alcohol-related offenses among these juveniles was substantially higher than the official charge records of the court indicate. This was due to the fact that seventy-seven additional contacts were made for which the officer did not refer the juveniles to the court.

Forslund and Meyers gave us a rare look at rates of juvenile delinquency on an Indian reservation. Unfortunately, they provided only descriptive information on their population and failed to consider legal and extralegal variables found previously to be important predictors of involvement in juvenile delinquency.[60] Also, by considering only one reservation in the state of Wyoming, they failed to acknowledge the importance of comparative samples of different tribal groups. Until more studies are conducted which include these methodological improvements, our understanding of what factors best explain American Indian youths' involvement in juvenile delinquency will be severely limited.

In summary, studies employing official records from the BIA or other tribal social control agencies have generally focused on selected Native American populations and failed to make important comparisons across different tribal groups. As Harring has noted, differences between various tribal groups are crucial factors to consider in accounts of American Indian criminality.[61] In addition, too few studies have provided longitudinal analyses of patterns of criminality among the various groups selected. To her credit, Minnis provided measures of a number of relevant extraneous variables to predict American Indian crime patterns in her study of the Shashone-Bancock tribe in Idaho, but her analysis is subject to the criticism raised earlier, i.e., that her measures of association among important variables failed to go beyond simple bivariate analysis.[62] Perhaps most importantly, these studies, like those utilizing official UCR data, failed to account for all known American Indian crime. That is, in no instance have these studies included all measures of American Indian criminality from both tribal and nontribal sources.

### Self-Reports of American Indian Involvement in Illegal Behavior

Morris Forslund and Virginia Cranston, in a continuation of an earlier study of official records on delinquency involvement among Wind River Reservation youth, conducted a self-reported delinquency study of ninth- through twelfth-grade students attending two high schools in the Wind River Reservation area in May 1972.[63] Data were gathered on 355 Anglo males, 315 Anglo females, 68 Indian males and 62 Indian females. The questionnaire surveyed twenty-nine delinquent behaviors ranging from felony crimes to minor offenses which, if committed alone, would be unlikely to result in adjudication of delinquency.

Their findings revealed that among those who had committed the offenses, there was a significant difference between Anglo and Indian males for seven of the offenses and between Anglo and Indian females for sixteen. Proportionately, Anglo males were more likely to have made anonymous telephone calls and drunk alcoholic beverages without the knowledge of parents or guardians, while Indian males were more likely to have been truant from school, taken things from desks or lockers at school, been involved in fighting behavior, and used drugs other than marijuana for pleasure. A significantly higher proportion of Indian females indicated that they had committed the offenses of truancy, running away from home, vandalism, minor theft, driving cars without license or permit, fighting behavior, and smoking marijuana in comparison to Anglo females.

In terms of frequency of involvement, similar results were reported except that there were no differences between Anglo and Indian males' use of drugs other than marijuana, and no differences between Indian and Anglo females for driving a car without a permit or license. However, Indian females were more frequently involved in disobedience at school, drinking without parental approval, and breaking street lights. Controlling for social class reduced the number of differences between Anglo and Indian youth delinquent involvement, although in other instances some differences emerged which did not appear in the total sample. Of the differences which did exist, however, all but one pointed to a higher proportion of Indian youths involved in delinquency. Moreover, while few differences were indicated among Indian and Anglo males on any social class level or for Indian and Anglo working-class females, both middle- and lower-class Indian females were found to be more frequently involved in delinquent behavior than their Anglo counterparts.

These researchers should be commended for being among the first to examine self-reported delinquency among Indian youth. Their study supports findings from previous research on other youthful offender populations in that a considerable amount of delinquency involvement was reported for both Anglo and Indian youth. Moreover, when social class was controlled in their analysis, Forslund and Cranston noted that many Indian and Anglo differences in delinquency rates were reduced. However, while their research included 130 Indian adolescents, larger samples are needed to draw meaningful conclusions concerning the actual involvement of Indian youth in delinquent behavior. Finally, with the exception of the sociodemographic variables of race, sex and social class, these researchers failed to include indicators of a number of variables that previous studies have found to be important determinants of American Indian criminality such as cultural conflict, isolation, and tribal membership.

Bruce Chadwick and his colleagues conducted a survey of the Seattle Indian community during the fall of 1972 to examine the type and extent of legal problems experienced by Indians living there.[64] Specifically, a list of three thousand Indians in King County was obtained through tribal rolls, community agency lists, public school records, arrest records, and subscriptions to a local Indian newspaper. From this list a random sample of two hundred adults was selected, of whom one hundred (50 percent) agreed to be interviewed by trained Indian interviewers. A comparison sample of one thousand whites was also selected from the telephone directory, and approximately 65 percent of these individuals responded to the survey. Although both civil and criminal matters were assessed, only the criminal justice questions will be considered here.

Respondents were asked to indicate how many times they had been arrested in the past year. The Indian sample reported 24 arrests per 100 persons compared to 4 out of 100 for the white sample. Chadwick and his colleagues contended that this self-report of arrests — a six-to-one ratio of Indian-to-white arrests — compared favorably to the ratio of arrests reported by Charles Reasons for the United States as a whole.[65] While the finding that one of every four Indians had been arrested in the previous year may demonstrate the need for crime prevention and rehabilitation programs designed for Indians, Chadwick and his colleagues also suggested that future research should assess the extent to which these arrest figures were the result of differential law enforcement practices.

Perhaps not surprisingly, the two samples differed in terms of socioeconomic status, with white respondents having higher education levels (12.1 vs. 11.1 years), occupational status, and annual incomes ($9,000 versus $5,000) than Indian respondents. Consequently, the authors controlled for level of socioeconomic status by examining the relationship between education, occupational status, income, and legal confrontations. Results indicated that the relationship between these measures of socioeconomic status and number of reported legal problems (both civil and criminal) were very small and statistically nonsignificant. Another factor thought to be an important predictor of legal difficulties was length of residence in Seattle. It was anticipated that persons who had lived in Seattle for a long period of time would be more familiar with the laws and economic practices of the city than those who had recently come from rural or reservation areas. However, the average length of time in Seattle for the Indian sample was fifteen years, and the relationship between this variable and legal difficulties was not statistically significant.

The study was also concerned with the utilization of local agencies to provide assistance in solving legal problems. Indians were nearly four times more likely than whites to use these services, although the number actually receiving aid did not approach the number reporting problems. Only 10 percent of the Indians who reported having been arrested in the past year had been represented by an attorney, and only 25 percent of those arrested who did not have an attorney believed that having one would have benefited them in their legal matters. One possible explanation for these figures lies in the fact that the majority of Indian respondents did not know about public agencies, with the exception of the public defender's office which provided legal resources to criminal defendants. Finally, the authors believed that more efforts were necessary to acquaint urban Indians with the existing opportunities for legal assistance, and that existing agencies should have more effective outreach programs to actively seek Indian clients.

It is perhaps unfair to compare Chadwick and his colleagues' study to that of typical self-report studies in criminology because of its larger emphasis on legal problems facing urban Indians, as well as whites. However, it does point out the difficulties for those who attempt to obtain self-report data on Indian populations. For example, the authors utilized a list of three thousand Indians in King County, while the census recorded that approximately eight thousand Indians resided in the area. This suggests that all possible respondents were not identified and, therefore, did not have an equal opportunity to be involved in the study. Moreover, their response rate of 50 percent was modest in comparison to most social science surveys, further highlighting the difficulties of obtaining an accurate measure of self-reported involvement in illegal behavior among Indian populations.

Gary Jensen and his colleagues have argued that a review of the literature on race and crime suggests that disproportionate rates of offending are actually a function of differential labeling of minorities by the criminal justice system.[66] However, these researchers also noted that research on alcoholism and alcohol-related health problems among Indian populations has demonstrated that differential labeling explanations do not account for the differences between Native Americans and other ethnic groups in terms of alcohol-related arrests. Rather, the latter studies suggest that there may be real behavioral differences in alcohol use among ethnic groups.

This reasoning led Jensen and his colleagues to posit that alternative theoretical perspectives may also be needed to explain differential involvement in deviant behavior among ethnic groups. For example, while some accounts of Indian drinking patterns are similar to traditional criminological explanations of deviance among general populations, stressing failure of socialization and lack of social controls (i.e., social disorganization), still other studies claim to have found a high tolerance of drunkenness among traditional Indian cultures.

In an attempt to address these conflicting hypotheses concerning Native American deviance, the researchers utilized a sample of youth from three Indian boarding schools representing the Navajo, Apache and Hopi tribes. Measurements of deviant behavior, defined as the rule violations among the three groups, were obtained.[67] The most common violation among the three groups was that involving alcohol use. There were, however, significant differences among the three groups in terms of alcohol use, with the highest rates for the Navajo youth, and the lowest for the Hopi youth. An examination of these differences in alcohol use within categories of family disorganization revealed that disorganization variables did not account for the tribal variations. Similar findings on an individual level of analysis also failed to support the notion that these patterns were a function of social disorganization. The authors noted that even when cultural values associated with acceptable drinking behavior were examined, their data provided no direct support for a cultural conflict interpretation of the observed tribal differences in alcohol use. Jensen and his colleagues concluded that although tribal variations in rule violations among the boarding school youth were persistent and significant, neither cultural deviance nor disorganization variables adequately accounted for these differences. They also urged future research to provide comprehensive tests which would include more refined measures of norms, values and behavior among both Indian and non-Indian populations.

Jensen and his colleagues should be given credit for their awareness of the importance of controlling for intragroup differences in studies of American Indian involvement in illegal behavior. Their findings concerning the differential rates of rule violations among the Apache, Navajo and Hopi youth add further support for this argument. Unfortunately, in spite of this methodological improvement over previous studies, the authors failed to account for why these differences existed, noting only that more accurate measures of integration into tribal society and culture might lead to a better understanding of Indian crime and delinquency.

Larry Williams and his colleagues conducted a study of self-reported arrests among American Indians in Seattle in 1972. Their primary goal was to identify factors which influenced either American Indian frequency of involvement in illegal behavior or their differential visibility to members of social control agencies.[68] The sample consisted of 96 out of 350 Indian respondents selected at random from a list of 4000 names obtained from tribal records, public school records, Indian organizations, service agencies, police records and the subscription list of a local Indian newspaper.

The dependent variable in the study was self-reported arrests, measured by asking respondents to estimate the number of times they had been arrested in the last five years. The independent variables in the study were categorized into three groups: background variables, personality variables and cultural variables. The background variables included age, sex, education, income, occupation, marital status, marital happiness, migration, social adjustment, and awareness of social agencies. The personality variables consisted of a number of widely used scales of self-esteem, anomie, personal control, tension and alienation. The cultural variables were degree of drinking problems, association with white people, involvement with Indian people, degree of Indianness and support for assimilation. The analysis was based on a stepwise multiple regression analysis that assessed the relative effect of each of the independent variables on the dependent variable, while controlling for the individual effects of the remaining variables in the regression equation.

Findings indicated that the largest single predictors of Indian arrests rates were the background variables of sex and age, explaining over 15 percent of the overall variance in the dependent variable. The other independent variables of social adjustment, drinking problems, tension, Indianness, marital adjustment, relative marital happiness and awareness of social agencies were significant predictors of self-reported arrests, but each variable only contributed a modest 5 percent or less to the overall variance explained by the final model. In total, these nine independent variables were found to be significant, and together explained approximately 36 percent of the variance in the dependent variable of self-reported arrests.[69]

It is important to note, however, that contrary to a number of previous studies which stressed the importance of cultural conflict in explanations of Indian criminality, this study found that when controlling for cultural and personality variables, background variables (which also have been important predictors of non-Indian criminality) were the most significant factors for self-reported American Indian arrest rates. These findings suggest that when controlling for race, similar demographic profiles describe both the typical Indian and non-Indian offender. Finally, given that studies of official arrest rates continue to indicate that Indian criminality is more problematic than that of whites, and at least as problematic as that of blacks, the authors suggested that future studies consider the possibility of an anti-Indian bias in the criminal justice system.[70]

Williams and his colleagues demonstrated that researchers are becoming more aware of the importance of multivariate analyses for controlling for alternative explanations of American Indian involvement in illegal behavior. However, the study also vividly demonstrated several methodological problems that researchers face in this area of criminology. For example, in order to determine more adequately what variables best explain American Indian criminality, or possibly their differential visibility to social control agents, sample sizes of more than ninety-six respondents will be necessary. Also, the study's response rate of approximately 28 percent was poor in comparison to most self-report surveys of general populations. This undesirable response rate suggests that other researchers should consider alternative methods of obtaining more representative samples of Indian populations, from both urban and rural areas, as well as from reservations and non-reservation settings.

Susan Robbins studied self-reported involvement in delinquent behavior among Seminole youth on three Florida reservations — Hollywood, Big Cypress and Brighton.[71] These reservations represent a diverse population, according to Robbins, in that Hollywood is extremely urban, while Brighton and Big Cypress are both fairly rural. Of the three reservations, Brighton is the most isolated. Robbins's main interest in the study was to assess the degree to which the variables of Travis Hirschi's social control theory — attachment, commitment and belief — accounted for Indian involvement in delinquent behavior.[72] Respondents were selected from the official Seminole tribal roll, and 129 Seminole youth completed anonymous, self-administered questionnaires. The sample consisted of 70 percent of all youth known to be living on the reservations.

The dependent variable in the study was an index of self-reported behavior based on seven items representing delinquent acts. Respondents were asked to indicate whether they had engaged in the following activities in the past: taken things worth less than five dollars; purposely damaged or destroyed property that did not belong to them; taken a car for a ride without the owner's permission; taken things of some value between five and ten dollars; broken into a building; physically hurt someone on purpose; and taken things worth more than fifty dollars. The independent variable of attachment, as outlined by Hirschi, represents the bond of affection and respect for significant others in society such as one's parents, teachers and friends,[73] and has been measured successfully in other studies of delinquency.[74] However, in this study an attempt was made to measure attachment in two dimensions, one to non-Indian persons and institutions, and another to conventional Indian persons. A second independent variable, commitment, according to Hirschi, represents the degree to which an individual is involved in conventional activities, and the extent to which that involvement would be jeopardized by engaging in illegal behavior.[75] The third independent variable, belief, refers to an individual's attitude toward the law which develops through attachment to parents and concern for approval from significant others.[76] Measures of these two independent variables conformed to those used in previous studies. The gender of the respondents was also included as an independent variable in the analysis.

The results indicated that all three reservations had high rates of delinquency. The Big Cypress Reservation had the highest delinquency rates, with 81.8 percent of the respondents indicating that they had engaged in some form of delinquency in the past. The Hollywood Reservation had a similar rate (79.7 percent), while the Brighton Reservation, the most rural and isolated of the three, reported the lowest rate (59.5 percent). Robbins stated that more males reported involvement in delinquent activities than did females. The data did not indicate a direct relationship between age and delinquency, although delinquent activity appeared to peak at around fifteen years of age.

Perhaps not surprisingly, Robbins reported that her attempt to measure attachment to persons within the Indian culture was unsuccessful.[77] She argued that the reasons may lie in the fact that child-rearing and socialization practices among Indians are quite different from those of non-Indians, and suggested that future efforts be conducted by individuals who were raised within the culture. The variable of attachment to non-Indian persons and institutions such as teachers, schools and police, however, was moderately to strongly related to self-reported involvement in delinquency across the three groups studied, although only three of the nine relationships presented were significant beyond the .05 level of analysis. Based on these measures of association, however, Robbins concluded that "most Seminole youth who respected the police, liked school, and cared what their teachers thought about them were somewhat less likely to be involved in delinquent behavior than those who did not."[78]

Findings concerning the variables of belief and commitment suggested that Seminole youth viewed law violations as wrongful behavior and perceived that sanctions for involvement in illegal behavior were likely to occur. For example, 92 percent of the youth believed that law violation was wrong. Moreover, 74 percent believed that they would be caught and punished if they committed a crime, and most believed that their parents would find out (85 percent). On the other hand, 69.5 percent of the youth indicated that they would not "get into trouble" for their involvement in illegal behavior. Robbins suggested that this finding points to a separate set of external constraints, one for the native culture and another for the society at large. In other words, "trouble" was caused by persons outside the native culture.

Bivariate relationships among the measures of commitment, belief and involvement in delinquent acts indicated moderate to strong relationships among the formal and informal threat variables and delinquent activity. Robbins argued that these findings suggested that Indian youth must employ "techniques of neutralization," which would reduce the effect of Hirschi's control variables, in order to engage in illegal behavior. She noted that one widely used example of these techniques is that of "blaming Indian problems on the injustices inflicted by the United States government."[79]

In conclusion, Robbins posited that her findings suggested that two distinct socialization processes work concurrently on the Indian child. Rather than partial or incomplete socialization in one society or the other, Seminole youth may be adequately socialized in both. In terms of the association between the control variables and delinquency, Robbins argued that it follows patterns of non-Indian expression as well as the pattern of very traditional Indian ways. Therefore, in order for Indian youth to engage in delinquent acts, they "must be relatively free of the controls of both Anglo and Indian society which act as deterrents to crime."[80]

Robbins's work is an improvement over previous studies on Indian delinquency in that she attempted to measure the degree to which a widely accepted theory of social control, as outlined by Hirschi, can account for involvement in illegal behavior among three different reservation samples of Seminole youth. Research should continue to assess the extent to which general theories of deviance and social control explain variations in American Indian rates of offending. Efforts such as these will help determine whether alternative explanations are needed to better understand American Indian crime patterns.

However, Robbins's study also suffers from a lack of methodological rigor in comparison to similar studies on general populations. For example, a recent study which focused on Hirschi's control theory variables, utilizing high school respondents, indicated that longitudinal measures of self-reported involvement in illegal behavior are necessary to establish the appropriate causal ordering among the independent and dependent variables.[81] Moreover, Robbins's analysis is problematic in that she failed to report the coding scheme used for her independent variables, thus limiting the interpretation of her results. Like so many other studies on American Indian criminality, she also based her conclusions on a relatively small sample from a single tribal group.

In addition, Robbins's study only provided a bivariate analysis of selected control variables and self-reported delinquency. As previously indicated, multivariate analyses are necessary to control simultaneously for alternative explanations of involvement in illegal behavior. A good example of this problem in her work can be demonstrated by considering one of her major findings. Robbins suggested that "techniques of neutralization" were intervening variables in the relationship between Hirschi's control variables and self-reported involvement in delinquent behavior, but she failed to provide any direct measure of these techniques in her research.[82]

In summary, self-reports of American Indian criminality, unlike their official counterparts, have the advantage of enabling researchers to identify both reported and unreported criminal activity, and provide some method of assessing whether official measures of involvement actually reveal differential visibility to social control agents. Not surprisingly, the two studies which examined this issue for both Indian and non-Indian samples reported only small differences, if any, among these two groups.[83] Moreover, the survey methods employed by self-report studies allow researchers to operationalize a number of theoretically important concepts to explain American Indian criminality such as differential social controls,[84] social class,[85] sociodemographic and social indicators of the population,[86] and other background characteristics such as parental drinking patterns.[87]

In spite of these advantages, self-reports of American Indian criminality also suffer from a number of methodological problems in comparison to current standards for these research designs.[88] For example, none of these studies has provided a longitudinal analysis of self-reported behavior. Evidence from recent longitudinal studies of self-reported behavior among general populations strongly suggests that employing measures of past behavior as an indicator of actual future behavior in causal models of involvement in illegal behavior produces spurious relationships due to misspecification of the causal ordering among their independent and dependent variables.[89] In addition, many of these studies also had other methodological problems such as low response rates,[90] samples with few Indian respondents,[91] and lack of comparisons between tribal groups.[92] Until more comprehensive research which incorporates these methodological refinements is conducted, our understanding of American Indian criminality will be restricted to simple descriptive and bivariate analyses of limited samples.

### Qualitative Studies of American Indian Criminality

Robert Kuttner and Albert Lorincz conducted a qualitative study of approximately one hundred urban American Indian women of Sioux, Winnebago and Omaha descent who were involved in prostitution during a five-year period beginning in 1965.[93] The major portion of the study was conducted in the "skid row" of Omaha, Nebraska. However, the geographical mobility of the subjects allowed for additional data to be obtained from Sioux City, Iowa, and the city of Chicago. The authors suggested that a sizable portion of Indian women over time were involved in a wide range of promiscuous behavior and prostitution activities, more so than UCR data would indicate (which according to Kuttner and Lorincz reported only 142 arrests for Indian prostitution in 1965). Limited economic opportunities both on and off the reservation, chronic alcoholism, tribal disorganization and a breakdown of regulatory mores were offered as possible explanations for involvement in these behaviors, although Kuttner and Lorincz argued that the problems of urbanization, which affect all economically disadvantaged minority populations, also played an important role.

Their results indicated that the behavior patterns exhibited by these Indian women could be classified into four general groups: normal promiscuity, extreme promiscuity, compensated promiscuity and professional promiscuity. The authors argued that these categories might be viewed as "evolutionary stages which mark the progression of the subjects from promiscuity to overt prostitution."[94] Rather than recruitment per se, involvement in prostitution was described as a gradual drifting through stages of promiscuity. However, to the extent that recruitment did occur, it was evident in interaction with blacks who were both involved in commercialized vice and living in ghetto areas which overlapped with Indian skid row communities.

Kuttner and Lorincz argued that alcoholism was the primary variable explaining the involvement of these women in this behavior. Unless they were staying with friends and family who could provide an adequate supply of alcohol, these women would frequent the skid row taverns daily. Drinking would begin early in the morning with money earned the previous day, until paying customers arrived later in the day. According to Kuttner and Lorincz, making large sums of money was not the goal of these women. Rather, most were satisfied with only being involved in the behavior long enough to pay for the day's drinking expenses. Attitudes toward the behavior were difficult to obtain, the authors suggested, because questions concerning these issues were typically met with statements which attempted to resolve what was assumed to be moral doubt on the part of the investigators. Self-esteem was maintained by rationalizations designed to show their superiority over potential economic and social rivals. In many instances, attitudes of family members were relatively unimportant, although in some cases they were simply unaware of when promiscuous behavior moved into the area of overt prostitution.[95]

For the most part, these Indian women are depicted as alcoholics who support their drinking habits through prostitution. With the exception of periods in which marriages or useful economic activities temporarily removed them from taverns, the social life revolving around the Indian (or skid row) bars continually brought these women back. There was also an absence of stigma and community rejection of these women.[96] These factors, along with limited educational backgrounds and few job skills, posed a difficult problem for those who would attempt to rehabilitate these women and provide legitimate economic opportunities for them. The authors noted that perhaps the best strategy would be to reduce the number of new recruits through early intervention programs, strengthened family support, and better educational and employment opportunities.

Kuttner and Lorincz shed light on a topic which has been overlooked by virtually all other studies of American Indian criminality. In this regard, their qualitative analysis provided a good model for more elaborate qualitative analyses of Native American involvement in prostitution behavior in the future. However, as James Inverarity and his colleagues have pointed out, quantitative analyses do provide the advantage of "imposing some constraints on overly creative imaginations."[97] Therefore, it is crucial at some point in the future that quantitative analyses also contribute to our understanding of this offense.

In summary, qualitative studies on American Indian criminality are few in number. The reason for this void in the literature may be linked to the fact that quantitative criminology has become a more preferred method of analysis over the past decade. However, the field of criminology has a rich tradition in qualitative research,[98] and more qualitative research is needed to contribute to our knowledge of American Indian criminality. In fact, given what little is known about American Indian crime patterns, and the continuing problem facing quantitative studies of obtaining large enough samples for meaningful multivariate analyses, it may be that qualitative methodologies will become the preferred strategy to study American Indian criminality.

### Summary of Research on American Indian Criminality

Unfortunately, virtually all of the studies to date on American Indian criminality have methodological shortcomings in comparison to current criminological research strategies employed to assess general patterns of crime. These shortcomings include small, unrepresentative samples, inaccurate measures of crime rates, simplistic bivariate analyses, lack of comparisons across different tribal groups, and a failure to control for important alternative explanations for involvement in illegal behavior. Nevertheless, it is beneficial at this point to identify those factors which continue to emerge from these studies as important variables to consider in future attempts to develop an etiology of crime among Native Americans. Moreover, several studies have provided strategies for possible future public policy decisions regarding Native American offenders.

Perhaps not surprisingly, a number of studies have indicated the importance of controlling for the frequency of drinking of alcoholic beverages when studying American Indian crime patterns.[99] Another group of studies has strongly pointed to the importance of social disorganization as measured by the degree of cultural conflict and/or the degree of marginality.[100] Still others have stressed the importance of several social structural and/or economic variables in explaining American Indian criminality.[101] For example, French and Hornbuckle argued that reservation status was a crucial factor to consider,[102] while Hayner noted that in addition to the degree of isolation, some indicator of the degree of relative economic deprivation among tribal groups was also an important explanatory variable.[103] Another study has emphasized the importance of selected demographic profiles of offenders, rather than race per se. Williams and his colleagues, for example, indicated that among their respondents, sex, age and marital status were the most important predictors of self-reported arrests.[104] Finally, several researchers have provided some timely information for possible policy decisions which might directly affect American Indians. Chadwick and his colleagues suggested that awareness of legal services can be an important predictor of criminal justice outcomes among American Indians, and recommended that more efforts be made by legal service agencies to make these services available to Indian clients.[105] Kuttner and Lorincz, on the other hand, suggested that early intervention programs, efforts toward strengthening family support, and providing more educational and employment opportunities would be important strategies to pursue in the future.[106]

**Future Research on American Indian Criminality**

This chapter has reviewed previous studies on American Indian criminality in an effort to determine what we do know about this issue, as well as to encourage more rigorous research so that we might know more in the future. However, any efforts in this area of criminological research will face several difficult tasks worthy of further consideration. For example, researchers will need to develop a method by which both official UCR data and BIA data on American Indian criminality can be utilized as a single indicator of the total incidence of known American Indian crime. In addition, efforts must be directed toward creating data bases which contain reliable indicators of American Indian economic, social and demographic conditions. These data could then be merged with comprehensive crime figures in order to more adequately assess multivariate relationships between these social structural variables and measures of involvement in criminal behavior over time at the aggregate level of analysis.

Individual-level studies of self-reported involvement offer another potential approach to understanding American Indian criminality. These studies typically provide researchers with the opportunity to generate truly random samples of various populations and operationalize theoretically derived variables which might not be capable of being measured at aggregate levels. However, as we have seen from previous studies of this kind, this area of research must develop methods to identify significant numbers of Indian respondents. It may be the case that studies such as these must be conducted at a national level in order to obtain representative samples of the total Indian population that are large enough to develop multivariate models from which meaningful generalizations can be made.

Another crucial avenue of research for studies on American Indian criminality is that which focuses on the various stages of the criminal justice process. Findings from a number of studies reviewed here which were conducted at single decisionmaking points in the sanctioning process have suggested that differential treatment of American Indian offenders may exist, although their methodological problems prevent us from making a definitive statement on this issue. What is needed are more studies such as those conducted on non-Indian offender populations which have employed measures of decisions made at various stages of the criminal justice process.[107] These studies allow researchers to assess the extent, if any, to which differential treatment of offenders at earlier stages of the process affects decisions made at later points in time. For example, it may be the case that the disproportionate numbers of American Indians incarcerated in state and federal prisons are not the result of overt discrimination at the sentencing stage. Rather, the differential visibility of American Indians to social control agents at the arrest stage may be the more significant variable to consider. In fact, more recent studies of non-Indian populations have suggested that certain factors in the process, such as the pretrial release decision, as well as contextual factors such as the geographical region in which the offender resides, may also play a crucial role in the differential treatment of offenders in the criminal justice system.[108] Studies of American Indian criminality must attempt to reach this level of methodological sophistication in order to adequately assess the degree to which differential treatment by the criminal justice system accounts for their disproportionate representation at various stages of the social control system.

Research on American Indian criminality at all levels of analysis should also more thoroughly assess those factors which can account for differential rates of offending within Indian populations. Several studies reviewed here have indicated that Native American crime cannot be viewed as a generic phenomenon.[109] Rather, researchers must attempt to identify situational and contextual factors that can account for these differences by utilizing comparative samples of Indian offenders across tribal groups.

Finally, research on American Indian criminality must address theoretically some of the anomalous findings posed by past research. For example, several studies reviewed here suggest that American Indian criminality, like that of other ethnic groups in the United States, is basically an urban phenomenon.[110] However, still other researchers argue that when reservation crime is also considered, the highest incidence of American Indian crime occurs in rural areas.[111] Moreover, there is some indication that, unlike most crime patterns, American Indian crime rates are positively related to economic wealth.[112] Future efforts must attempt to resolve theoretical issues such as these in order to better understand American Indian criminality. Ultimately, alternative theories may be necessary to explain these differences, given that a majority of the criminological theories today assume that typical "street crime" is in many respects a result of the complexities of urban life, and is motivated by a lack of economic resources.

### Social Justice, Public Policy, and American Indian Criminality

Data on American Indian criminality suggest this racial group has a disproportionate involvement in crime. This conclusion has been documented in both empirical research and official criminal justice figures reviewed here. Although the most recent criminal justice statistics indicate that arrest rates for black Americans are the highest of all ethnic groups, American Indian arrest rates are still two times the rate of white Americans and nearly four times the rate of Asian Americans. When all substance abuse-related offenses are examined, Native Americans have the highest rates of arrest. American Indians are arrested at twice the rate of white Americans and six times that of Asian Americans. When only alcohol-related offenses are examined, American Indian arrest rates are approximately two-and-a-half times that of whites and blacks, and seven-and-a-half times that of Asian Americans. Perhaps not surprisingly, Hispanic rates in these categories are very similar to those of American Indians.[113]

Rates of imprisonment for American Indians follow similar patterns. Although American Indians comprise only 0.6 percent of the total U.S. population, the most recent incarceration data reveal that American Indians make up approximately 2 percent of the federal and 1 percent of the state prison populations. These figures also indicate that although black Americans have the highest rates of incarceration, Native Americans are confined in federal and state institutions at a rate that is more than two times that of white Americans, and six times that of Asian Americans.[114]

Because data on criminal justice sentencing outcomes are more difficult to ascertain due to the lack of a systematic reporting system like that for arrest and imprisonment rates, comparisons among American Indians and other population groups on this indicator of criminal justice outcomes are more problematic. Efforts to assess the sentencing outcomes of American Indians, as demonstrated in this chapter, can be found only in very limited quantities in research findings published by various governmental agencies and professional journals. However, conclusions drawn from the limited number of studies available do suggest that American Indians experience differential treatment by the criminal justice system in comparison to other population groups.

The major problem with all of these sources is that most fail to control for the relevant legal and extralegal factors that previous scholarly work on other racial groups has found to be important predictors of criminal justice outcomes. Findings from the majority of these studies indicate that although minorities (particularly blacks, based on the volume of findings about this group) have experienced more contact with social control agents, a large portion of this experience has been the result of more frequent involvement in serious crimes, which is highly correlated with more severe dispositional outcomes. Therefore, a number of scholars argue that although minority groups may be disproportionately represented in arrest, conviction and incarceration rates, this finding can be explained by legal and extralegal variables such as prior criminal record and socioeconomic status.[115]

In spite of these findings, several sociological theories of law, particularly those of conflict and labeling, hypothesize racial bias in the criminal justice system. Conflict theories typically account for this bias in the criminal justice system by arguing that laws are created by those groups in society who maintain, or have access to, power.[116] These groups influence the process of creating law in such a way as to criminalize those behaviors which adversely affect their interests, and to de-emphasize, or to ignore altogether, those behaviors which positively affect them. Therefore, according to conflict theorists, the disproportionate representation of minority groups in the criminal justice system is accounted for by the fact that the behavior in which these groups are more likely to participate, because of their positions in society, is defined by the powerful as illegal. On the other hand, those behaviors in which the powerful are more likely to engage, and which are equally or, perhaps, even more costly in terms of harm to society and the environment, are typically handled either in an administrative format, through various regulatory agencies, or simply viewed as outside the realm of social control agencies in general.

Labeling theories pose the problem of bias in a somewhat different framework, although their analyses ultimately rely on some notion of a dominant group's ability to use its power and resources in society to avoid criminal sanctions.[117] Labeling theorists argue that the primary question for criminology is why some groups are reacted to differently than others. They argue that all members of society engage in behavior which could be labeled as deviant, but only certain groups are the object of societal reaction (i.e., actually caught, punished and treated as deviant or criminal by society). In fact, one primary indicator of power in this analysis is the ability of an individual or group to elude or reject the criminal label. According to labeling theories, the behavior of minority group members is more often the subject of the legal sanctioning process, and therefore, as indicated by official criminal justice statistics, these groups have higher rates of involvement in crime.

Still another approach to the understanding of the differential treatment of minority groups in the criminal justice system is an internal colonial model. Although it primarily has been used to account for the status of blacks in the United States, and other groups in the Third World, it recently has been employed to account for the general status of American Indians in the United States,[118] and in particular their involvement with the criminal justice system.[119] This model suggests that a dominant group comes to control a subordinate one on the basis of the former's ability to destroy the culture and social organization of the subordinate group, as well as to obtain control of the latter's economic resources. The dominant group further enhances its power over the subordinate group by creating, and then playing upon, stereotypes of the subordinate group which depict them as embodying characteristics which are devalued and despised by the dominant group. In its advanced stages, the internal colonial model posits that the dominant group enlists members of the subordinate group into societal roles which further subjugate them. In the case of the criminal justice system, this process results in members of the minority group joining the lower ranks of the social control agencies in positions which allow them to arrest fellow minorities as violators, bring them into the formal legal system, and actually participate in their punishment as guards and other correctional agents. This co-optation of subordinate group members further enhances the power of the dominant group, while simultaneously creating an illusion that the colonial power has opened society to the members of the colonized group. It has been suggested that tribal law enforcement agencies under the direction of the BIA are examples of how the co-optation process continues to work in Indian communities today.[120]

Although the most appropriate theoretical model to explain American Indian criminality will only be determined by future research efforts, empirical evidence of the ability of the Anglo-American legal system to undermine the traditional way of life for American Indians continues to be readily present. One example can be found in the case of the use of peyote by American Indians who are members of the Native American Church. Although the use of peyote in religious ceremonies has been documented in earlier times, the modern version of the practice can be traced to the creation of the Otoe Church of the First Born in the state of Oklahoma in 1909, which evolved into the Native American Church by 1918. Since this time, opposition to the use of peyote has spread and state laws prohibiting its use have been created. As a result, legal cases over time have focused on attempts by social control agents to arrest, detain and incarcerate American Indians who use peyote in their religious practices as members of the Native American Church.[121] This treatment of American Indians who practice the peyote religion demonstrates the ability of Anglo-American law to produce a "chilling effect" on American Indian culture.

The persistent legal assault on American Indian culture is further evidenced by the treatment of American Indian offenders incarcerated in state and federal prisons. Numerous efforts to bring religious practices (which are analogous to those used by dominant religious groups in the United States) into the prison have been met with much opposition by correctional authorities. American Indians who wear their hair in traditional lengths have been subjected to disciplinary procedures by prison officials.[122] The use of sweat lodges and other aspects of American Indian religion have also been the subject of legal cases, although in some instances, these efforts have resulted in favorable decisions which allowed limited participation of American Indian prisoners in their religious practices.[123]

Still another example of the legal conflict between Indian culture and that of the dominant white society can be found in the regulation of traditional hunting and fishing activities of the tribes. The states of Washington and Oregon were the sites of a number of legal battles over these issues in the late 1960s and early 1970s. Confrontations between tribal members participating in annual fishing activities, local and state police agencies, and citizen groups resulted in the arrests of a large number of American Indians on charges that these tribal members were violating gaming and fishing laws. American Indians were also charged with more serious offenses during some of these confrontations, but it was apparent that the arrests were the result of the increased hostilities brought about by the confrontations with local and state police concerning Indian fishing activities.[124]

More recently, Indian tribes in northern Wisconsin have been involved in similar confrontations with local and state officials and citizen groups concerning their rights to fish and hunt off tribal reservations based on nineteenth-century treaties which have been upheld in recent federal court decisions.[125] Although most of these confrontations have resulted in the arrests of whites who have attempted to disrupt the fishing and hunting activities of various tribal groups in the area, the extent to which American Indians have experienced racial bias from the fallout of these activities in the form of increased surveillance, arrests and convictions for nonfishing activities is difficult to determine. Considerable media coverage of these activities, and the establishment of several antitreaty rights groups such as PARR (Protect Americans' Rights and Resources), have heightened the tensions in the area, and threaten to disrupt the annual fishing and hunting activities of the tribes.

The establishment of tribal courts has been hailed as one possible method by which American Indians might not only regain control over the regulation of the behavior of tribal members, but also exercise jurisdiction over a wide range of conflicts between Indians and non-Indians. Although some variation of tribal courts has existed for a long period of time, more recent efforts have focused on what happens to Indians who commit crimes in Indian country.[126] However, there are several problems associated with these efforts. Tribal courts are an invention that is inherently foreign to the traditional Indian way of life. In other words, the establishment of tribal courts can be viewed as still another example of the continuing effort of the dominant society to impose its value system and form of social organization upon Indian people. A second concern is that tribal courts systems have severely limited jurisdictions. In accordance with statutory law, most of the serious offenses committed by Indian defendants are handled in federal courts. The few offenses over which tribal courts do have control are minor criminal and/or civil matters. Therefore, tribal courts are rarely in a position to provide an alternative forum for Indian defendants accused of "ordinary crime." Still another concern that has been raised is the lack of due process rights for the accused. Tribal courts are typically staffed and operated by Indians who have very little knowledge of the American judicial system and how it operates. Therefore, many of the common features of American jurisprudence such as the right to have an attorney represent the defendant in legal proceedings, a trial by jury, and the right of appellate review may not be present in Indian tribal courts. Tribal courts have also been accused of preferential treatment of defendants with relatives in various official positions in the tribal legal systems.[127]

Nevertheless, these examples serve to highlight the degree to which Indian ways have been subjugated and destroyed by laws of the dominant society which seek to control culturally and spiritually sanctioned behavior. It is in this sense that American Indians' ability to achieve social justice has been severely limited. Future public policy decisions must take into account the historical conditions under which American Indians have attempted to survive, and provide this unique American racial group with the resources and power necessary to regain control over their lives and those of future generations. Whether the current policy of self-determination will allow American Indians to realize complete and independent control over all aspects of their legal, social and political lives is open to debate. That which has been presented here does point out, however, that social justice for American Indians who have had personal experience with the American criminal justice system has not been actualized, and that future public policy decisions must begin to take into account the fact that many aspects of American Indian criminality today are directly linked to the failed policies of the past.

# NOTES

[1] This chapter will not focus on a number of legal issues which have been systematically addressed in a wide body of academic and popular sources of literature. First, it will not focus explicitly on federal Indian law. Several widely cited accounts of this area of law have already been done. See, for example, Felix Cohen, *Handbook of Federal Indian Law* (Charlottesville, VA: Michie: Bobbs-Merrill, 1982); and Vine Deloria, Jr., and Clifford M. Lytle, *American Indians, American Justice* (Austin, TX: University of Texas Press, 1983). Native American civil law issues have also been examined by several widely respected legal scholars, and will not be of concern here. Also see Deloria and Lytle, ibid, pp. 193-215. In addition, literature on traditional systems of Indian justice, which have received considerable scholarly interest in the last few decades, will not be pursued in this study. See Harold S. Colton, "A Brief Survey of Hopi Common Law," *Museum Notes*, Museum of Northern Arizona, 7: 6 (December 1934): 21-24; Richard F. Van Valkenburgh, "Navajo Common Law II: Navajo Law and Justice," *Museum Notes*, Museum of Northern Arizona, 9: 10 (April 1937): 51-54; John Philip Reid, *The Primitive Law of the Cherokee Nation* (New York: New York University Press, 1970); John L. Dickson, "The Judiciary History of the Cherokee Nation From 1721 to 1835," unpublished Ph.D. dissertation (Norman, OK: University of Oklahoma, 1964); Elmer R. Rusco, "The Pluralistic Basis of American Indian Law," in Laurence French, ed., *Indians and Criminal Justice* (Totowa, NJ: Allanheld, Osmun, 1982), pp. 39-52; Charles F. Wilkinson, "Basic Doctrines of American Indian

Law," in French, ed., ibid., pp. 75-92; and Deloria and Lytle, op. cit., pp. 110-138.

In addition, the historical, philosophical and religious bases of traditional forms of Indian jurisprudence, which also have received widespread attention in recent years, will not be considered. For information on these subjects, see Laurence French, "Introduction: An Historical Analysis of Indian Justice," in French, ed., op. cit., pp. 1-17. Finally, because of the considerable attention devoted to alcohol abuse and suicide among Native Americans, these two forms of social deviance will not be of primary concern in this chapter. For example, see Stephen J. Kunitz, Jerrold E. Levy and Michael Everett, "Alcoholic Cirrhosis among the Navajo," *Quarterly Journal of Studies on Alcohol* 30: 3 (September 1969): 672-685; Edwin M. Lemert, "Drinking among American Indians," in Edith Lsansky Gomberg, Helene Raskin White and John A. Carpenter, eds., *Alcohol, Science and Society Revisited* (Ann Arbor, MI: University of Michigan Press, 1982), pp. 80-95; Lyle Longclaws, Gordon E. Barnes, Linda Grieve and Ron Dumhoff, "Alcohol and Drug Use among Broken Head Ojibwa," *Journal of Studies on Alcohol* 41: 1 (January 1980): 21-36; Joan Weibel-Orlando, "Indians, Ethnicity, and Alcohol: Contrasting Perceptions of the Ethnic Self and Alcohol Use," in Linda A. Bennett and Genevieve M. Ames, eds., *The American Experience with Alcohol: Contrasting Cultural Perspectives* (New York: Plenum Press, 1985), pp. 201-226; Martin D. Topper, "Navajo 'Alcoholism': Drinking, Alcohol Abuse, and Treatment in a Changing Cultural Environment," in Bennett and Ames, eds., ibid., pp. 227-251; and Jack Bynum, "Suicide and the American Indian: An Analysis of Recent Trends," in Howard M. Bahr, Bruce A. Chadwick and Robert C. Day, eds., *Native Americans Today: Sociological Perspectives* (New York: Harper & Row, 1972), pp. 367-376.

[2]Morris Janowitz, "Sociological Theory and Social Control," *American Journal of Sociology* 81: 1 (July 1975): 82-108.

[3]Leonard D. Savitz, "Black Crime," in Kent S. Miller, ed., *Comparative Studies of Blacks and Whites in the United States* (New York: Seminar Press, 1973), pp. 467-516.

[4]Hispanics, at least until recently, have also been overlooked. For example, see Gary LaFree, "Official Reactions to Hispanic Defendants in the Southwest," *Journal of Research in Crime and Delinquency* 22: 3 (August 1985): 213-237.

[5]Sidney Harring, "Native American Crime in the United States," in French, ed., op. cit. note 1, pp. 93-108; and Phillip A. May, "Contemporary Crime and the American Indian: A Survey and Analysis of the Literature," *Plains Anthropologist* 27: no. 97 (August 1982): 225-238.

[6]Harring, ibid.

[7]Federal Bureau of Investigation, *Uniform Crime Reports for the United States: [Year]* (Washington, D.C.: Federal Bureau of Investigation, U.S. Department of Justice, [published annually]).

[8]For example, see Sue Titus Reid, *Crime and Criminology* (New York: Holt, Rinehart and Winston, 1988).

[9]Harring, op. cit. note 5.

AMERICAN INDIAN CRIMINALITY

[10]Ibid.

[11]Division of Law Enforcement Services, Bureau of Indian Affairs, U.S. Department of the Interior, Washington, D.C.

[12]Deloria and Lytle, op. cit. note 1, pp. 161-192.

[13]Ibid., pp. 175-178.

[14]Harold G. Grasmick and Donald E. Green, "Legal Punishment, Social Disapproval and Internalization as Inhibitors of Illegal Behavior," *Journal of Criminal Law and Criminology* 71: 3 (Fall 1980): 325-335; and Harold G. Grasmick and Donald E. Green, "Deterrence and the Morally Committed," *The Sociological Quarterly* 22: 1 (Winter 1981): 1-14.

[15]Wesley G. Skogan, "The Validity of Official Crime Statistics: An Empirical Investigation," *Social Science Quarterly* 55: 1 (June 1974): 25-38.

[16]John P. Clark and Larry L. Tifft, "Polygraph and Interview Validation of Self-Reported Deviant Behavior," *American Sociological Review* 31: 4 (August 1966): 516-523.

[17]Norman S. Hayner, "Variability in the Criminal Behavior of American Indians," *American Journal of Sociology* 47: 4 (January 1942): 602-613.

[18]Lewis Meriam, technical director, et al., *The Problem of Indian Administration*, the Meriam Report (Baltimore, MD: Johns Hopkins Press, published for the Brookings Institution, 1928).

[19]Hayner, op. cit. note 17, p. 613.

[20]Ibid.

[21]Hans Von Hentig, "The Delinquency of the American Indian," *Journal of Criminal Law and Criminology* 36: 1 (May-June 1945): 75-84.

[22]Ibid., pp. 82-83.

[23]Omer Stewart, "Questions Regarding American Indian Criminality," *Human Organization* 23: 1 (Spring 1964): 61-66.

[24]Charles Reasons, "Crime and the American Indian," in Bahr, Chadwick and Day, eds., *Native Americans Today*, op. cit. note 1, pp. 319-326.

[25]Laurence French and Jim Hornbuckle, "An Analysis of Indian Violence: The Cherokee Example," *American Indian Quarterly* 3: 4 (Winter 1977): 335-356.

[26]Ibid., p. 336.

[27]Marvin E. Wolfgang and Franco Ferracuti, *The Subculture of Violence: Towards an Integrated Theory in Criminology* (London: Tavistock, 1967).

[28]French and Hornbuckle, op. cit. note 25, p. 353.

[29]John Hagan and Kristin Bumiller, "Making Sense of Sentencing: A Review and Critique of Sentencing Research," in Alfred Blumstein, Jacqueline Cohen, Susan Martin and Michael H. Tonry, eds., *Research on Sentencing: The*

*Search for Reform*, vol. 2. (Washington, D.C.: National Academy Press, 1983), pp. 1-54.

[30]Archie Randall and Bette Randall, "Criminal Justice and the American Indian," *The Indian Historian* 11: 2 (Spring 1978): 42-48.

[31]Ibid., p. 43. Also see Tables 3 and 4, p. 48.

[32]Donald Black, "Production of Crime Rates," *American Sociological Review* 35: 4 (August 1970): 733-748.

[33]Edwin L. Hall and Albert A. Simkus, "Inequality in the Types of Sentences Received by Native Americans and Whites," *Criminology* 13: 2 (August 1975): 199-222.

[34]In a multiple regression analysis, additional controls for type of previous offense, military service and type of discharge, number of dependents, and average degree of harshness of the sentencing judge were included.

[35]Also see Randall and Randall, op. cit. note 30. Although these researchers did not control for important legal and extralegal variables, they provided some tentative evidence of a disproportional representation of Native Americans in both the state and federal criminal justice systems based on courtroom observations of the bail decisions in Spokane District and Superior Courts for two months (April and May) in 1976, and state and federal prison admission data for selected years. For example, while Indians made up only 4.7 percent of the population of the state of Washington (compared to 76.02 percent for whites and 16.64 percent for blacks), 10.86 percent of all Spokane court appearances were for Native Americans, while 5.43 percent were for black defendants and 80.62 percent for white defendants. Native Americans also accounted for 21.05 percent of all pretrial detainees during this period, compared to 8.77 percent for blacks and 64.91 percent for whites. This differential treatment was further indicated by the disproportionate numbers of those detained prior to disposition of their cases: 86 percent of Indians, 71 percent of blacks, and only 35 percent of whites. Looking at the prison admission data, Randall and Randall reported that the average length of sentence in federal prisons during 1972 for Indians was 47 months, compared to 41.2 months for whites and 56.4 months for blacks (the average for all offenders was 45.6.), while in the state of Washington during 1970, Native Americans made up 5.41 percent of all admissions, compared to 18.9 percent for blacks and 71.19 percent for whites.

[36]Bert H. Swift and Gary W. Bickel, *Comparative Parole Treatment of American Indians and Non-Indians at U.S. Federal Prisons* (Washington, D.C.: Bureau of Social Science Research, 1974).

[37]Also see Randall and Randall, op. cit. note 30. These researchers also reported data on parole decisions at the state and federal levels. Among federal prison parolees from 1970 to 1972, 42.9 percent of Native Americans had their parole revoked, compared to 28.4 percent of whites and 33.1 percent of blacks. For the state of Washington, 1957-to-1959 data on adult parolees indicated that 47 percent of the Native Americans who were released during this period had their parole revoked, compared to 38 percent of the whites and 34 percent of the blacks. However, as mentioned previously, these figures are descriptive

only, and fail to control for important legal and extralegal variables which might affect parole decisions.

[38]Tim Bynum, "Parole Decision Making and Native Americans," In R. L. McNeely and Carl E. Pope, eds., *Race, Crime and Criminal Justice* (Beverly Hills, CA: Sage, 1981), pp. 75-87.

[39]Ibid.

[40]See Judith R. Blau and Peter M. Blau, "The Cost of Inequality: Metropolitan Structure and Violent Crime," *American Sociological Review* 47: 1 (February 1982): 114-128; and Michael J. Hindelang, "Variations in Sex-Race-Age-Specific Incidence Rates of Offending," *American Sociological Review* 46: 4 (August 1981): 461-474.

[41]Hayner, op. cit. note 17; Von Hentig, op. cit. note 21; Reasons, op. cit. note 24; Stewart, op. cit. note 23; French and Hornbuckle, op. cit. note 25; and Randall and Randall, op. cit. note 30.

[42]Hall and Simkus, op. cit. note 33; and Bynum, op. cit. note 38.

[43]Jerrold E. Levy, Stephen J. Kunitz and Michael Everett, "Navajo Criminal Homicide," *Southwestern Journal of Anthropology* 25: 2 (Summer 1969): 124-152.

[44]Wolfgang and Ferracuti, op. cit. note 27.

[45]Ibid.

[46]Levy, et al., op. cit. note 43, p. 126.

[47]Howard S. Erlanger, "The Empirical Status of the Subculture of Violence Thesis," *Social Problems* 22: 2 (December 1974): 280-292.

[48]Mhyra S. Minnis, "The Relationship of the Social Structure of an Indian Community to Adult and Juvenile Delinquency," *Social Forces* 41: 4 (May 1963): 395-403.

[49]Comparisons with 1960 data for the state of Idaho revealed that mean room occupancy at Fort Hall was 2.81 times that of the state as a whole, and that there were 2 rooms per house compared to 4.2 per house statewide. Comparisons of living conditions with Spokane Indians and whites in contiguous counties also revealed some startling contrasts. Only 6.2 percent of the Shashone-Bancock households had phones, compared to 32.5 percent for Spokane Indians and 68.5 percent for whites; 18.5 percent of the households had a bathroom, compared to 32.5 percent for Spokane Indians and 83.2 percent for whites; 19.2 percent had indoor plumbing, compared to 42.5 percent for Spokane Indians and 94.2 percent for whites; 63.8 percent had electricity, compared to 95 percent for Spokane Indians and 99.1 percent for whites; and 56.2 percent had television, compared to 80 percent for Spokane Indians and 73.5 percent for whites.

[50]One example of the lack of economic opportunities is related to the availability of land. Respondents indicated that the most important problem on the reservation was the inheritance and utilization of land. Federal government allotment policies and subsequent inheritance practices have resulted in heir-

ship problems and land fractionalization. Water problems and lack of farm machinery also contributed to the land utilization problem.

[51]Minnis, op. cit. note 48, p. 401.

[52]Ibid., Table 5, p. 402.

[53]Ibid., p. 402.

[54]Ibid., p. 403.

[55]Ibid.

[56]Morris A. Forslund and Ralph E. Meyers, "Delinquency Among Wind River Indian Reservation Youth," *Criminology* 12: 1 (May 1974): 97-106.

[57]See R. Hale Andrews and Andrew H. Cohn, "Ungovernability: The Unjustifiable Jurisdiction," *Yale Law Journal* 83: 7 (June 1974): 1383-1409; Susan Datesman and Frank Scarpetti, "Female Delinquency and Broken Homes: A Reassessment," *Criminology* 13: 1 (May 1975): 33-55; Peter Kratcoski, "Differential Treatment of Delinquent Boys and Girls in Juvenile Court," *Child Welfare* 53: 1 (January 1974): 16-22; and Katherine S. Teilmann and Pierre Landry, "Gender Bias in Juvenile Justice," *Journal of Research in Crime and Delinquency* 18: 1 (January 1981): 47-80.

[58]Forslund and Meyers, op. cit. note 56, p. 100.

[59]Ibid., p. 102.

[60]Michael J. Hindelang, Travis Hirschi and Joseph G. Weis, *Measuring Delinquency* (Beverly Hills, CA: Sage Publications, 1981).

[61]Harring, op. cit. note 5.

[62]Minnis, op. cit. note 48.

[63]Morris A. Forslund and Virginia A. Cranston, "A Self-Report Comparison of Indian and Anglo Delinquency in Wyoming," *Criminology* 13: 2 (August 1975): 193-197.

[64]Bruce A. Chadwick, Joseph H. Stauss, Howard M. Bahr and Lowell K. Halverson, "Confrontation with the Law: The Case of the American Indians in Seattle," *Phylon* 37: 2 (Summer 1976): 163-71.

[65]Reasons, op. cit. note 24.

[66]Gary F. Jensen, Joseph H. Stauss and V. William Harris, "Crime, Delinquency, and the American Indian," *Human Organization* 36: 3 (Fall 1977): 252-256.

[67]Actually, Jensen and his colleagues also presented findings on Native American criminality based on two additional sources of data: Uniform Crime Reports for 1970 and a survey of southern Arizona high school students. Similar to previous studies, the researchers presented 1970 UCR data on Indian crime rates for all offenses which placed the Indian arrest rate several times higher than that of blacks and whites, with an even more pronounced disparity when alcohol-related offenses were examined. For these crimes, Indian arrest rates were seven to twenty-two times greater than those for blacks or whites.

The researchers also provided an urban-rural breakdown for alcohol- and non-alcohol-related crimes, as well as total crimes by racial categories. According to these figures, the Indian arrest rate was four times greater than that for whites in urban areas, and two-and-a-half times greater in rural areas. In comparison to blacks, the Indian rate for non-alcohol-related crime was only slightly higher in urban areas, and only twice as high as the black rate in rural areas. In fact, black arrest rates in urban areas exceeded those for Indians for common instrumental crimes such as larceny, burglary and robbery, violent interpersonal crimes such as murder and assault, and sex offenses. The second data source was a self-report study of delinquency among a sample of 1,700 southern Arizona high school students. The findings from this study further supported Jensen and his colleagues' argument concerning differential alcohol use. The most striking difference in self-reported delinquency among their sample was that for involvement with alcohol and drugs. Indian youths reported approximately three times as many drinking incidents than either Anglo or Chicano youths. Similar differences were also noted for involvement with marijuana and other illegal drugs. Unfortunately, only twenty-one Indian students were included in the sample, making generalizations from this analysis problematic.

[68]Larry E. Williams, Bruce A. Chadwick and Howard M. Bahr, "Antecedents of Self-Reported Arrest for Indian Americans in Seattle," *Phylon* 40: 3 (Fall 1979): 243-252.

[69]Ibid., pp. 249-251.

[70]Also see Stewart, op. cit. note 23; and Reasons, op. cit. note 24.

[71]Susan P. Robbins, "Anglo Concepts and Indian Delinquency: A Study of Juvenile Delinquency," *Social Casework* 65: 4 (April 1984): 235-241; and Susan P. Robbins, "Commitment, Belief and Native American Delinquency," *Human Organization* 44: 1 (Spring 1985): 57-62.

[72]Travis Hirschi, *Causes of Delinquency*, (Berkeley, CA: University of California Press, 1969).

[73]Ibid.

[74]Raymond Paternoster, Linda E. Saltzman, Gordon P. Waldo and Theodore G. Chiricos, "Perceived Risk and Social Control: Do Sanctions Really Deter?" *Law and Society Review* 17: 3 (1983): 457-479.

[75]Hirschi, op. cit. note 72.

[76]Ibid.

[77]Robbins, "Anglo Concepts," op. cit. note 71. She suggested that attachment as defined by Hirschi might be a cross-cultural concept to examine delinquency, although many of the definitions utilized did not measure Indian attachment adequately. Qualitative interviews she conducted with tribal members and other youth suggested that cultural differences in terms of expressing feelings easily might explain the inability of traditional measures of attachment to apply to this tribal group. Robbins argued that "future efforts to explicate and operationalize measures of Indian attachment must address the nature of this expression and identify specific persons to whom youths are attached," and that "operational definitions that are based on dominant soci-

ety norms" may "have little applicability in Indian culture." Ibid., pp. 240-241.

[78]Ibid., p. 238.

[79]Robbins, "Commitment, Belief," op. cit. note 71, p. 61.

[80]Robbins, "Anglo Concepts," op. cit. note 71, p. 241.

[81]Paternoster, et al., op. cit. note 74.

[82]Robbins, "Commitment, Belief," op. cit. note 71, p. 61.

[83]See Forslund and Meyers, op. cit. note 56; and Forslund and Cranston, op. cit. note 63.

[84]Robbins, op. cit. note 71.

[85]Forslund and Cranston, op. cit. note 63; and Chadwick, et al., op. cit. note 64.

[86]Williams, et al., op. cit. note 68.

[87]Jensen, et al., op. cit. note 66.

[88]See Paternoster, et al., op. cit. note 74.

[89]Ibid.

[90]Chadwick, et al., op. cit. note 64; and Williams, et al., op. cit. note 68.

[91]Jensen, et al., op. cit. note 66; and Robbins, op. cit. note 71.

[92]Chadwick, et al., op. cit. note 64; Williams, et al., op. cit. note 68; and Robbins, op. cit. note 71.

[93]Robert E. Kuttner and Albert B. Lorincz, "Promiscuity and Prostitution in Urbanized Indian Communities," *Mental Hygiene* 54: 1 (January 1970): 79-91.

[94]Ibid., p. 83.

[95]Venereal disease was a major problem, although treatment was generally obtained only as a result of arrests and subsequent routine health checks. Contraception was generally not used, perhaps for the most part because of a known high rate of infertility among the prostitutes.

[96]For example, in terms of formal sanctions, police regulation consisted of requests for identification cards. Even those who were obviously over age twenty-one were picked up by police if they were without cards. However, attempts by vice officers to engage in these efforts were frequently unfruitful, because bar patrons who recognized them would subsequently alert the women before the vice officers entered the establishments. As a result, it appeared that most of these women had never been charged with prostitution.

[97]James Inverarity, Pat Lauderdale and Barry C. Feld, *Law and Society: Sociological Perspectives on Criminal Law* (Boston: Little, Brown, 1983), p. 271.

[98]See Clifford R. Shaw, *The Jack-Roller: A Delinquent Boy's Own Story* (Chicago: University of Chicago Press, 1930); Elliott Liebow, *Tally's Corner: A Study of Negro Streetcorner Men* (Boston: Little, Brown, 1967); and Eleanor M. Miller, *Street Woman* (Philadelphia: Temple University Press, 1986).

[99]Stewart, op. cit. note 23; Levy, et al., op. cit. note 43; Kuttner and Lorincz, op. cit. note 93; Forslund and Meyers, op. cit. note 56; Forslund and Cranston, op. cit. note 63; and Jensen, et al., op. cit. note 66.

[100]Hayner, op. cit. note 17; Von Hentig, op. cit. note 21; and French and Hornbuckle, op. cit. note 25.

[101]Hayner, op. cit. note 17; French and Hornbuckle, op. cit. note 25; Forslund and Cranston, op. cit. note 63; Chadwick, et al., op. cit. note 64; and Williams, et al., op. cit. note 68.

[102]French and Hornbuckle, op. cit. note 25.

[103]Hayner, op. cit. note 17.

[104]Williams, et al., op. cit. note 68.

[105]Chadwick, et al., op. cit. note 64.

[106]Kuttner and Lorincz, op. cit. note 93.

[107]Candace Kruttschnitt and Donald E. Green, "The Sex-Sanctioning Issue: Is It History?" *American Sociological Review* 49: 4 (August 1984): 541-551; LaFree, op. cit. note 4; and Martha A. Myers and Susette M. Talarico, "Urban Justice, Rural Injustice? Urbanization and Its Effect on Sentencing" *Criminology* 24: 2 (May 1986): 367-392.

[108]Ibid.

[109]Hayner, op. cit. note 17; and Jensen, et al., op. cit. note 66.

[110]Reasons, op. cit. note 24; and Jensen, et al., op. cit. note 66.

[111]Robbins, op. cit. note 71; and Harring, op. cit. note 5.

[112]Hayner, op. cit. note 17; Harring, op. cit. note 5; and Minnis, op. cit. note 48.

[113]Ronald B. Flowers, *Minorities and Criminality* (Westport, CT: Greenwood Press, 1988), especially pp. 105-118.

[114]Ibid.

[115]While self-report studies have suggested that the true incidence of crime among various subgroups of the population is more equally distributed than official statistics indicate, the lack of such studies among American Indian populations makes any meaningful discussion of this issue difficult for this racial group.

[116]Ian Taylor, Paul Walton and Jock Young, *The New Criminology: For a Social Theory of Deviance* (New York: Harper Torchbooks, 1974); and George B. Vold and Thomas J. Bernard, *Theoretical Criminology*, 3d ed. (New York: Oxford University Press, 1986).

[117]Ibid.

[118]C. Matthew Snipp, "The Changing Political and Economic Status of American Indians: From Captive Nations to Internal Colonies," *American Journal of Economics and Sociology* 45: 2 (April 1986): 145-157; and C. Matthew Snipp, "American Indians and Natural Resource Development: Indigenous Land, Now Sought After, Has Produced New Indian-White Problems," *American Journal of Economics and Sociology* 45: 4 (October 1986): 457-474.

[119]Harring, op. cit. note 5.

[120]Ibid.

[121]Since there are several excellent reviews of the origins of the church and case law concerning attempts by local, state, federal and even tribal governments to prohibit the use of peyote, no attempt will be made here to provide a detailed account of these issues. See Paul E. Lawson and Jennifer Scholes, "Jurisprudence, Peyote and the Native American Church," *American Indian Culture and Research Journal* 10: 1 (1986): 13-27; and Weston La Barre, *The Peyote Cult*, 4th ed. (New York: Schocken Books, 1975).

[122]Robert S. Michaelson, " 'We Also Have a Religion': The Free Exercise of Religion Among Native Americans," *American Indian Quarterly* 7: 3 (Summer 1983): 111-142.

[123]Laurence French, "Contemporary Indian Justice and Correctional Treatment," in French, ed., op. cit. note 1, pp. 179-186.

[124]Alvin M. Josephy, "The Great Northwestern Fishing War: The Clashes Over Native American Fishing and Hunting Claims," in *Now That the Buffalo's Gone: A Study of Today's American Indians* (New York: Alfred A. Knopf, 1982), pp. 171-211.

[125]See *Lac Courte Oreilles Band of Lake Superior Chippewa Indians* v. *State of Wisconsin*, 653 F.Supp. 1420 (W.D. Wis. 1987).

[126]Deloria and Lytle, op. cit. note 1.

[127]Samuel J. Brakel, "American Indian Tribal Courts," in French, ed., op. cit. note 1, pp. 147-162.